Media Raves
No B.S. Business Success

INC. magazine included the first edition of this book in its list of 100 BEST BUSINESS BOOKS.

From the *Houston Business Journal:* "The *No B.S. Business Success* book delivers hard-nosed advice for real-life entrepreneurs who must meet payrolls, satisfy customers, and battle bankers and bureaucrats."

From Rich Karlgaard, Contributing Editor/Publisher, *Forbes* magazine, Forbes.com. Seen weekly on *Forbes on Fox*, Fox Business News TV: ". . . . there are even paragraphs of your writing that are as good as novelist Tom Wolfe's. And I should know. I published an original 7,500 word piece by Mr. Wolfe."

What Readers Say About this Book

"There is more truth about the entrepreneurial experience in this book than in an entire MBA program."

—Dr. Herb True, Adjunct Professor, Notre Dame University

"I met you in person at a book signing where I purchased several of your No B.S. books including Business Success. I started reading them that evening and couldn't put them down, devouring them by 3 A.M. They changed my way of thinking overnight. I scrapped my old business plan and came up with a new marketing approach . . . I accomplished more in the next 4 days than in the first year and a half, since startup."

—Chris Orlando, Orlando Home Improvement

"In a world focused on lack, insecurity, and doubt, your words are a shining beacon of hope!"

—Dr. Chris Bonn, Women's Wellness Center of Ogden

"In the first two chapters of *No B.S. Business Success*, you did such a great job of describing how I've been feeling . . . ."

—Susie Nelson

"Even Donald Trump could learn from your *No B.S. Business Book* and other No B.S. books!"

—Kristi Frank, Entrepreneur/competitor on *The Apprentice*
(See video interviews with the author, Dan Kennedy,
and Kristi Frank at www.NoBSBooks.com)

And about the Glazer-Kennedy Insider's Circle™ Experience

"I never realized that there are others who think and feel as I do. I feel a lot more confident knowing that, while I may not be like 'normal' people, that's something to embrace! Your books like *No B.S. Business Success* . . . the tele-seminars . . . the local Chapter meetings in my area . . . I walk away with such a 'can-do' attitude and a rush of ideas relevant to my business I never would have thought of on my own. I swear I can see the light bulb on top of my head come on, just like in the cartoons!"

—Kathee Italico, President, Memory Lane Photo Productions

"There is something magical about a Kennedy seminar. I've been with you for 23 years, and I'm still scratching the surface. Just when I think I must have heard it all, I discover more about 'doing business on my terms.' Just when I get that down, I learn about 'selling to the affluent.' There is no end to business improvement with you..."

—Dr. Greg Nielsen, D.C.

For a FREE GIFT including free trial membership in Glazer-Kennedy Insider's Circle™ see pages 266–267

No B.S.

BUSINESS SUCCESS

IN THE

NEW

ECONOMY

- Adapt to New Business Realities
- Gain Extreme Marketplace Advantage
- Profit From New Economy Customers

Dan S. Kennedy

EP
Entrepreneur.
Press

Publisher: Jere L. Calmes
Cover Design: David Shaw
Production and Composition: Eliot House Productions

This publication is designed to provide accurate and authoritative information in regard to the subject matter covered. It is sold with the understanding that the publisher is not engaged in rendering legal, accounting or
other professional services. If legal advice or other expert assistance is
required, the services of a competent professional person should be sought.

Library of Congress Cataloging-in-Publication Data
   Kennedy, Dan S., 1954–
      [No B.S. business success]
      No B.S. buisness success for the new economy/by Dan Kennedy
        p.   cm.
      Previously published under title: No B.S. business success.
      ISBN-10: 1-59918-361-7 (alk. paper)
      ISBN-13: 978-1-59918-361-9 (alk. paper)
      1. Success in business. I. Title.
   HF5386.K2765 2009
   658.4'21—dc22   2009014599

Printed in Canada
14 13 12 11 10 09   10 9 8 7 6 5 4 3 2 1

The old economy is shattered and gone forever.

It's never coming back as it was.

While some time-honored, reliable business strategies and skills continue to have their place—are even more important than ever—they must be combined with new, more creative and agile thinking and more tough-minded and disciplined methods in sync with the realities of the New Economy and the demands of its consumers and clients.

Welcome to The New Economy

Well, it's not like we shouldn't have seen this coming.

Problem: We are monstrously over-stored. The same stores every few miles. The joke about Starbucks was it had reached the point they were opening new Starbucks in the Men's Rooms in existing Starbucks. Me-too, same-as, indistinguishable chain stores, chain restaurants with zero differentiation right across the parking lot from one another. Simply, much, much more than the market could support. Implosion certain destiny.

Problem: There are far too many over-lapping brands. Should there ever have been Cadillac pick-up trucks when GM also has Chevy and GMC trucks? Other than to perpetuate jobs locked in by union contract, could the existence of Pontiac and Buick and Chevy and Cadillac and GMC possibly be justified? Not unique to GM, though. Many other companies sinned similarly. And it seems everybody wanted to play in everybody else's sandbox, sacrificing their very identities to their detriment. Starbucks added egg, cheese, and meat breakfast sandwiches (that ruined the coffee aroma in their stores) while McDonalds hurried to add lattes and gourmet coffee while Subway added pizza while Dominos Pizza added sub sandwiches, your pharmacy added clothes and lawn furniture, Wal-Mart added iPhones. It's a damn mess. That must be cleaned up.

Problem: Everybody already owns too much stuff. How many cars, TVs, computers, games, remodeled kitchens, backyard decks can consumers consume before they need a break? Above all else, the recession was made and extended by demand problems.

Problem: Worst of all, salesmanship perished and service went to hell in a handbasket, as free-flowing, easy, excess credit and the latest in a series of fools' bubbles (this one with theoretically never-ending multiplying of property values so homes became ATM's, not investments) enabled countless companies with poor sales practices, lazy and inept salespeople, sloppy over-staffing, casual management, and abysmal customer service to prosper, or at least seem to prosper. Truth is, consumers welcomed a good excuse to stay home and stop buying and *punish*.

Imagine a very loosely held together, giant ball of yarn with dozens of loose ends poking out all over the place. It wouldn't matter much which of the loose ends you gave a good tug; the entire ball, really *pile* of yarn would implode and collapse and unravel. So it has been with the economy. It really wouldn't have mattered if it had been too many sub-prime mortgages issued to poorly qualified and irresponsible borrowers, based on inflated equity with no regard to the borrowers' ability to pay, then bundled together in inventive investment packages or if it had been sudden skyrocketing of gas prices or if it had been the weight of mass-multiplied, poorly regulated hedge funds or accelerating disappearance of old-style manufacturing jobs sent overseas or just about any other loose end you might name—any one given a good yank would have been enough. Of course, when several got pulled hard in different directions at the same time . . . .

Incidentally, the real estate bubble was visible far, far in advance of its bursting. In 2003, an outstanding book on the subject, *The Coming Crash in the Housing Market* by John Talbott, a former vice president at Goldman Sachs and real estate economist, very accurately predicted both the mortgage meltdown and real estate crash we've recently experienced—and reading it saved me some money. Authoritative articles began appearing pretty frequently from 2004 on, like the one on July 26, 2004, in the *Financial Times*, headlined

"Party Over—Turn Off The Housing Boom Lights," and stating that "the end is near in use of exotic type mortgage money". We should have seen this coming. Some of us did. I began foretelling in earnest of 2007–2008 in my *No B.S. Marketing Letter* and other publications in 2004.

What has been painfully revealed are extreme, systemic weaknesses and flaws and vulnerabilities—and gross excesses—throughout our socio-economic, financial, and political systems, papered over for a while, but worsening like undiagnosed disease all the while until, finally, we got slapped in the face with a monster recession. It's not my first rodeo. I built my first businesses during the Jimmy Carter recession, with tight credit, double-digit interest and inflation and unemployment rates, and gas shortages and gas lines. These things may very well be avoidable, but these things happen. For people seeing it firsthand for the first time it is terrifying and can be paralyzing. But it's not the first time and it won't be the last time traumatic change has replaced an old economy with a New Economy.

From Monster Recession to New Economy

For people who respond boldly, creatively, intelligently, and responsibly, grand and glorious new opportunities, greater in scope, more powerful for rapid wealth creation, and more accessible to all are being presented by the emerging New Economy. With honest Darwinism, the herds are being thinned, the weakest eaten, and the strongest stepping over carcasses in the street en-route to bigger and better things. You choose whether to lie down and be stepped on or to move forward—quickly—because moving forward is the only way not to be stepped on. The once generous and cheery economy is going through a very irritable and unforgiving mood. Conditions are harsh.

There are new opportunities. They have new requirements. There are also evergreen, time-honored, wholly reliable success principles most business owners and entrepreneurs have drifted from, neglected, or forgotten that must be restored as governing priorities. This book, *No B.S. Business Success for the New Economy*, and its brother *No B.S. Sales Success for the New Economy* are about all of those things: new opportunities, new requirements, neglected principles to be restored.

Let me briefly describe the emerging New Economy as it directly affects entrepreneurs. Here are the new realities:

1. All the power has returned to the customer and he knows he has it.

2. The customer's tolerance for anything ordinary—ordinary products, services, expertise, experiences, for the banal and commonplace, and certainly for incompetence—is zero.

3. Money will be spent more judiciously, so it will be attracted only to businesses offering much more appealing and complete value propositions, with superior reputations, unique positioning, exceptionally effective marketing to tell their story, and outstanding customer service before, during, and after the sale. A more cautious consumer, striving to be sensible and responsible, will be judging you and trying to determine if your company is worthy of his trust before he buys from you. You will be under greater scrutiny.

4. You must genuinely earn your right to your customers' interest and support by providing well-matched, specialized, even customized product, service, and value propositions. People now have the opportunity, power, and awareness to demand what is specifically for them and precisely matched to their needs,

interests, and desires. They are not going to be on buying sprees, buying whatever is in your wagon that you want to sell.

New Economy Customers will not be as tight-fisted as recession customers, but they will be extremely demanding.

The New Economy will not be as grumpy and harsh as the recession economy, but it will not be generous or forgiving either.

Business success in The New Economy will be earned, not given. Businesses must be better. Businesspeople must be much better.

Contents

CHAPTER 5

CHAPTER 6

CHAPTER 7

FOREWORD
By Brian Tracy

You are about to get into a business championship fight. In this book, you will be knocked around, and many of your most cherished ideas will get punched and stomped on. Like a roller coaster, your stomach will drop and you might have trouble breathing. But don't worry, you'll arrive safely at the other end.

In my years as a consultant and business speaker, I've written 28 books, translated into 20 languages, and produced more than 300 audio and video learning programs. I have a good understanding of the importance and value of good business ideas.

My friend Dan Kennedy is unique, a genius in many ways. I have always admired his ability to see the vital truths in any business, and to state these realities with straight language and clear definitions.

Dan has written a timeless book, with ideas, insights, and methods you can use immediately to get better, faster business results.

His approach is direct. His ideas are controversial. His ability to get results for his clients is unchallenged. When you read, learn, and apply what you discover in the pages ahead, your business life, and your income, will change forever.

Put up your mental tray tables. Put on your conceptual seatbelts. You are entering an area of considerable turbulence. But you will come out of this experience a better businessperson than you ever have been. You will arrive at your destination of business success and profitability faster than you ever thought possible.

Good luck, and bon voyage!

—Brian Tracy

Brian Tracy is one of America's most sought after and popular professional speakers, author of dozens of business books, and a visionary thinker about business trends, opportunities, and strategies. www.briantracy.com.

PREFACE

Just a spoonful of sugar helps the medicine go down.

—R. SHERMAN, FROM *MARY POPPINS*

Welcome to what I sincerely hope is the most truthful, blunt, straightforward, non-sugarcoated, no pabulum, no holds barred, no-nonsense, no B.S. book you have ever read on succeeding as an entrepreneur.

I wrote the first edition of this book back in 1993, and since then I've personally heard from thousands of readers, from all over the world. You saw a few of their comments on the opening pages of this book. It struck a chord with entrepreneurs—the chord of authenticity. No college classroom theory, no baloney. Real world truths from somebody who succeeds day in, day out, as an entrepreneur, working without a net. Since then, a lot has happened in my life, business and personal. For example, I've sold two businesses I built up, walked away from a very important and lucrative nine-year business relationship, made planned, continual evolutionary changes in my other businesses, gone through a divorce after 22 years of marriage, re-married the same woman several years later, been diagnosed diabetic, and more. I'm pleased to report I'm happier than I've been in many years, and am living the life I set out to live. Anyway, all these changes, new experiences, what I've learned from my clients certainly warranted a complete updating of this book.

I wrote that last paragraph for the updated edition published in 2004. But in just a handful of years since then, a whole lot has changed in the business world too. The once mighty have fallen, the credit and banking system is in collapse and under recreation, a new eagerness for massive government interference in every aspect of business as well as everyday life has permeated America, and an entirely new economy—THE New Economy— is emerging, with new rules, new restrictions, new obstacles, and new opportunities. Many business owners have spent recent months wandering around, moaning "Oh, my God—what do I do *now*?" A lot of businesspeople and investors were caught unaware, for no good reason; the entire scenario was easily forecast. Many are moving into The New Economy weary and wounded or in stubborn denial, and may or may not survive. Others are striding in confidently and boldly, ready to put the recession well behind them and re-make themselves and their businesses as changed conditions and opportunities require. Whatever scars you may carry from the recession in progress or easing, whatever position you are re-starting or starting from, you can count on three things:

First, there will always be successes.

Second, the *principles* that make business success possible have not changed and will not change. Strategies and tactics and applications, yes. Principles, no. Switching from typewriter to PC has not altered the writing of a successful book. Switching from one kind of economy to another has not altered the fundamental ways in which successful entrepreneurs approach business. I did not change a single one of the **No B.S. Eternal Business Truths** first placed in the first edition of this book 16 years ago. They are evergreen. Some even more relevant in The New Economy. I have changed some of my advice about applying these Truths, but not the Truths themselves. And you should draw some confidence from how well these principles have stood the test of time and withstood the storms of the most recent period.

Third, I won't B.S. you in this book. As the umpire says, I'll call 'em as I see 'em—based on 35+ years on business battlefields, before, during, and after recessions. Experience in my own businesses, with hundreds and hundreds of private clients—almost all from-scratch millionaire and multi-millionaire entrepreneurs, and with the tens of thousands of Glazer-Kennedy Insider's Circle™ Members, who interact with me day to day. Nothing in this book comes out of a university's ivory tower or protected, pleasant tree-lined campus; it all comes from the blood-splattered business battlefield. This book is not a book report drawn from other books by a student and spectator; it is an in-the-trenches report. If you are living the life of the entrepreneurial business owner, you will hear its ring of authenticity loud and clear.

It is a personal book, me talking straight with you, as if I was consulting with you, and as if we were sitting around at the end of the day on my deck, watching the sunset, enjoying adult beverages, and just hanging out. Because it is personal, along the way I'll be telling you quite a bit about me and about my business life, past, present, and future. None of this is about bragging. I have no need for that or interest in doing it. What I share, I tell you so that you understand the basis for the advice and opinions I dispense.

I have occasionally been introduced as The Professor of Harsh Reality. This does NOT mean I'm negative. If anything, I'm one of the most optimistic, positive-minded people you'll ever meet. However, I do not believe in confusing positive thinking with fantasy. And the word "optimism," like many words in our perplexing English language, has more than one meaning. There's a mammoth difference between earned, deserved, justified optimism and wild-eyed, blue-sky, stubborn optimism. One of the biggest optimists I've ever known had brief peaks of amazing entrepreneurial success but could never sustain them, more frequently had shockingly deep lows of entrepreneurial failure, acted with appalling irresponsibility as a business owner and organizational leader, abused investors, spent five years in a state penitentiary, and is ending his life broke and estranged from family and friends—enormous talent and know-how wasted. His self-destruction is tragic. Extreme, but then, I see a great deal of business tragedy caused by the same basic disease: a refusal to deal with "what is."

I've discovered that I'm most successful when I have a firm grip on what is and least successful when caught wrestling with what ought to be. Creating your own reality of choice is what being an entrepreneur is all about, but it has to be built on solid ground not fairy dust.

If you are already in business for yourself, this book will help you go forward into The New Economy more astutely, efficiently, productively, and confidently. I think you'll also catch yourself nodding as you go along, saying to yourself, "This guy has been where I live." Sometimes there is value in just finding out you're not alone! In fact, the very first "success education" that I was ever exposed to, in my early teens, was a set of recordings titled "Lead the Field" by Earl Nightingale, in which he gave me badly needed permission to violate the "norms" I saw around me, with his dramatic statement:

> *"If you had no successful example to follow*
> *in whatever endeavor you choose,*
> *you may simply look at what*
> *everyone else around you*
> *is doing*
> *and do the opposite, because –*
> THE MAJORITY IS ALWAYS WRONG."

That may not be a precise, verbatim quote; it is as I recall it and have it stored in my subconscious as a primary guiding principle. This, for example, led to my strategy of deliberately questioning all industry norms and deliberately violating most of them, and encouraging my clients to do the same. It also led to my coining of the term "Mediocre Majority" to succinctly describe the vast undistinguished middle of any industry or profession. Anyway, Earl said a lot of things I had been thinking but had never heard anyone validate, and that gave me a great boost of confidence and conviction. Maybe some of my words, here, will do the same for you.

Most entrepreneurs tell me that, because of this feeling they get from this book, they are instantly eager to share it with other entrepreneurs. Please do so! If you want some place to send them, refer to www.NoBSBooks.com. There you and anyone you direct there will find on-demand video interviews of me hosted by Kristi Frank, who competed on Donald Trump's *The Apprentice* television show, free excerpts and previews from many of my books, additional free resources, and more.

If you have not yet started in business but intend to, this book might scare you off. If it does, consider it a favor; you're too easily spooked to succeed anyway. The entrepreneurial arena and The New Economy is no place for the timid, nervous, or easily worried to come and play. If it doesn't scare you off, it will help you avoid many pitfalls and problems and help you cope with those that can't be avoided. It will not cover the basics. There are plenty of books out there on the basics and we're not going to cover the same ground all over again. This is not a how-to-start-a-small-business book. This is a go-for-the-jugular success book.

As I said earlier, I am not a fuzzy-headed academic, pocket protector and wingtip shoes accountant, or other theorist, although there are plenty of these pretenders writing business books. I'm also not a retired authority who runs a business in my memory. I've been on the firing line meeting a payroll, battling the bankers and bureaucrats, struggling to satisfy customers, and solving real business problems. Over the years, I've arrived at a point where my own business is engineered to meet all my lifestyle preferences—for example, only one employee, in a distant office, not underfoot; no set hours; no unscheduled phone calls. But still, I deal with clients and vendors and real business life just like you do. I am invested in and advising several different businesses including start-ups, including a software company that earned a spot on the *Inc.* 500 list of fastest growth companies two years in a row, and a chain of upscale men's barber shops. I also work very hands-on with clients in a wide variety of businesses, as well as being "the consultant to the consultants"'—I advise over 50 different leading marketing and business consultants, each exclusively serving a different business or professional niche, in total in direct, hands-on relationships with over one million small business owners. I am still on the front lines myself and I am behind the scenes and intimately involved with a broad diversity of businesses. I live with independent entrepreneurs every day of my life—like some daring researcher in the wild, not just observing, but living with the lions and tigers and bears. I want you to know this because I think it makes this book more valuable to you.

I'll never forget taking over a company with 43 employees, never having managed more than 2 people in my life. I grabbed every management book I could get my paws on and sucked up all the experts' advice. Then, after a couple of months of getting my brains beat in every day by my employees, I started to look critically at the credentials of those "expert" authors. Most of them had never—I repeat, *never*—managed a workforce. These geniuses spewing out creative management, non-manipulative management, Japanese management, open-door management, and everything-else management wouldn't have survived a week in the real world. I resent those authors to this day. And it's a shame that a lot of college kids get that management theory; that is, fantasy sold to them as reality. So, I chucked all their books, rolled up my sleeves, used my common sense, and started finding out what really works and what doesn't.

Ever since then, I've looked at every new business book with suspicion. Most won't pass muster because most can't pass the real-experience test. I was originally motivated to write this book largely because reading most of the other books written for and sold to entrepreneurs turned my stomach. I am just as sickened by most of the most current crop.

I also want you to know that there are a lot more things I haven't got a clue about than there are things I understand, and, in this book, I have not dealt with any of the many things I'm in the dark about. Everything in here is based on my own expensive experience. It may not be right. You may not agree with it. But at least you should know that I didn't swipe it out of somebody else's book, give it a jazzy new psychobabble name, and pass it off as a new miracle tonic.

I also know you can't eat philosophy. So, while there is a lot of my own philosophy in this book, its primary job is showing you how to make more money then you ever imagined possible, faster than you can believe possible. This is a book about getting rich. If that offends you, please put this book back on the shelf or take it back to the store and get a refund. Spend your money on milk and cookies instead. You'll be happier. In fact, I'd like to quickly clear up a big misconception about what being an entrepreneur and owning and building a business is all about. The purpose is <u>not</u> to employ people, <u>not</u> to do social good, <u>not</u> to pay taxes. A lot of liberals think those are the purposes of business. Nuts to them. The purpose of being an entrepreneur is to get really, really rich, and reward yourself for taking on all the risk and responsibility with exactly the kind of life and lifestyle you want. Facilitating that is the sole aim of this book.

Before getting into the "meat," on the next few pages you'll find a brief description of my business activities past and present, and what my current business looks like. I think you'll benefit more from the book if you understand where I'm coming from; however you can choose to skip these pages if you like and jump right to Chapter 1. Your choice.

Finally, I'd like to explain the Mary Poppins quote at the top of this Preface. *Mary Poppins* was one of the first movies I got taken to see in a theater as a child. If you've seen it, you can probably call up the scene of Julie Andrews and the children singing the "just a spoonful of sugar helps the medicine go down" song. It's a lovely thought. Or, as she would say, "loverly." In real business life, however, the emotional need for spoonfuls of sugar is very dangerous. How well you can take medicine—i.e., deal with reality—has a great deal to do with how successful you are as an entrepreneur.

There's a legendary book you've hopefully read by Napoleon Hill, titled *Think and Grow Rich*. In that book, he enumerates 17 success principles adhered to in common by the hundreds of history's greatest entrepreneurial achievers he studied, interviewed, and worked with, like Andrew Carnegie, Henry Ford, Thomas Edison, and so on. Of the 17 principles, the one everybody seems to like the least and ignore the most is "Accurate Thinking." I believe it to be the most important one. So this book, my book, is heavy on that principle. It is medicine without the accompaniment of sugar.

Finally, let me say that, when I graduated high school, my parents were flat broke. I started with no family money. I didn't step into a family business. No one handed me anything on a silver platter. At age 55, I am semi-retired, a multi-millionaire, free to live precisely as I choose, indulging my interest in horseracing, all made possible through the kind of thinking, attitudes, habits, and strategies I've laid out in this book. I have been blunt, forthright, and held nothing back.

With that said, I still hope you not only profit from this book, but enjoy reading it. And I welcome your comments, thoughts, or questions. You can communicate with me directly by fax, 602-269-3113.

Best,
Dan S. Kennedy

Other Notes from the Author

1. For those of you who are gender or political correctness sensitive, an explanation to head off letters: I have used "he," "him," etc. throughout the book rather than awkwardly saying "he or she," "him or her." I do not mean this as a slight to women, only as a convenience. I'm not getting paid by the word.

2. In many instances, I've been able to use the names of actual companies and individuals, the details of actual case histories and examples throughout the book. In a few cases, individuals' names have been withheld on request.

3. The first edition of this book was published in 1993 by another publisher, Self-Counsel Press. A revised and updated edition was published in 1995. The next edition, published by Entrepreneur Press in 2004, preserved approximately half of the original text with only statistics or time-altered information revised, but also has about 50% brand new material. Now this FOR THE NEW ECONOMY edition has preserved all that was evergreen but again revised or added about 50% new material.

A Look at the Author's Business Activities

Dan Kennedy is a multi-millionaire serial entrepreneur who has started, bought, built, and sold a number of businesses, and developed a large, loyal international following as an author, speaker, consultant, and coach.

His business adventures have included ownership of an advertising agency; interests in a cosmetic company with retail locations and independent distributors; an award and trophy company conducting all its business via mail-order and selling in volume to the U.S. Army, Navy, Air Force, Marines, Boy Scouts of America, and over 200 of the Fortune 500 companies; and a seminar company training over 20,000 dentists and chiropractors. He once bought a publicly held custom manufacturing company "no money down," took it through a nearly successful turnaround and Chapter 11 Reorganization, and ultimately sold its manufacturing operations to a competitor while retaining its publishing assets for a new business.

His publishing business based around his *NO B.S. MARKETING LETTER* was sold in 2003, and now operates as Glazer-Kennedy Insider's Circle LLC, providing information and membership benefits to over 20,000 business owners; online information to over 250,000; publishing his *NO B.S. MARKETING LETTER*, the most widely subscribed to newsletter about direct marketing, marketing, and entrepreneurial strategies and a portfolio of other newsletters, audio programs, online courses, and other resources; and supporting over 150 local Chapters and Kennedy Study/Mastermind Groups throughout the United States and Canada. Information about this organization can be found via the Free Gift Offer and website on pages 272–273.

As of this writing, Dan is easing his way toward semi-retirement. He has one elite, private business coaching group of his own—with 20 participants each paying a $34,000.00 yearly fee; a reduced schedule of 20 private consulting days a year; and he continues creating marketing campaigns and writing copy for ads, direct-mail campaigns, websites, infomercials, etc. for a stable of clients, many with him for 5 to 20 years, and occasionally accepting a new client. He very selectively accepts equity in startup companies. He rarely accepts speaking engagements anymore except at Glazer-Kennedy Insider's Circle™ conferences for its Members.

CHAPTER 1

THE DECISION AND DETERMINATION TO SUCCEED

*Men are anxious to improve their circumstances,
but are unwilling to improve themselves.
They therefore remain bound.*

—JAMES ALLEN, *AS A MAN THINKETH*

Contrary to a great many textbook assertions, having the best product, the better mousetrap, a whiz-bang new idea, the top location, the best market, the smartest accountant, the neatest bookkeeping system, or a ton of capital—or all of them together—does not ensure success. On the other hand, having the worst product, a mediocre mousetrap, a silly idea, a bad location, a weak market, an accountant who can't count, a shoebox and paper bag bookkeeping system, or no money—or all of these things together—does not ensure failure.

I have seen people succeed under the most improbable conditions. I've also seen people who have everything going for them still manage to screw it up. In all of these cases, it's the person making the difference. That's why there really are no business successes or failures; there are people successes and people failures.

For an extended period of time, the incredible dysfunction and dereliction of duty of CEOs running some of America's corporations and business institutions as well as literally hundreds of thousands of small business owners was concealed by a wildly over-generous economy fueled by stupid credit. Businesses that were manufacturing debt far more than anything else seemed to be prospering and the buffoons and criminals running them were widely accepted as successful. The inevitable bursting of multiple bubbles—unchecked, outrageous real estate appreciation, easy money and foolish credit, and public corporation values so far out of whack with incomes or legitimate assets they seemed to defy all laws of economic gravity—replaced a Santa Claus economy with a violently angry Grinch one. People who only appeared to be successful because it was just about impossible not to appear that way were stripped naked and shown to be losers. If you strip away all the layers of deceit, of stupidity, or irrational exuberance, of poor business practices, of abusing customers and investors, what you eventually get to, behind every business failure, is a person who has failed himself and those around him, by failing to adhere to fundamental principles of successful achievement.

In short, every outcome is the product of someone's decisions.

We'll get to the decisions about marketing, sales, and management required to make a business perform profitably, in a sustainable manner. But first, here, let's confront the most basic of all decisions: the decision to succeed.

A Matter of Personal Decision

Entrepreneurial success, like most things in life, is mostly a matter of decision. A partnership, friendship, intimate relationship, or marriage that succeeds or fails, a book that gets written or remains a jumble of notes in a drawer, the garage that gets cleaned out Saturday or put off until next week—these are all the result of decision. Or, to be more accurate, decisions. Decisions, for example, of self-reliance and personal responsibility, or of not waiting for better or ideal timing or circumstances, help from others, or a muse's delivery of just the right mood.

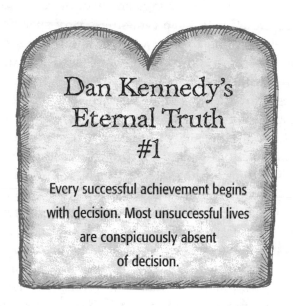

Dan Kennedy's
Eternal Truth
#1

Every successful achievement begins with decision. Most unsuccessful lives are conspicuously absent of decision.

Most people go through life making decisions by default, choosing only from narrow options dictated by others or by evolving circumstances. One millionaire friend of mine grew up in a very small town where, as he put it, there were two career options: working at the factory or raising pigs and chickens. With only a few exceptions, everybody he went to school and graduated with chose one of those two options. Stayed there, did one of those two things, died there. He left. Many people go through life as if confined by tall barbed wire fences and armed guards in whatever "place" they find themselves. Business owners do this too. They create and organize a business to be a certain thing and operate in a certain way, then act as if some law exists forbidding its change. In approaching their businesses this way, they might

4 @ NO B.S. Business Success

as well be stuck in that small town with a profound belief in only two options—the factory or the farm.

The New Economy mandates a much more willing and creative approach to constant change and evolution and reccurring reinvention in order to keep a business very specifically and currently relevant to the customers able and willing to support it. Agile businesses—run by mentally agile leaders—can prosper as never before. But domination purely by size or brand stature or longevity is entirely a thing of the past. The best recent object lesson: General Motors, a giant no longer relevant to its customers, run as if things like longevity or brand status mattered, as if size ensured continuation. Staying relevant requires constant change, and there is nothing less tolerated in The New Economy than the irrelevant. The economic power has returned to consumers and they know it. Consumers have been spoiled like indulgent billionaire parents' prodigies with so many customized, specialized, niched choices that they now expect to get things that are clearly and uniquely for them. Satisfying them en masse is nearly impossible. But you are not locked into any business definition or model, any product mix, any pricing formula, any set of stay-in-place limitations, so if you decide to do so, you can be morphing to meet your customers' greatest interests day to day.

I am often amused when traveling, and asked what I do, and I describe it as best I can, then I get the envious sigh, the gee-I-wish-I-could-do-that, and then the laundry list of complaints and dissatisfactions from the person about his present career or business or life. I'm amused because he apparently does not know he can change all that by decision. Similarly, when traveling and asked where I lived, and I answered "sunny Phoenix" (where I lived for over ten years), I'd often get the envious sigh, the gee-I-wish-I-lived-there-instead-of-in-X, then the litany of unpleasant things about their home city. This amuses me because apparently they haven't noticed the highway signs in their town pointing the way out.

It's amazing how people spend their lives in prisons entirely of their own making, the key dangling right there in the lock, no jailer in sight.

I find it very hard to work up much sympathy for most of these sad-sacks. I remember listening to a 40-or-so-year-old guy working behind the counter at a neighborhood convenience store where I sometimes stop for coffee complaining loudly, even poetically about his miserable job, low income, and lousy lot in life. I asked where he lived and which way he drove to work. After he answered, I asked if he'd noticed that everyday, twice a day he drove past the public library, a gigantic repository of help for changing your career, your finances, your life—all free. As you might guess, I might as well have been speaking Martian. If pressed, I assure you, he'd tell you he was too busy or too tired to read, or didn't like to read, or had bad eyesight when he was in school, or some other pitiful excuse. Pfui.

Truths That Aren't, That Hold You Back

Successful entrepreneurs learn to be much more assertive, proactive, and creative in making decisions to change things as they prefer, to make things happen. If you are to succeed as an entrepreneur, you have to break free of your old reacting and responding mode and switch to the assertive, proactive mode. **You have to reject the entire idea of limited choices.**

As an entrepreneur you need to reject every single piece of programming you've ever received about limited options or prerequisites for exercising certain options. Limitations, rules, industry norms—these are for other people, but not for you. Reject any idea that removes any option from your table.

Just for example, that certain options exist only for people with particular education, licenses, or certifications. Sure, you can't just up and declare yourself a heart surgeon or airplane pilot. But you can certainly be the CEO, and you can certainly make as much money as you choose.

Here's a little jolt: one of the highest-paid marketing consultants and coaches working only with restaurant owners who I helped start in business, a man who is paid millions of dollars a year from those owners for his advice, has never worked in, managed, or owned a restaurant. For four years, I had the largest business training company serving dentists and chiropractors, working with over 10,000 doctors, but I am neither a DC nor DDS. The current owner of one of the most successful independent movie studios, who has prospered by bringing comic book characters to the big screen, in partnership with giants like Warner Brothers, did not work as script writer, camera man, grip, film editor, or actor, did not go to film school, did not apprentice in Hollywood before starting his movie production company. He owned a chain of dry cleaning stores. He liked comic books. And he proved adept at raising money from investors. The man who created one of the world's largest ad agencies from scratch was a door-to-door salesman and a short order cook. Traditional qualifications matter if entering and trying to climb a ladder controlled by others inside a corporate organization but they do not matter at all in the entrepreneurial arena. Not at all. Only what you decide and do matters.

This is a very disconcerting thought for people who have gone to great pains to secure academic or other credentials, i.e. the approval of others, or to build resumes. These people hate hearing this, resent it, resist it. Still, the marketplace is unimpressed by anything but the doing.

You also need to reject limiting definitions. Single-function businesses are dinosaurs, with rare, notable, and generally unsustainable examples. Yes, there is such a thing as a gourmet cupcake bakery that makes and sells nothing but ungodly priced cupcakes—which reminds me of an old John Belushi skit from *Saturday Night Live* about the Scotch tape store, into which customers kept coming asking for paper clips or pens. The cupcake store exists. Let's see how it's doing in five or ten years. It won't be there as is at all. It's a fad, like the pet rock.

The most successful "restaurant owner" that I know does not think of herself or define herself that way, although it is true that she owns a restaurant. But it is merely "the Bat Cave" for an aggressively marketed private party catering business, a wine school and wine tasting society, an e-commerce business selling her recipes, spices, prepared food items, and party planning "coaching" worldwide. The restaurant itself is open only ten nights a month to the public, about the same to members only, for prix fix dining experiences. How would you *define* this business?

WARNING:
Your Entry Point to Entrepreneurship May Be a Handicap to Overcome

For many people, the decision to pursue the entrepreneurial lifestyle is the by-product of an evolving dislike for their jobs, frustration with their bosses, or a sudden loss of employment. They may be downsized, forced into early retirement, or just get fed up one day and tell the boss to "take this job and shove it." The employees-turned-entrepreneurs out of default or disgust lug a lot of mental and emotional baggage with them. The habits, attitudes, and behaviors that work for the employee in the corporate bureaucratic environment do not work well at all in the entrepreneurial environment, and must be left behind. The reason why so many new businesses fail is that the owners were unable to leave their old attitudes behind.

There is no "doing enough to get by" in the entrepreneurial world.

Clinging to narrow and traditional definitions—the equivalent of corporate job descriptions—can get you killed.

And in The New Economy, there is no place to hide and a harsher, brighter spotlight is shining on your every decision and every move.

Personally, I've only held one job in my entire life, for one year, immediately out of high school. I secured a territory sales position with a national book publishing company, that was supposed to be for a college graduate with sales experience. I got it through a combination of bluster, white lies, and agreeing to work on "free trial" for three months, no pay, no company car. Although I excelled at the work itself, by year's end my sales manager and I agreed I was fundamentally unemployable. Thus I became entrepreneurial. However, I'd always intended to be my own boss, and I was very fortunate to have some preparation for it in youth, as my parents had been self-employed my entire life. While other kids were still reading comic books and filching their fathers' *Playboys*, I was, too, but I was also reading *Think and Grow Rich*, listening to Earl Nightingale tapes, working in the business, riding with my grandmother on job deliveries to clients, and writing up my list of life goals. This is not a mandatory prerequisite. I know plenty of wildly successful entrepreneurs who came from much less helpful backgrounds. But I did have the edge of clear intent from the start of my adult life, and little time to acquire the bad habits of thought and behavior that most long-time employees of other people have to shed when switching to entrepreneurship.

Anyway, I think, to succeed, you not only must make a firm and committed decision to do just that, you must also decide to give up long-held attitudes and behaviors that fit fine in your previous environment but do not work well in entrepreneurial life. Although I don't swim, I imagine it'd be tough to swim across a good-sized lake insisting on clinging to a boat anchor. Letting go of anchors from your former life as you dive into entrepreneurial waters is essential.

Why Trying Doesn't Work

Some people think and talk in terms of "trying" a business or "trying" out the entrepreneurial experience. Before achieving major success in business myself, I went through considerable agony, corporate and personal bankruptcy, stress, embarrassment, humiliation, and near-starvation. If I'd been just "trying," just taking a test-drive, I'd have quit. And make no mistake about it; my experience is the norm among ultimately successful entrepreneurs.

Rich DeVos plunked down millions to buy the NBA franchise, the Orlando Magic, apparently to indulge himself. Many years, for as long as I can recall, Rich, and his lifelong partner Jay VanAndel, appeared on the annual *Forbes* magazine list of the 400 richest men in America. Certainly many have envied DeVos' ability to buy a professional basketball team! What guy wouldn't love to own his own pro sports team?

But I wonder how many envied Rich and Jay when they were barely surviving in business, bottling a liquid cleanser in a decrepit gas station, delivering drums of the gunk cross-country to their few distributors in their own pickup truck, being laughed at by friends and family, in the earliest days of creating Amway. I wonder how many times they thought about quitting, but didn't.

I am not in their league although I've always found them inspiring. But I do own 20 to 25 racehorses at any given time—that eat while I sleep. I drive some of them myself, professionally, in over 100 harness races a year. I travel by private jet 90% of the time. I most recently indulged myself by buying a couple classic cars. My wife and I have two homes. We take a number of vacations each year. Consider all this a metaphor for whatever life you or others might envy. Many envy mine. Such envy, so-called class envy, is often exploited by politicians and has been most ruthlessly and shamefully exploited by President Obama.

But it's not a matter of "class" at all. There's no such thing as a "rich class." There are people like me who decided to get rich and made decisions others are not willing to make in order to do so, and make decisions others are not willing to make everyday to stay wealthy. Many people do not envy my work schedule at all when they discover how much I work, how disciplined my approach to my work is, and how hard I drive myself, day in, day out. Many people do not envy the massive amount of on-going gathering, processing, studying, organizing of information that I do. In fact, forget envy; they outright state they wouldn't consider working as I do. Even fewer would go through everything I've gone through so far to create and sustain this life.

My friend Jim Rohn, one of this lifetime's greatest success teachers, says that if you follow any highly successful businessperson around for a week—if you can keep up—you'd see the mystery of his success solved. You'd say, "Well, it's no wonder he's so successful. Look at ALL the things he does." In my experience, most people given such opportunity, also wind up saying, "Well, I would never do ALL that." Not couldn't. *Wouldn't.* And most would definitely quit the first time they ran

Yes, I Have Definite Political Opinions

I don't think you can separate personal and political philosophy. I find almost all highly successful businesspeople who've created their own success stories from scratch share a very clear political viewpoint. I write about mine in a column published weekly at www.BusinessAndMedia.org and in a special content section at the DanKennedy.com site: DanKennedyPolitics.

up against a really ugly and miserable set of circumstances, like the recent recession. And *that* is why only about 5% of the entire U.S. population earns over $250,000.00 a year. Not for lack of opportunity. Simply because they decide not to. Any other explanation is nonsense. And any attempt to re-distribute wealth by government hand to those whose decisions are incompatible with wealth and do not cause wealth is doomed to failure, as history has repeatedly demonstrated.

It's worth very seriously questioning whether or not your own decisions are compatible with success and are the kinds of decisions that cause success, and whether or not you are willing to make and live by these essential decisions.

Keeping Faith with Your Commitments

To succeed as an entrepreneur requires decision and determination—total, unwavering commitment. To keep faith with this commitment, you have to develop and embrace attitudes, habits, and behaviors that are markedly different from those of most of the people you've known. You have to cut down on time spent with people who are not supportive of your entrepreneurial ambitions. Time spent hanging around fearful people, doubtful people, skeptical people, people not themselves committed to successful achievement, can impair your ability to succeed.

You mean I have to change my friends?

Probably. And the books you read. And the television programs you watch. And a whole lot more. We cannot help being and becoming a product of the ideas we associate with most, of the books and magazines we read, the tapes we listen to, the TV we watch, and the people we spend time with.

As thick-skinned as I believe I am and as much of an independent thinker as I pride myself in being, I admit that my performance and determination vary in relationship to what I'm reading, what

I'm listening to, and who I'm hanging around with. Earl Nightingale brilliantly summarized all this: "We become what we think about most." If you are going to become an exceptionally successful entrepreneur, that is what you must think about most.

Another way to look at this is in terms of passion. The most successful entrepreneurs I know are passionately involved with entrepreneurship in general and their businesses in particular. They're in love being with entrepreneurs, excited about their products or services, "on fire" with enthusiasm, and that gives them superhuman powers.

This is one very good argument for belonging to entrepreneur groups, coaching programs, and peer advisory groups, so you have regular contact and share ideas and information with like-minded entrepreneurs who validate, support, and encourage you. You can greatly accelerate your entrepreneurial success and decrease your aloneness, and isolation-related stress by associating with other progressive entrepreneurs. In such an environment, you are continually challenged by the others' achievements and progress. The other members as well as a top-notch business coach running the group can call you on your B.S. You can derive personal motivation from recognition unavailable anywhere else—after all, who but kindred spirit entrepreneurs can understand and appreciate your making the difficult decision to axe a non-productive employee or your success with a new ad campaign? Being part of the right group of progressive, creative, and tough-minded entrepreneurs can make a huge difference.

You cannot immunize yourself against the influences of the ideas in the people you associate with. There is no vaccination to protect you from limiting, unproductive, antibusiness, or anti-success thinking. For this reason, you must immerse yourself in associations that are in harmony with your goals and aspirations.

This doesn't mean that you must socialize only with other entrepreneurs. I have friends who are college professors, corporate executives, actors, athletes, office workers, and so on, but I choose

GKIC Membership

GOOD NEWS! There are Glazer-Kennedy Insider's Circle™ Chapters meeting regularly in over 150 areas throughout the United States and Canada, facilitating exactly this kind of support for more than 10,000 entrepreneurs every month. You can find a Directory at DanKennedy.com, or if you take advantage of my Free Gift Offer on pages 272–273, and there is a Chapter in your area, you'll automatically receive an invitation to a meeting.

them carefully. They do not have negative attitudes about business people; they do have interesting ambitions within their careers or tied to others' outside interests that can be stimulating. But, frankly, there are very few of these in my life. I call them "civilians," and I imagine that I think of them much like a career military officer thinks of civilians. They cannot possibly understand me or what I do. Because my primary interests in life are business, success philosophy, and politics and theirs are pastimes that distract from such thinking, we have little as common ground. An enjoyable evening now and then, a trek to the theater together, a Super Bowl party, fine. Regular association, mind-numbing and tedious at best, harmful at worst.

Unfortunately, you are going to discover that the majority of nonentrepreneur civilians have a number of set-in-cement biases against and frustrations with you, the entrepreneur. Here are some of the big ones you'll run up against.

ACCUSATION: You're a Workaholic

Most entrepreneurs I know experience great conflicts between their commitment to business and other aspects of their lives:

marriage, family, civic activities, and so on. Having two failed marriages in my background, I'm hypersensitive to this conflict, and I'm always working on ways to handle it more effectively. The fact—and it is fact—that the line between "work" and "play" is thoroughly blurred for the true entrepreneur, and the corollary fact that the entrepreneur's business life is often, frankly, bluntly, more important to him than his personal and social life is a huge source of befuddlement, annoyance, and tension for those around him. If you read a lot of biographies of great entrepreneurs, you'll find this a common thread. Read the Buffet bio *The Snowball* just as example. The vast majority of people casually familiar with Warren Buffet view him as a kindly, wise owl, an elder statesman, a *pater familias* for investors. But being married to him or a child raised in his household would, if this book is to be believed, give you a very different sense of the man.

It's convenient and easy for others to label the determined, passionate entrepreneur as a workaholic—a diseased, neurotic addict guilty of neglecting non-work responsibilities, of not loving his or her spouse or family, of being a self-absorbed ass. It's convenient and easy, but overly simplistic, and certainly not very helpful.

In reality, the constantly working entrepreneur may be saner and happier than the critics. Most people detest their jobs, yet they continue going to them day after day, month after month, year after year. They spend the lion's share of their lives doing things they find boring and unfulfilling, but lack the guts to do anything about it. They live for weekend escape. They spend five days a week as prison inmates and hope for two they may enjoy. Isn't that sad? By contrast, the successful entrepreneur manages to create and stay involved in work that is so enjoyable and fulfilling that he no longer thinks of it as work, and that provides exceptional financial rewards as well.

The lovers, friends, parents, and others who throw around the workaholic label secretly resent their own "stuckedness" and try to make themselves feel better by attacking you, by making you feel guilty or odd.

We could dismiss the critics as jealous, resentful, and unreasonable just as easily as they label us as workaholics. However, no one wants to go through life married only to a business in general. We need mates, family, and close friends. And they won't all be involved in our businesses or even in business. We don't get to choose our families and, besides, some diversity in social life is healthy and necessary. So, better understanding of ourselves and others, recognition of the special problem we present to others, and creative efforts at preserving relationships are all very important.

The Blurred Line

*O*ne of the ultimate object lessons in this is Richard Branson, founder of Virgin Airlines, and all the other Virgin companies and brands. He told *Fortune* magazine: "I don't think of work as work and play as play. It's all living."

The typical entrepreneur is constantly initiating new projects, even new businesses, to justify the long day, to keep the game alive. They are not just motivated by desirable end results; they're equally motivated by the enjoyment and thrill they derive from the whole process of business. They love the "action." If this is workaholism, I'm guilty.

But, also, thanks to divorces, aging, long conversations with wiser people, and many other factors, I'm developing an appreciation for balancing that passion with other passions, so that I'm less guilty. And I've discovered a very odd secret. A difficult one for everybody raised on "work ethic" like me, but here it is:

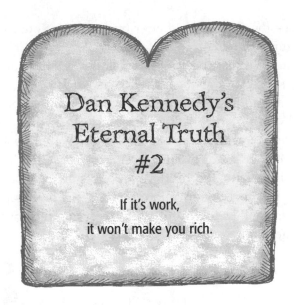

Dan Kennedy's
Eternal Truth
#2

If it's work,
it won't make you rich.

out-working everybody else on the planet is NOT the best path
to success as an entrepreneur. As a matter of fact, figuring out
how to work less—if focused on highest value and highest yield
work—is far more useful. Over the past ten years, I've been systematically shedding businesses and responsibilities, cutting
back on involvements, each year warning my CPA and tax advisor to anticipate a significant drop in my earnings. But the
opposite has occurred.

My Platinum Inner Circle Member and client Ron LeGrand
has this saying:

The Less I Do, The More I Make

Ron is a hugely successful real estate investor and entrepreneur, juggling literally hundreds of projects.

You have to be very careful about how you interpret this particular adage. You can't take it literally, cut your work hours in

half, sleep in a hammock, and expect your income to leap up. But there are many applications of this idea that work brilliantly. For example, the less you do that others could do, thus the more you do that only you can do, the more you make. Or, the less you do that feels too much like uninteresting, unfulfilling work and the more you do that feels like fun, the more you make.

Succeeding in business is a real magic trick. Succeeding in business and having a good life is an even greater, more challenging, more worthwhile trick. Since anything and everything is possible for the determined person, why not set your sights on the very best?

Some entrepreneurs manage to involve those close to them in their work-absorbed behavior. Tom Monaghan, founder of Dominos Pizza, gratefully tells of his wife's patience when he would always choose a pizza joint to check out whenever they were traveling or on vacation. Some fortunate couples share the same entrepreneurial passion and have that work for them.

But what if you're making the big transition from employee to entrepreneur with a spouse who is happy with your old behavior? Or what if you're involved with someone who cannot survive in a relationship dominated by your entrepreneurial passion?

Some of these relationships end. If yours is to survive, you need to be very aware of the strain that your new entrepreneurial personality, passion, and lifestyle is going to create and take proactive, preventive steps to make up for it, then hope for the best but be prepared for the worst.

PERCEPTION: You're a Wild-Eyed Risk Taker, a Riverboat Gambler. Have You Lost Your Mind?

One of the things that frightens many people and their loved ones about choosing the entrepreneurial lifestyle is the risk. It's interesting that our society chooses the cautious "be careful" as a means of saying goodbye to a friend. We don't say "be success-ful" or "be happy," we say, "be careful."

The true entrepreneur prefers to be adventurous and "fail for-ward" all the time. Running a business *is* a risk, but it needn't be foolhardy. I rarely make a decision without considering every-thing from the best-case scenario to the worst-case scenario. I try to expect the best and insure against the worst.

Most people see things as black or white: someone is either the meek and mild Clark Kent or the strong and daring Superman. They try to see themselves instantly turning from Kent to Superman and have understandable difficulty conceiving and believing in such a miraculous transition.

Such dramatic overnight makeovers rarely occur. People grow into and with their new roles. You *can* start from where you are and grow to where you want to be. Anxiety about the risks inherent in business is natural. But the real objective of the entre-preneur is to *manage* risk, not to *take* risk.

Everybody manages risk every day. For example, statistics indicate that the risk of having a home fire during a lifetime is very high. Some people sensibly manage this risk by installing smoke and heat detectors, checking the batteries periodically, keeping an escape ladder in the hall closet, devising and rehears-ing an escape plan with the kids, having surge protectors for major appliances, and so on. This is thorough risk management.

Other people just install a smoke detector and forget about it. They are managing the risk to a lesser degree.

Still others do nothing at all. They *take* the risk.

The successful entrepreneur deals with carefully calculat-ed, measured risk. He demands accurate, complete information from associates and advisers and welcomes input and ideas from credible sources. But he also knows when to stop and avoid the paralysis of never-ending analysis.

There's a balance between two little and too much caution. In J.R.R. Tolkien's book *The Hobbit,* the wizard Gandalf offers Bilbo Baggins an opportunity to go on a great adventure with the potential of acquiring great riches at the end. Bilbo responds with his perspective on adventures: "Nasty disturbing uncomfortable things! Make you late for dinner."

Somewhere between the extremes of unbridled risk and Bilbo's total aversion to adventure you will find your balance as an entrepreneur. As you gradually develop that sense of balance as a risk manager and decision maker, you'll find that you can function without much stress or anxiety.

As an aside, let me give you an important observation about how entrepreneurs get into trouble more often than not: failing to gather readily available information before making decisions and commitments. As a consultant, I can usually stump most clients with just three questions about the history of their planned business ventures. Very few people bother to do any homework. They merely have an idea and act on it, like a child grabbing candy from a grocery store shelf on impulse.

I'm unceasingly amazed at the people who start businesses without even studying the history of the industry they've chosen to enter. Far too many entrepreneurs fritter away far too much time needlessly inventing and experimenting when they could be implementing, because they don't know much about anything that happened before yesterday!

Information gathering is a very important task for the entrepreneur. I realize it sounds dull, feels slow, but nevertheless, the quality of information you amass and consider will have a great deal of impact on the outcome of your decisions. At www.NoBSBooks.com/free, I've posted A *Guide to Research Sources for Entrepreneurs,* which you can download free of charge. It's on the internet so we can periodically update it.

BIG LIE: The Price of Entrepreneurial Success Is Just Too Much to Pay

For some, that's a true statement. For others, it's a big lie. There are some people who really will be happier and more productive in non-entrepreneurial roles. But there's also great misunderstanding about the price of success.

Every lifestyle, every choice has its price. The person who follows the old model of staying in a good job with a good company for 40 years pays the price in boredom, frustration, and quiet desperation of unfulfilled, untested potential. Today, people who try to stay with that model often pay an even higher price: after many years of service, a merger, acquisition, down-sizing, bankruptcy, or even disappearance of an entire industry puts long-time employees out on the street. They must tackle a dynamic, tough job market with outdated skills and face the future without the financial security they believed was guaranteed to them for their loyalty and longevity. Entrusting your success to others in corporate bureaucracies is increasingly risky business.

Then there are the legions of "gray people." I don't mean aging; I mean pallid, pasty, near dead looking. Every morning they march off to a job they have no interest in doing well and derive nothing from but an unsatisfactory paycheck. Every night they come home bored and boring. The price they pay is huge, but it is a slow, almost invisible dying. If you look close, though, you can see it in their eyes.

Yes, entrepreneurial life exacts a high price. Often in ways everyone around you dislikes intensely. As chief cook and bottle washer, you've got nobody to call in sick to. While the employee leaves at 5:00 whether work is done or not, you can't; if there's a deadline looming, you must meet it, even if that means skipping dinner, your kids' school recital, sleep.

In one interview, the daughter of Dave Thomas, founder and developer of the Wendy's fast food chain, was asked if her father came to her school events. She said she doubted if he even knew where her school was! Yes, the entrepreneur's family pays a price too.

However, I know plenty of fathers who are physically home every night and every weekend but mentally and emotionally elsewhere. Or who are constantly concocting excuses to get away from their families. Like golf, a game that clearly would never have been invented if marriage hadn't been invented first.

The reality is this: you don't get to choose a life without a price. There are options, but each has a different price.

There are two sides to the price of entrepreneurship. As an example, consider illness or death in the family. My father was ill in his later years, and there was some real risk he might be suddenly rushed to the hospital and die without much warning. I knew, if I was en-route to a speaking engagement or in a distant city honoring a speaking commitment, that I would not "stiff" the seminar promoter; I would honor my contractual commitment and my father would wait. That never happened. When the time came that he was rushed to the hospital, I was able to drop what I was doing, buy a ticket without blinking, and fly across country for a good, lengthy final visit. I also supported him financially, entirely, for over ten years.

The person in a "normal" job gets family leave. The entrepreneur does not. The employee has one boss, the entrepreneur many. In many ways, it is easier for the employee to do the things in family life generally regarded by most people as correct and appropriate, but it is quite often the "odd man out" entrepreneur in the family that everyone else turns to, to get out his checkbook and pay the bills the others can't. His willingness to pay the price for entrepreneurial success is what makes it possible for him to pay the tab in family crisis or tragedy. When financial crisis arises in the family, nobody calls the *poor* relative.

The upshot of this is, you the entrepreneur must be prepared for, and be rather thick-skinned toward, the criticism of the non-entrepreneurs in your life about the price they perceive you pay for your success.

The Decision of Autonomy

When you depend on others, you collect and store up excuses for failure like Harry does. Harry doesn't like his too-small, indisrepair house. He doesn't like his five-year-old, mechanically ailing car. He doesn't like the pile of bills in the kitchen drawer. He hates his job. He doesn't respect his boss. But wait, the one thing he does have going for him is a book of excuses. He opens it up and sighs with relief: *This sorry state of affairs isn't my fault. My mother liked my brother more and that gave me an inferiority complex. We grew up on the wrong side of the tracks. My family couldn't afford to send me to college. . . .* And on and on and on.

This is called burying yourself in B.S. If you really want to be a success in business, you need to be *emotionally* independent before you can ever become *financially* independent.

To succeed as an entrepreneur, you must set aside your neediness for acceptance from others. Immunity to criticism is a "secret" shared by <u>all</u> the highly successful entrepreneurs that I know.

To succeed as an entrepreneur, you have to set aside your "Book of Excuses" once and for all. Making money as an entrepreneur and making excuses are mutually exclusive, wholly incompatible.

I feel fortunate to have discovered a lot about this very early in life.

If I ever got an allowance, it stopped when I was still a little kid. I don't remember it. I do remember earning my spending money very early on. I picked strawberries and packaged tomatoes at the greenhouses behind our community, cleaned stalls at a nearby stable, and washed and waxed cars. I soon figured out that selling was easier than manual labor. So I spent my teen years selling. I sold business printing and advertising specialties, Stuart McGuire shoes, a new plasticized, reusable carbon paper, and became involved in a multi-level marketing company.

In my early experiences in direct and multi-level sales, I quickly found out that most of my distributors (even though they were 5 to 25 years older and more "mature" than I was) could not be relied on even to have the appropriate literature, samples, and other materials with them at presentations! If I wanted prospects handled properly, I had to take steps to make up for the others' lack of organization, discipline, and reliability; I had to have extra supplies on hand. This business taught me the importance of self-reliance, and the futility of relying on others.

The sooner you arrive at accepting 100% responsibility for everything, the more successful you'll be. Go take a look in the mirror. There's the man or woman—the *only* man or woman— who can make you happy, thin, rich, famous, or whatever it is that you aspire to. Dr. Phil can't *make* you thin, McDonalds doesn't *make* you fat.

The power you need and can have as an entrepreneur comes from eschewing all excuses. Never blaming the economy, the government, the competition, the timing, your parents, your school, or anything or anyone else for anything. Ultimate power comes from accepting total responsibility. When you believe as I do that circumstances control other people but not me, then circumstances won't control you either.

A very common occurrence in America in recent years has been Wal-Mart coming into a town, and lots of little mom-n-pop businesses rolling over and dying. Their owners blame Wal-Mart. There have been protest marches. Books written. Much hand wringing about behemoth Wal-Mart destroying small businesses left and right. All utter and total B.S. And here's the proof: there are small businesses who have thrived when Wal-Mart came to their towns. Why? Because they didn't embrace the excuse for failure. They re-engineered their businesses to do what the giant won't, to compete in a different way.

Bill Glazer, President of Glazer-Kennedy Insider's Circle™, is a case in point. In his former life, he was a retailer. When he began, in downtown Baltimore there were 14 competing menswear stores, each independently owned. As giant national chains entered the market, 13 of those stores closed. The last store standing, one of two thriving stores owned by Bill, ably withstood heavy, direct competition from the giant discounter, Mens Wearhouse. In fact, his stores enjoyed double-digit annual growth while his industry went flat, and his stores consistently generated per square foot profits 250% higher than the industry average. How could this be?

For one thing, Bill is an ingenious, aggressive marketer, who violated his industry norms, made extensive use of direct-mail, and overall developed such unique and effective marketing he was able to package it and sell it to thousands of other retailers for their use. Another, he is extremely disciplined, so he insisted on his salespeople performing; booking appointments by phone with customers rather than standing around waiting and hoping for somebody to walk in. But possibly of greater significance is his *attitude* about competition, his conviction that he can always reposition his own business and out-maneuver the big behemoths or anyone else. He approached his business from the standpoint of someone totally and completely in control of results—not someone with results subject to the control of others.

Entrepreneurial success requires a very, very strong sense of autonomy. My dictionary says "autonomy" means "self-governing." Simple. Good. It says a lot.

Free Gift

Bill contributes to my *No B.S. Marketing Letter* and all other Glazer-Kennedy resources, and provides expert coaching to our Members on "outrageous advertising that is outrageously successful." You can meet Bill via one of the FREE Webinars provided to new Members, as part of my FREE GIFT to readers of this book. The complete offer is on pages 272–273 or you can go directly to FreeGiftFrom.com/business.

For example, it says you make your own rules. You feel free to ignore or violate or, at the very least, challenge and test all established norms of your industry. To ignore competitive pricing and, instead, devise a marketing system that has you selling in a competitive vacuum—which happens to be my specialty as a marketing strategist and consultant. You decide to do business on your terms, to fit your preferences, which I talk a lot about in this book's sister-book, *No B.S. Time Management for Entrepreneurs.* It says you organize and operate your business to meet your objectives, to suit your preferences, as discussed in great depth in *No B.S. Ruthless Management of People and Profits.* Andrew Carnegie, one of America's first from-scratch billionaires and the inspiration for the all-time bestselling book on success, *Think and Grow Rich,* spoke of the need for a secret sense of superiority. The sense that ordinary rules and restrictions are for ordinary people, not you. This explains why so many super-successful entrepreneurs quite literally change the entire industry or profession they are a part of.

It also means you govern your own thoughts and emotions, and do not let others dictate how you should think or what you should believe.

The truly legendary mega-entrepreneurs I admire and have studied exhaustively were or are intensely self-governing.

Walt Disney, for example, violated the established, universal, ironclad amusement park industry "rule" of multiple entrances and exits. Against all expert advice, he designed Disneyland with but one entrance and egress. Although he did not do so for purely mercenary reasons, it's impossible to estimate the enormous volume of souvenir merchandise sales that occur precisely because everyone must "walk the plank" past the stores and merchandise carts to get out of the park. In many other ways, as Disneyland, then Disney World developed, Walt insisted on building based on his beliefs, often in direct opposition to how things had always been done before.

Walt was one of the great "Unreasonable Men"—a description that fits most terrific entrepreneurs. My friend and speaking colleague, Mike Vance, who worked closely with Walt for many years, tells the true story of Walt being told by a waitress that "something didn't seem right" about the Bayou Restaurant—then abruptly shutting the entire thing down, shooing away all but a few of the customers, sacrificing revenue and creating havoc, then conducting an impromptu focus group to get to the bottom of what "didn't seem right." It turned out to be the absence of fireflies, which Walt demanded be fixed by importing fireflies. Time and time again Walt drove his bean-counter brother crazy, demanding things be done, often expensive and difficult things, to achieve the exceptional authenticity the parks are famous for.

Walt put Disneyland in a location no one thought could possibly work.

The cliché "he walks to the beat of his own drum" applied magnificently to Walt. As it does to Trump.

Donald Trump is so famous he needs only one name, Trump. Like Cher. Most established experts in commercial real estate development avoid branding their properties with their name, as the traditional industry belief has been that doing so made it difficult to attract top tenants or to later sell the property. Trump has been sharply criticized and ridiculed for slapping his own name on every building he develops. However, he says that as soon as the Trump name goes up on one, its value pops up by 10% to 15%. Trump is much maligned, criticized, made fun of, and has certainly had his downs as well as ups, but he has also made himself fabulously wealthy and into a famous and valuable brand.

> "Sam Walton was less afraid of being wrong than any man I've ever known."
>
> —DAVID GLASS, RETIRED CEO, WAL-MART

GKIC Invitations

Invitations to Glazer-Kennedy events like the ones featuring George Ross from The Trump Organization and Ivanka Trump, Gene Simmons of KISS, Peter Shea of Entrepreneur Media, etc. are available to Members. The entry door is at www.FreeGiftFrom.com/business. Discussions about my books that I had with Kristi Frank from *The Apprentice* can be viewed on-demand at www.NoBSBooks.com.

I appeared as a speaker on a program with The Donald, and we have had his right-hand man and chief negotiator, George Ross, Ivanka Trump, and Bill Rancic and Kristi Frank, competitors from *The Apprentice*, as speakers at Glazer-Kennedy Insider's Circle™ annual SuperConferences. I have quizzed them all for insider info and insight, with all the answers verifying my observation that Donald Trump is autonomy on steroids.

Men like these *are* self-governing. They break rules, re-write rules with impunity, daring and, often, even arrogance. With some it is blatantly apparent. With others, masked—such as with Buffett.

This attitude can have its costs. It is, itself, risk—risk of embarrassment and humiliation, risk of accumulated envious and resentful enemies eager to celebrate a fall. But this attitude seems at the core of every extraordinarily successful entrepreneur I know. Many could easily be clinically diagnosed as narcissists and have considerable difficulty with relationships. Most live with constant peer disapproval, criticism, and conflict. This is the price tag of so consistently getting their own way and getting things accomplished beyond the bounds—often even beyond the imaginations—of 99.9% of the population around them.

Mental Toughness Required

The autonomy you develop will stand you in good stead when your business hits some of the rough roads. Which it will.

One sad truth about business is that you never finish with the same people you start with. Partners, friends, key employees, and others will fall by the wayside for one reason or another as you go along. You will outgrow some. Others will become jealous and resentful of you. I can assure you that, at some point, you will have to make a decision that will be very unpopular with everybody around you. Then you will ultimately decide that the only indispensable person in your business is you.

Recently, a member of one of my coaching groups came to grips with his need to get rid of a soured employee. He procrastinated for over a year, tolerating her bad attitude, sabotage of his authority with other employees, and almost constant criticism of his ideas. He argued with me that she was indispensable. She'd been with him for 13 years, knew his business inside and out. She managed the office, interacted with clients, and he relied on her daily. He had erred in letting this one person become so apparently indispensable, but it ultimately turned out she wasn't quite as indispensable as she or he thought. In the two months immediately following her departure, the number of new clients dramatically increased, revenues increased, other employees stepped up to the plate. She had been blocking the flow of money into the business just as surely as if a giant boulder had been placed in the doorway. This is a situation all too common; the business owner reluctant to rid his business of a person who has long ago morphed from asset to liability. Turning blind eye and deaf ear to this is mental *weakness*.

I once had to end a 5-year relationship with a business partner who had been my closest, best friend. At another time, an 11-year working relationship with a lawyer who had become a friend and who had gone through many battles with me also had to be ended. I've had to fire long-time employees who I liked personally. And

I've had to put my foot down, have a confrontation, and endure temporary anger and tension in the work environment. But, ultimately, business cannot be run by committee or consensus. You're it. Being *it* is not always fun. But always necessary.

I have also fired clients, and encourage my clients to let exceptionally troublesome or unprofitable customers go. I have killed pet projects, and encourage my clients to welcome the swift sword; to get out of bad situations sooner rather than later, with only egg on their faces and disappointment in their minds rather than blood all over the floor and a gaping hole in the bank account. Any mental weakness, squeamishness, hesitation, or procrastination over tough decisions will be costly and can be fatal. One of the worst things you can possibly do in business is be late.

Hey, That's Not Fair!

A lot of people respond to their various handicaps, problems, and disappointments with the complaint "It's just not fair." And it sure isn't. For starters, we don't get to pick our parents. There's a flaw in the system right there! Next, most of us aren't movie-star gorgeous. The U.S. tax system is grossly unfair to small business owners and job-creators. And we're being threatened with that being made worse. Often, business owners are confronted by unfair competition on a slanted playing field here at home and in the global marketplace. Injustice abounds. But all this pales in comparison to the biggest injustice and mystery of all, the frequency with which bad things happen to good people.

Donald R., an honor student, a considerate, courteous young man, and talented athlete, had an accident on the high school trampoline, landed on his back across the frame, and wound up paralyzed in both legs and in both arms for life. He had to make a choice. He could have retreated into isolation, devoted his life to self-pity and bitterness, and lived as a helpless invalid. Most people would have been sympathetic. What happened to him was so unfair. Instead, Donald R. learned to focus the entire force of his personality through his voice so he could use the telephone, the only tool that lets him travel anywhere in the world while wheel-chair bound, to become an enormously successful businessman.

At first dialing with a pencil clenched in his teeth, he became one of the most proficient telemarketers in his chosen industry. He supported himself with dignity. He made the money to have a beautiful home custom built with every imaginable conven-ience and gadget to help him function as if he wasn't handi-capped. He became an inspiration to others in his field and to other handicapped people. He was influential in his community, generous to good causes, completely productive, and proud. He enjoyed an active social life and a happy marriage.

There is no argument that Donald got dealt a lousy hand. Bad things *do* happen to good people, and sometimes we have little or no control over such things. However, we *can* control our reactions to the cards we are dealt. After Donald had his accident, he dumped a few cards, drew a few new cards, and changed his hand by choice. I knew Donald personally many years ago, when I was in direct sales, and marveled at the decisions he made, the autono-my he insisted on, the success he achieved. When you think about what stops most people in their tracks and ends most people's ambitions, Donald's obstacles were Mt. Everest vs. others' pebbles.

For several years, I appeared on a number of seminar-events where Christopher Reeve was another of the speakers. Imagine suddenly being dealt his hand. Going from a physically impos-ing, athletic, dynamic actor known to many as "Superman" to someone completely immobilized, wheelchair captive, totally dependent. He still chose to pursue a multi-faceted career as a professional speaker, author, actor, and producer, even though the very act of getting out of bed was a Herculean project. He is no longer with us, but in the years he was, he organized an important nonprofit organization that continues his advocacy, compelling the medical establishment to reluctantly reconsider its position on certain spinal cord injuries as irreversible, and promoting research needed to find new treatments, cures, and technologies for persons with such injuries.

That's why there are always people who pull themselves out of the worst ghettos in America to become successful, prominent businesspeople, top athletes, and good family men and women. Oprah Winfrey is just one example of someone who proves this point. She emerged from the horror of child abuse; she began her career inauspiciously, but made herself into the top female talk show host in America, a talented actress, and a savvy entrepreneur. This is why we can never accept the idea that success is predetermined by genetics, upbringing, environment, or education. It's why it is so hard to gift success. Because decisions made have more impact than any other factor.

We choose our reactions. We decide what happens next. Complaining, whining, and proclaiming the unfairness of the situation does nothing to improve it.

I'm sort of an unjustified success. I'm woefully unqualified for just about everything I do.

As I recall, I got a C in high school speech class and probably deserved worse. I had a rather severe stuttering problem three different speech therapists failed to cure. If you had seen me stuttering and stammering as a kid, you wouldn't have wagered a nickel on my future as a professional speaker. Incredibly, I rose to success and prominence, including ten consecutive years on the biggest, seminar tour in America, a tour envied by other speakers that included dozens of cities each year, audiences as large as 35,000, and appearances with former U.S. Presidents, world leaders, Hollywood celebrities, famous athletes, and other top speakers. By any reasonable appraisal, I didn't belong there. I chose to be there.

The fact that I earn a large income as a writer would be a heart attack-sized surprise to my English and journalism teachers. In total, I've had 13 books published. My first business book, *The Ultimate Sales Letter,* has become something of a bible for advertising copywriters, and has been continuously available in bookstores since 1991. That kind of longevity is rare. My books have been translated in 8 different languages, published in 21 different countries.

Over the years I've talked to a lot of people *thinking about* writing a book. Many hold back because they feel they aren't qualified. That's a double whammy; a self-image deficiency, and an inaccurate appraisal of the way the marketplace works. Others have written books but not done what is necessary to market them. Mostly, everybody's waiting for somebody else to discover them, certify them, anoint them, invest in them instead of deciding to make what they want to happen, happen.

I'm also responsible for the sale of tens of millions of dollars of merchandise each year through the advertising that I create, but I have no formal training in that field. As a direct-response advertising copywriter, I've earned over a million dollars a year in fees and royalties year after year. How did that happen? Choice.

I could go on with other resume items, all the result of decision, not of qualification.

Personally, I prefer being an unjustified success rather than a justified failure.

For years, one corner of my office was graced by a huge, stuffed Yogi Bear. He was there to remind me of his favorite saying: "I'm smarter than the average bear." He was lost in a cross-country move somehow, but the choice remains: to be smarter than the average bear. I'm not necessarily better educated, or better qualified, or better capitalized, or better connected. But "street-smarter." Go-ahead, I say, run your best at me. I'll keep figuring out new ways to win faster than anybody else can manufacture new obstacles! *That* is the attitude of the entrepreneur who makes it big.

Some cynic once said, "There is no justice. Only power." As an entrepreneur, you have tremendous opportunity to acquire the power of control over all aspects of your life. I'm not talking about the kind of power you lord over everybody, bullying power, brute power. I mean the power to arrange your life as you desire it to be. To associate with people you really enjoy and benefit from being with, to earn an income truly commensurate with your contributions, to live where you most want to live, to travel or to stay home. Your finances are not controlled by some corporate bureaucracy or the whim of a boss. You write your own paycheck.

I have, for example, arranged my business affairs so that I can take many mini-vacations, linked to business travel, as well as extended vacations without worry. I can work at home and let my office run itself. I never have to sit in rush-hour traffic. I get to pick and choose clients and projects. I can demand all my clients travel to me, so I am in the home city where I stable and race my horses, so I can drive professionally in over 100 harness races a year. When most business owners hear this and get to see "inside" the way I conduct my business, they instantly produce the list of 99 reasons why they could never create such autonomy for themselves. Sadly, the ability to create that list is of only minimum wage value. An idiot could create *that* list. Given enough time, a monkey with a typewriter might. It's the person who decides to create the strategic plan for getting what he really wants in life via his business that stands apart from the masses and therefore becomes powerful, independent, and rich.

You get power by deciding to have power.

Renegade Millionaire System

A much more in-depth, advanced discussion of autonomy is included in my Renegade Millionaire System. For information, visit www.RenegadeMillionaire.com.

CHAPTER 2

THE *REAL* ENTREPRENEURIAL EXPERIENCE: CODE RED

I'm only an average man, but, by George, I work
harder at it than the average man.

—THEODORE ROOSEVELT

The entrepreneur suffers more bureaucratic fool-
ishness than you can possibly imagine until you deal
with it firsthand. As an entrepreneur, you are drafted
into service without compensation as a bookkeeper and tax col-
lector for at least three different governments (federal, state, city)
and for at least a dozen different taxes, some dealt with twice
monthly, some monthly, some quarterly, and some annually.
There is nothing that politicians and bureaucrats understand less
or that costs and frustrates entrepreneurs more than this enslave-
ment to government.

Some years ago, I had one friend, an owner of a small retail
business, who got so angry over all this that one day, when his
mail was filled with more letters from government agencies than

anything else, he had a heart attack, tax notice clutched in hand.

Former Senator and Presidential candidate George McGovern bought a bed-n-breakfast as a retirement adventure. Subsequently, in an article he wrote for *Inc.* magazine, he confessed that he was overwhelmed with the nonsensical, outrageous government interference in his business. He said, had he understood this when in the U.S. Senate, he'd have voted very differently on a large number of issues and laws. McGovern subsequently filed bankruptcy and publicly blamed much of it on the burdens government layered on his business. He even noted: "A critical promotional campaign never got off the ground because my manager was forced to concentrate for days at a time on needlessly complicated tax forms for both the IRS and the state of Connecticut."

This points out the fatal flaw of a noncitizen government, taken over by professional politicians lacking real world experience.

If you've read Ayn Rand, as most entrepreneurs have and all entrepreneurs should, you can certainly see the events of her visionary novel *Atlas Shrugged* marching toward us with frightening and depressing speed and apparent inevitability. Very recent events have made this book much more timely— and frightening. But its underlying message is that those of us who choose to be the producers of wealth and creators of business better shed any thoughts of appreciation or even fair treatment by the government or the population at large we support, and live as we see fit for our own satisfactions. We should expect and accept undue interference and opposition as the reality and recognize it is our willingness to triumph against it—a willingness most couldn't muster on their best day—that makes our success possible.

As entertainment, at the conclusion of this chapter, you'll find a "legal document" that I created and published in my *No B.S. Marketing Letter.* Feel free to copy it and share it with any other business owner you think might enjoy it. It speaks to the litigious and regulatory intensive environment in which we operate. A little entrepreneurial humor.

Government interference and idiocy—tax upon tax, regulation upon regulation—is only one of the many severely annoying, emotionally challenging distractions from productivity that the entrepreneur confronts hour by hour, day by day. There are also employee problems, vendor problems, financing problems, customer problems, and competitor problems. On top of all that, there are the times when nothing's going right and red ink is flowing all over the checkbook like blood.

How You Respond to Pressure Determines Your Success. High Tolerance for Stress and Pain Is a Skill Successful Entrepreneurs Are Paid For.

You might think entrepreneurs are paid for creating or inventing, making or providing exceptionally appealing products or needed and valued services, or for managing and growing and expanding their businesses effectively, or for building up equity within a business. But these achievements are actually possible only for the entrepreneur who masters the management of problems. Who can, again and again, pass the tests of creativity and will placed before him.

Almost every legendary entrepreneur is severely tested at one time or another, one way or another.

When I interviewed Tom Monaghan of Dominos Pizza years ago, he talked about going from "entrepreneurial wiz kid" to "village idiot" overnight. Trump has nearly gone broke more than once. Bill Gates spent years mired in federal anti-trust litigation. Should you attempt anything of real significance or expansiveness, you too will be tested.

In The New Economy, the tests will come more frequently, more quickly, more furiously. Regulatory changes took away telephone prospecting and a large part of tele-marketing, broadcast faxing, and broadcast voice messaging or "robo-calling," all marketing media relied on by hundreds of thousands of businesses—and some businesses did not survive the loss or never recovered from it. As I write this, at least 11 states' legislators are contemplating do-not-mail regulations similar to the do-not-call laws, these laws are potentially paralyzing to businesses' growth and outreach to new customers. A change in federal law streamlining the unionization of workers in smaller businesses is gaining steam in Congress; local laws placing all sorts of food ingredient restrictions and disclosure requirements on restaurants are proliferating; and I could go on and fill ten pages with the list of other threats. Add to this the constant, rapid changes in technology, fast-changing consumer demands, the commoditization of product and service categories by the internet, liberalizing of global trade thus multiplying imported goods in every imaginable category—even food. Again, I could continue. **The New Economy Entrepreneur lives in a heightened, high-threat environment.** If the government had a color-coded chart for it, every day would be Code Red.

> "The only thing you can be certain of in business is that problems you have not thought of are headed your way."
>
> —MARK BURNETT, CREATOR OF SURVIVOR AND THE APPRENTICE; AUTHOR, JUMP IN!—EVEN IF YOU DON'T KNOW HOW TO SWIM

To be very candid, I am pleased that I have done most or all of my creating and building and have accumulated sufficient wealth that I do not need new earned income. One of the few good things about approaching 60 wealthy, instead of being 30 years old, is that I will not be battling to build businesses in the current and foreseeable conditions, which I view as more difficult and daunting than any I dealt with. I do not envy the entrepreneur on his way up. The New Economy Entrepreneur will, in my opinion, have far greater need—and more daily need—for extreme mental and emotional toughness and resilience than his predecessors. I pride myself in being a "stress camel"—able to endure enormous heat and keep moving forward over great distance without even a sip of relief. You'd better be. To say something encouraging, The New Economy also offers opportunities that are greater than ever, media and technology conducive to faster speed of startup and growth than anything that existed before, and a no-boundaries marketplace accessible to all. But with that comes a whole new level of threat, hazard, and pressure. How you personally respond to threat, hazard, pressure, and crisis will have a great deal to do with your success.

A while ago, one of my long-time clients had built up a $20-million-a-year-plus company, but through a sequence of mis-judgments, others' greed, partner disputes, and attempting to go public, he lost control not only of his own company but all the intellectual properties he had personally created over a decade that made the business possible. Ultimately, he was unceremoni-ously escorted by security guards out of his own building.

While many would panic or rail against the injustice or roll up in a ball and die, he is a true entrepreneur. He methodically went to work on the problems, but also instantly went to work creat-ing an entirely new business, new products, new opportunities. He operated simultaneously on multiple tracks, all aimed at the same chief objectives. In only a few months, he had settled the dispute, re-acquired all his products and publishing rights, and developed a new, fast-growing, much more profitable company.

I think one of the secrets to success is that, no matter what, you have to crawl out from under, set aside, and ignore all the bureaucratic B.S., the million little irritations and problems, even crisis in order to keep the process of getting, serving, and satisfy-ing customers as your number-one priority. This is easier said than done. There's so much of the other that entrepreneurs and their typically small, over-worked staffs can too easily fall into the trap of viewing the customer as an interruption and obstacle to getting the necessary work done.

Sometimes, when the problems are overwhelming, resilience and determination are the only resources and pride is the only immediate reward. You'll be hard pressed, for example, to find an entrepreneur who hasn't had the experience of meeting the payroll by the skin of his teeth, having nothing left over to take home to the family, having to tell the kids they can't afford this or that, taking calls at home from personal bill collectors, and then lying awake at night, staring at the ceiling, wondering if, at next paycheck time, it will be any different. But pride can keep you going. And keeping going is the only way to get anywhere!

There is the axiom: it is difficult to remember your objective of draining the swamp when you are up to your ass in alligators. But that is exactly what is required of the entrepreneur.

Even when I was at the helm of an ill-advisedly acquired, deeply troubled, money hemorrhaging, chaos and crisis riddled corporation, I pulled myself out of the alligator-fighting for at least one hour every day, to re-focus on the objectives, to get something done that was positive and productive and goal directed.

Take a Trip Down Lonely Street

Whether you're winning or losing at the moment, the isolation of the entrepreneurial experience is surprising and dangerous.

For some, the loss of social community is significant. This was expressed in an article in *Entrepreneur* magazine by Beverly Bernstein, who left a job with Mattel Toys to start her own consulting business. After two years, her business was booming and she was earning twice her old salary, but she missed the camaraderie of the corporate workplace. "When you start your own business, you don't have the same collegial relationships as when you work inside a company," Beverly explained. "I missed the laughter and the interchange of ideas. I missed the energy. And I miss them." The danger in this is hiring people you can't really justify having, hiring friends or making employees into friends.

For many, the absence of "sounding boards" produces uncertainty, self-doubt, indecisiveness, and procrastination. The entrepreneurs in my coaching groups have always talked about the isolation they often feel. They lament having no one of like mind and common understanding to test their ideas on, brag to about their victories to or to discuss their problems with, and cite that as a great benefit of being in one of my groups. They can't have open and frank discussions that, in any way, reveal anxiety or weakness with employees or associates, nor can they too happily celebrate their successes. Civilians, i.e., nonentrepreneurs, can't understand them at all.

Even isolation inside a business or its industry or profession can be creatively paralytic. Too often, the owners of hardware stores only attend conferences with other retailers, only read their industry's trade journals, only pay attention to what their direct competitors and peers are doing. If they grow their company, they tend to hire people with experience inside their industry. All this reinforces the way things are and avoids questioning it. Specific to marketing, I call it "marketing incest," and tell people it works just like real incest; with each generation, everybody gets dumber. And dumber.

As an employee, many decisions are made for you, many more are arrived at through consensus. A social environment with friendship is provided. And, at the end of the day, if there's work yet undone, in most cases, you go home, shrug it off on the way, and pretty much ignore it. All that changes dramatically when you own the business. I doubt there's anything as totally absorbing as the entrepreneurial experience. Pro athletes and their coaches certainly live their businesses, but they have off days, even off seasons, and rest periods. They get paychecks and they don't have to worry about attendance, network viewership, merchandise sales, and budgets. The entrepreneur has to play the game *and* run the business.

It's even difficult to maintain your regular social life. People you used to enjoy getting together with suddenly seem different; their concerns and conversations trivial; their daily experiences so different from yours that there's no longer any common ground. In many cases, their attitudes are so different from yours you can't afford to be around them. Bill Glazer, President of Glazer-Kennedy Insider's Circle™, says that the entrepreneur is the loneliest person in the world. He knows. He's been one his entire life, and has coached and consulted with thousands.

In The New Economy, this isolation can be harder to bear emotionally, as the pressures are greater; more hazardous intellectually, as the pace of change is accelerating and the need for legitimate ideas and information accelerating with it.

One way or another, the successful entrepreneur carefully forms and maintains alliances and associations that give him some relief from the loneliness of his role and access to open exchange of ideas and experiences. This is not new. Industrial revolution leaders like Carnegie, Edison, Firestone, and Ford created formal "master-mind alliances." But it is much more necessary at today's pace than then. Within the Glazer-Kennedy organization, comprising more than 25,000 Members throughout the United States, Canada, and more than a dozen other countries, we facilitate strategic and supportive association as many ways as we can. There are over 150 local Chapters and Kennedy Study/Mastermind Groups meeting regularly, there is an international group (called Peak Performers) coming together for multi-day meetings several times a year, two international conferences that include roundtable discussion groups and meet-the-expert discussion groups, and online communities. In this "place," participating entrepreneurs can be confident of a common ground—understanding and use of my marketing and

You're Invited

If there is a Glazer-Kennedy Insider's Circle™ Chapter meeting in your area, you're invited to obtain a Free Guest Pass and experience a meeting for yourself. I'm confident you'll be impressed with our Certified Independent Business Advisor, the caliber of the business owners participating, and the value of the information, ideas, and training provided. You can find a Directory at www.DanKennedy.com and directly contact the Advisor in your area. Note: this is NOT an ordinary networking group. There's a lot more to this than swapping business cards and giving your "elevator pitch"! This is a multi-faceted support program for entrepreneurs. Also, you can experience all Membership Benefits FREE for a trial period, by registering at www.FreeGiftFrom.com/business.

business methods, and can easily and efficiently meet other entrepreneurs to form on-going relationships and alliances with, drawing on them from all over the country and beyond. In Chapter 47 of my *No B.S. Ruthless Management of People and Profits,* I talk about the six Support Circles every entrepreneur needs; without all the explanation there, I've reproduced the illustration here in Figure 2.1. What we provide to Glazer-Kennedy Insider's Circle™ Members provides Circle #5 and facilitates your development of #2 to #4, to some extent #1, and #6. But you have to make this a priority, to organize your own Support Circles, from all resources and sources that might be available to you.

I'm an Overnight Success—After 30 Years

It is only in the last 20 years that I've experienced substantial, consistently increasing success in my businesses. Most of the

FIGURE 2.1: Support Circles

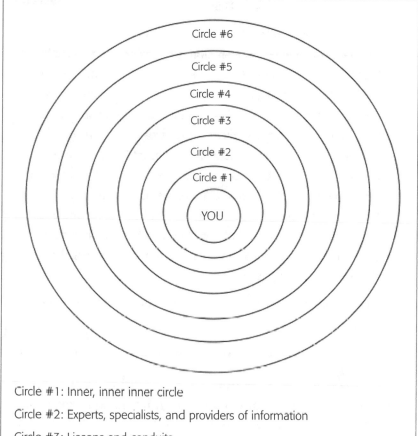

Circle #1: Inner, inner inner circle

Circle #2: Experts, specialists, and providers of information

Circle #3: Liasons and conduits

Circle #4: High performance, high reliability vendors and suppliers

Circle #5: "Looser" group mentors, consultants, coaches, peers, and colleagues

Circle #6: Your Dialogue with the Dead

wealth has been collected only in the past ten. There were many years of struggle. There is a common, popular idea that most entrepreneurs deeply resent: that they are sudden, even

"Blessed"

If you were born in the United States or Canada or another country where free enterprise flourishes, if you were born healthy, you were blessed. But attributing what anyone does with their life to unearned gifts, pre-destiny, divine providence, or random good fortune . . . well, here's a favorite story, in abbreviated form. A minister driving through a rural area on a sunny day comes upon a strikingly beautiful, magnificent farm. Tall rows of corn as far as the eye can see in one direction, lush fields extending to the horizon in the other. The farmer is near the fence, by his tractor, taking a break, so the minister stops his car and goes over to him, on impulse, and says, "Sir, God has blessed you with an extraordinary farm that stands apart from all your neighbors as the crown jewel of this entire area."

"That's true," the farmer said slowly, "but you should have seen this place when He had it all to himself."

overnight successes—ignoring the many years of struggle and sacrifice, of labor in oblivion. If you now make a seven-figure income as I do, you are looked upon by so many as "lucky" and "fortunate" or even "blessed," ignoring the years when there was no luck to be found and an income preceded by a minus sign. Sometimes entrepreneurs going through tough times are discouraged by this. They fall into the trap themselves of thinking that others they see riding high got there easily and quickly, and they wonder "why them and not me?" Truth is, there are virtually no overnight successes. Almost every successful entrepreneur I've ever noticed and researched or gotten to know has been revealed as someone who stumbled and bumbled and crawled through a great deal of darkness before winding up in the spotlight.

In the darkest days, I would run around all day telling employees, associates, vendors, and investors not to worry, that I knew what I was doing, that everything would be okay. Then I would lock myself in the bathroom, look in the mirror, and call myself a liar. Not a day went by that I didn't have to convince myself to continue. I have personally had some very public flops in business. Over the years, getting to work closely with hundreds of from-scratch multi-millionaire entrepreneurs, I've come to realize we all have had those times. You can't afford to fear them or resent them or ever feel you are experiencing them but other successful people have somehow avoided them.

Consider, for example, the speaking career part of my business. From 1991 through 2001, I was one of the featured speakers on tour with famous motivational superstar Zig Ziglar and many "celebrity" speakers on heavily advertised all-day events, addressing tens of thousands of people in each city, in about 25 cities each year, often selling $70,000.00 to $150,000.00 or more of my books and audio learning programs per hour. This contributed to my being sought out and given other top speaking opportunities, helped raise my speaking fees, and made me the envy of many of my peers. As a result, more than one professional speaker has said to me, "You lucky dog."

Attributing it to luck is an insult.

I started speaking in 1977. In one year, I gave free talks, selling tickets to my own seminars, in over 100 real estate, insurance, and other sales offices, often to groups of just 3, 5, or 10 people. Sometimes people were inattentive or downright rude; while I spoke, they answered their phones, read their newspapers, and slurped their coffee. It didn't help any that I wasn't a very good speaker. In my first 10 years of speaking, there were plenty of horror stories. Seminars where hardly anybody showed up and I lost money. Tough, tough audiences. I went on tours of five cities in five days, driving from city to city to make it to each. Grinding, grueling travel. Countless motel rooms with defective air-conditioning, heat, or plumbing. I could go on. But every business has its own version of such an obstacle course, to brutally separate the weak from the strong. Fortunately, I made pretty good money even during the worst of these learning experiences and times required to develop my skills and strategies. I've bought dinner with change scrounged from seat cushions once or twice but I've never gone without dinner.

In publishing, I had two big, costly, painful failures before getting it right the third time. That was with the business built around the *No B.S. Marketing Letter*, which has led to the Glazer-Kennedy Insider's Circle™ empire, on which the sun literally never sets.

It's worth noting that countless great companies built by celebrated entrepreneurs flirted with extinction on at least one occasion while being built. If you devour autobiographies and biographies of great entrepreneurs, as I do, and as I advise, you'll find this very much their shared experience. Federal Express nearly ran out of cash and closed its doors—strung along by pilots using their own credit cards to buy fuel for the airplanes and famously rescued at one point by founder Fred Smith's casino winnings. Newman's Own, the food products company created by actor Paul Newman, that lives on after his death and provides millions to worthy charities, nearly ended before it began, when no company would agree to manufacture or distribute the products—even though Paul obviously brought great star power to the project. Tom Monaghan almost had Dominos Pizza die in his hands—twice.

After all, if it was too easy, everybody'd do it, and it'd be devalued.

Every "overnight success" knows there's no such thing.

Even with Success, There Is Failure

Because the entrepreneur is always innovating, experimenting, and pioneering, there's always failure mixed with success: the new ad, the new products, or the new service that doesn't work—or worse.

A friend of mine, Ted G., sold his company early this year for more than $6 million. He started it ten years ago with $1,000.00. The day he strolled into the bank with the $6 million check, he felt that he was a pretty smart, successful, even heroic fellow. A month later, he put together a seminar, promoted it with a major advertising campaign, and lost about $40,000.00. The three days that he worked, teaching that seminar at a loss, he didn't feel so smart, successful, or heroic.

I know what this is like. In the past, I've gone bankrupt, personally and corporately. I've had my cars repossessed. I've gone from a new Lincoln to a 15-year-old Rent-a-Dent, paid for weekly in cash. I have had so little that had a burglar broken into my apartment, he might have left a donation. As a result of the

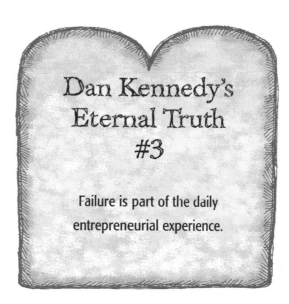

Dan Kennedy's
Eternal Truth
#3

Failure is part of the daily
entrepreneurial experience.

bankruptcies, I was criticized, reviled, and sneered at by professional peers, persecuted by my own trade association, and humiliated beyond belief. To give it all its best spin, let's summarize it as prolonged, profound financial embarrassment.

Today, I say with great gratitude, things are much, much better. But even at the height of success, there's failure. For example, one of the things I do in my direct marketing consulting business is create strategy and write copy for national print ad campaigns, large direct-mail campaigns, even TV infomercials. While my batting average is much better than most, there are still failures before a success—we call those "tests," and sometimes even irredeemable failures. A client may have put up $200,000.00 to $500,000.00 or even more and I may have hundreds of hours invested in a project that tests so miserably there's nothing left to do but dig a large hole in the backyard, shove the work in, say last rites, and walk away. That is not easy to do.

Personally, I can show you a portfolio of print ads that have run profitably, month after month for years; single sales letters

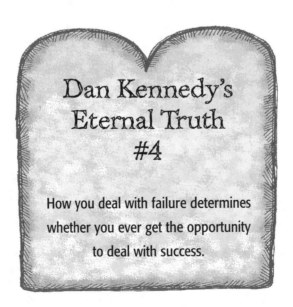

Dan Kennedy's
Eternal Truth
#4

How you deal with failure determines
whether you ever get the opportunity
to deal with success.

that have produced millions of dollars for my companies and for clients; infomercials that have literally made people millionaires. But for every wildly successful project I might show you, there are a number of flops. Almost every success has its foundation parked on a graveyard concealing the bones of failure.

The need to shake it off, regroup, and bounce back, to pick yourself up, dust yourself off, and start all over again, is universal and reoccurring in the entrepreneurial experience.

The flip side, using my speaking business as an example, is standing there on-stage in front of 10,000 people, basking in their laughter and applause, sending them stampeding to the book and resource tables, doing more business in 60 minutes than some stores do in 60 days. In my other businesses, I glory in big orders and unsolicited letters of praise in the mail; planning a new promotion, implementing it, and seeing it work; solving a tough problem; and closing a big sale, negotiating a big contract. My fees often range from $100,000.00 to $1,000,000.00 per project.

I don't think there's anything like the "high" of entrepreneurial success, of taking the germ of an idea and nurturing it, step by step, embellishing it, developing faith in it, implementing it, making it work, and turning it into tangible, substantial rewards. As of this writing, I'm assisting with the development and launch of a nationally franchised chain of upscale men's barber shops using a membership model, which have been christened with my name. The business is Kennedy's All-American Barber Club™ and you can see it at www.KennedysBarberClub.com. My associates and I have every reason to anticipate a huge success and watching that develop will be exciting.

However, there is still the chance of embarrassing failure. The acquisition of the existing shops and their complete makeover to our business model and preparation for franchising required major investment, with franchising beginning against a suddenly, rapidly expanding recession, stock market crash, bank failures, credit crunch, and mass retail store closings turning good, viable retail and mixed use centers from good locations to bad virtually overnight. Not ideal circumstances. But if we pull it off, we will create great businesses, second businesses, and investments for thousands of shop owners, we will make our master-area franchisees rich, we will establish an exciting new concept within its industry, we'll establish a platform—customers in membership in a lifestyle club—on which to grow additional businesses. And we'll have a grand success story. Many will probably call it an overnight success. It will be a thrill. And that is, in large part, what the best of the entrepreneurial experience is: conceiving something, believing in something, and bringing it from idea in womb to life.

It's a kind of glory. Songwriters and musicians talk about the experience of driving down the road, fiddling with the radio, and suddenly hearing their own song come on for the first time. Most pull over to the side of the road and listen in awe to what they've wrought. We entrepreneurs get that same kind of a jolt when we see our commercial on TV, our ad in a magazine, our new storefront, our product on the store shelf. Most people never experience anything like this.

And sometimes you make it big. Imagine being Bill Rosenberg, a high school dropout who started a little business in 1946 with $2,500.00 saved from working 2 or 3 jobs at a time, 7 days a week, 12 hours a day. He has seen his little business grow into the nationwide chain, Dunkin' Donuts®. Imagine the thoughts he has had, seeing another location open. Seeing thousands of franchise owners at their conventions.

Imagine being my clients, Bill Guthy and Greg Renker, now unable to flip through TV channels anywhere in America, anytime day or night, and not land on one of their own infomercials, all combined generating over a billion dollars a year. Their business built by the lowly TV infomercial involves Hollywood celebrities of every generation, from P. Diddy and Jessica Simpson to Vanessa Williams to Victoria Principal and Susan Lucci to Regis Philbin.

They started humbly. Bill was in the audiocassette manufacturing business, making product for others. Neither had any particularly relevant background or experience that would suggest likely success in creating infomercials.

Imagine being my client, Dr. Chris Tomshack, once an ordinary chiropractor who had grown to dislike his practice and consider leaving his profession altogether. Instead, he reinvented almost everything about it, from advertising to operations, and wound up creating such a "perfect practice" it begged to be replicated; he is now CEO of a nationwide organization of over 250 franchised chiropractic and weight loss clinics bearing his HealthSource® brand. Or my client Michael Gravette. In the early days of his business, to save desperately needed money his wife raided dumpsters for empty boxes to pack and ship their products. Today, his company, Safety Technology.com, has thousands of independent distributors, retail locations, and online affiliates selling millions of dollars of his personal, home, and business security products.

This is the glory. But behind virtually every entrepreneurial glory, there's an investment of plenty of blood and guts. Never think otherwise.

What Ultimately Separates Entrepreneurial Winners from Losers?

There's a sign on my office door that reads: "Whatever it takes."

That is the entrepreneur's job description: holding your paychecks; loaning money to your business; working long hours; having to sell and motivate constantly; dealing with bankers, lawyers, unresponsive vendors, and other difficult folks. The list could go on. **Entrepreneurial life is the solving of the never-ending stream of problems**. People who go into business for themselves because they think they will have fewer problems than they had in their previous jobs wear down and wear out quickly.

Carter Henderson, author of the book *Winners*, observed, "To be in business is to be assaulted by relentless adversity and crisis; it comes with the territory." **The characteristic that tends to distinguish the winners from the losers is the relentless conversion of problems to opportunities, negatives to positives.**

Now, I don't mean classic "positive thinking" methodology. I don't believe that whistling in the dark does much to protect you from the bogeyman. If he's there, whistling won't help. For 30 years I've warned people to watch out for the misguided, militant Positive Thinkers who want everyone to be two of the monkeys: See No Evil, Hear No Evil.

That's how you wind up with a Fannie Mae and Freddie Mac and subprime lending collapse, an anvil dropped on your head, all your money stolen, misdiagnosed by doctors, etc.

There's a vast difference between earned, deserved, justifiable optimism and foolish, unwarranted, dangerous optimism. Optimism can be virtue or vice, like most things, depending on application. There are, incidentally, plenty of wildly optimistic people who are always dead broke. The single biggest optimist I have ever known was broke far more than rich, occasionally incredibly successful but unable to sustain it, dangerously denying of reality, completely irresponsible as a business owner and leader of an organization, did five years in a state penitentiary for stubbornness, and is ending his life in a sad state of affairs, estranged from family and friends, and broke. But he was the poster boy of unbridled optimism.

I'm not talking about *that* kind of thinking. Instead I'm talking about an automatic, action-oriented response that instantly dissects crisis and creates new opportunity. That "entrepreneurial reflex" makes all the difference. Will you be dead-tired or energized at the end of every day? Glum and depressed or good-humored and optimistic? Effective or paralyzed? This "reflex" makes those distinctions.

The Good News

As an entrepreneur, you do get a very special entitlement: you can depend on there being a new door to open whenever another door slams shut. In his book *Think and Grow Rich*, Dr. Napoleon Hill wrote: "In every adversity lies the seed of an equal or greater achievement."

Just about every really terrific thing that has occurred for me has come out of something really terrible. You may think I'm being a Pollyanna, but if you will dig for it, you'll find great opportunity in every adversity. In my seminars for entrepreneurs, one of the key principles I teach is:

<u>All</u> News Is Good News.

This is very difficult to accept at face value. Yet, if you closely examine your own history as I have mine, you will probably find as I have that every event that seemed negative or tragic at the time was an essential bridge to something better or to a new opportunity. Entrepreneurs understand this, their "entrepreneurial reflex" of resiliency is based on it. Resiliency is not a character trait that you either have or don't have. It's a cultivated habit of thought and business practice, based on lessons learned from your own past experience and the experience of others. It becomes reflex through repetitive use.

In The New Economy, it will be *the* great divider between the successful and unsuccessful, because more change, more challenge to old ways, more disruption, and, yes, even more crisis is likely to occur more often at a faster pace than ever before. The internet removed all geographic boundaries from business, and that was good news for the woman in the small Iowa town who baked the most amazing molasses brownies but only sold them to a few local restaurants—now she ships them to customers all over the world who order from her website. But the removal of geographic boundaries is a two-way street. It permits every local merchant in that small town to be challenged by distant competitors. The local bookshop is now up against Amazon.com, the shoe store up against zappos.com. And the conventional barriers to business startups that made it possible to garner and protect market share, that made men like Buffett rich by buying good, long-established companies because of that market share, are fast disappearing. This threatens the capture and keeping of "territory." It threatens yours.

If you are successful, you'll get no peace or rest. Somebody will be coming at you every minute. Not just from across town or even across the country but from fast-developing, distant nations teeming with people with unmitigated ambition and new ideas. Add to this, the new power taken by government as its opportunity from crisis, from the recession, to interfere in private industry to an extent and to extremes far beyond anything ever seen or contemplated in this country. This means that things you rely on for advertising, marketing, selling, or satisfying customers or even for your primary competitive edge may be suddenly taken away from you, restricted, taxed excessively, or otherwise interfered with. Do-Not-Call, Do-Not-Fax laws; trans fats bans; all installment finance contract law and its certainty put into question by the Obama administration's empowerment of bankruptcy judges to erase principal balances owed to lenders in mortgages; these are a few fairly recent examples and harbingers of many things to come.

There are also big threats. Consider that the relatively brief, but huge surge in gasoline prices of 2008 almost instantly put a variety of kinds of businesses in extreme financial jeopardy. Or how quickly the recession revealed giant manufacturers, huge banks, name brand retail chains to be houses of cards, dependent on ever escalating debt rather than profits to continue. And the domino effects up and down the food chain and sideways from each of the system shocks we witnessed. Well, the future is pregnant with such threats. We are dependent on others for our oil. A world war might originate from any number of global hot spots. Another, bigger 9-11 or 9-11-like attack on U.S. soil. Such things can drastically alter your customers' behavior, your industry, the economy in a heartbeat. All this makes you a promise: that you will be barraged with more challenges to your business' prosperity and your success, coming at you at a faster pace, from more diverse places than business owners have ever had to cope with before. So entrepreneurial resiliency will be the most valuable of powers.

So here's the resiliency question: **If "X" happened, what would we do?**

Sometimes the answer to that turns out to be superior to your Plan A, in place only because "X" hasn't happened.

Immediately after 9-11, a number of my clients saw business just about halt. Some sat paralyzed and waited for quite some time until their particular customer group returned to its spending and investing. Others were more agile. One was inspired by the necessity, by their phones suddenly not ringing, to make a major shift in their business that has subsequently been worth millions of dollars and made their company infinitely better than what it was, and this is a direction they might never have gone without the impetus of that tragedy.

For years I have operated my office without a receptionist, with limited and controlled "live" access hours thus shielding my staff from constant interruption and dramatically increasing their productivity. However, that all started as "Plan B," when my mother, the receptionist, was hospitalized, then died. As an emergency, temporary measure, we went to Plan B. It quickly became clear Plan B should get a promotion to Plan A. The interesting thing is, I could have been on Plan B at least five, maybe ten years sooner, and used my mother's time and ability as an employee much more profitably, and I wonder how much money was lost/could have been made. Today, and for the past several years, my office phone is *never* answered live.

I got into the coaching business on a serious level as an answer to sacrificing the income from lots of speaking gigs I no longer was willing to travel to do. I did one primarily to replace the income of the other. But couldn't I have done that three, five, seven years earlier, if I'd asked: *if I was confined to a wheelchair and couldn't travel to speak, what would I do?*

It is actually embarrassing to use 20/20 hindsight and see how many times I might have made much faster progress toward my overriding goals by much more frequently using the Plan B question. I suppose it's inspirational, and a wonderful testament to the free enterprise system, that someone as big an idiot as I am can do as well as I have. That's the drawback to writing up information like this; you wind up rubbing your own nose in your idiocy. Not even a dog'll do that.

Anyway, here's the incredibly provocative exercise: 1) make a list of as many individual things you do rote, the person you rely on, the business methods you use, etc.; 2) ask the Plan B question regarding every single one of them; 3) repeat same exercise at least once a year.

FIGURE 2.2: Legal Document

IMPORTANT LEGAL NOTICE

You are about to consume food substances in this restaurant which contain calories, fat, sugar, salt, carbohydrates, artificial flavors, preservatives, and other ingredients which may be, in some way, harmful to your health. Consuming inordinately large quantities of these food substances in this establishment or elsewhere or in combination thereof may make you fat. Consuming spectacularly excessive quantities may, in fact, make you clinically obese or, in plain English, so incredibly fat short people huddle under your blubber as shade on hot days. Also, eating these food substances may contribute to diabetes, cancer, heart disease, blindness, deafness, numbness, and tingling in limbs. You may have allergic reactions to these food substances. You may choke on a sandwich like Mama Cass. In short, eating can kill you any number of ways. It is a dangerous and harmful thing to do. If you consume food substances in this establishment identified as "dessert," these warnings are treble true. Especially dangerous and potentially harmful are desserts identified on our menu as "Chocolate Death Cake" (hint, hint, hint) and "Banana Fudge Mountain." We make no representations whatsoever as to the nutritional value of the food substances we serve; to the contrary, it is our opinion that the food substances we serve have no redeeming nutritional value at all. Further, certain of the food substances we serve have ingredients and/or combinations of ingredients which may be or may in the future be judged to be addictive. The owners, investors, employees of, landlord of, and vendors to this establishment accept absolutely no responsibility or liability for whatever results you may experience as a result of eating here, including but not limited to, obesity and related adverse health conditions. If you have any concerns about these matters, please use your pudgy fingers to push the buttons on your cell phone and consult your physician and/or attorney before eating.

FIGURE 2.2: Legal Document, continued

WAIVER OF LIABILITY

"I, _____, hereby acknowledge that I have read the above Legal Notice carefully and understand it completely, and I certify that I am not an idiot. Further, I warrant that I will not, in any way, at any time, attempt to hold this establishment responsible or liable for any health or medical conditions I may have or develop in the future, including but not limited to obesity and related conditions. I also hereby prohibit any member of my family or any other individual, organization, or entity from attempting to hold this establishment responsible or liable as noted above on my behalf. I firmly and clearly state that I am fully and completely responsible for whatever I pick up and stick into my pie hole."

Signature: _____

Print Name: _____

Witness Signature: _____

Witness Name: _____

Disclaimer: this document is provided for entertainment purposes only, is not intended as a substitute for actual legal advice, and should you need a legal document for this or any other purpose, the services of a competent legal professional should be sought. Its author and/or publisher accepts no responsibility or liability for your use or mis-use of this document provided for entertainment purposes only.

From: www.dankennedy.com

CHAPTER 3

HOW DO YOU KNOW
IF YOU HAVE A REALLY
GOOD IDEA?

A hunting party was hopelessly lost, deep in the woods. "I thought you were the best guide in all of Canada," complained one of the hunters. "I am," said the guide, "but I think we're in Michigan now."

The late Wilson Harrell, entrepreneur and business consultant, had a unique way of testing a new product, service, or business idea. He called it the "Well, I'll be damned!" test. Harrell suggested taking a sample of your idea to at least 20 potential buyers (but not friends, relatives, or neighbors!) to see how they react. If they don't say, "Well, I'll be damned" or "Why didn't I think of that?" you do not have a winner.

If most of the people do say the magic words, ask them other questions such as, What would you be willing to pay for this? If it were available at that price, would you definitely buy it? Maybe buy it? Why? How would you use it? Do they think it's such a good idea they might want to invest in it? Why? Why not?

He described a loose type of "focus group," and it does have value. Even better, I've encouraged inventors to get even a primitive version of their product made, set up at a swap meet, hang a microphone around their neck hooked to a loudspeaker, and try to sell it, just like the slicer-dicer guy does at the county fair. If you can't sell it there, you probably can't sell it on TV or in print ads or off store shelves either.

The point is that, one way or another, you have to get the actual marketplace's assessment, preferably early rather than late, at as little cost as possible.

This brings us to the most important rule of entrepreneurial marketing I can think of:

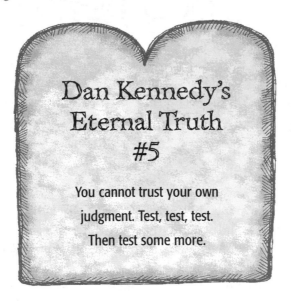

Dan Kennedy's
Eternal Truth
#5

You cannot trust your own
judgment. Test, test, test.
Then test some more.

Are entrepreneurs impatient by nature? Maybe so, but successful entrepreneurs must learn to be patient sometimes. Testing is one of those times. Anytime you can, any way you can, test.

Ask Your Customers

There is a classic story about a famous supermarket, Stew Leonard's, which I recall getting from Tom Peters, author of the now-classic business book, *In Search of Excellence*. As I recall, the supermarket's management regularly met with groups of customers over coffee and doughnuts to ask them what they liked, what they didn't like, what they wanted done differently, what they thought of a new product or service. It was this group that solved a mystery for them and rescued them from their own creative misfire. Customers had expressed a desire for more fresh fish, so the store had ramped up its early morning purchasing of fresh fish from the docks, rushing it to the store, neatly packaging it and displaying it with signage and identifying it as Fresh Fish—but sales did not improve. In conversation with customers, it was revealed that many didn't accept it as Fresh, signage be damned; it didn't look fresh, like at the fish market. So the store created a separate place, with open trays instead of glass cases, beds of ice, the fish not neatly cleaned, not put on trays and wrapped, and sales soared. They had erred in "over-serving" by prettying up and packaging the fish, sanitizing the experience. Now, many years after hearing this story, with a full appreciation for the importance of the buying experience to the customer, I can tell you the problem was twofold. There was the problem of some customers not even believing the fish fresh. But the other, bigger problem is that the customers wanted the experience of picking out fresh fish at the fish market down by the docks, but without having to go down there. The experience you create and deliver matters a whole lot.

The supermarket managers may never have figured this out without direct dialogue with their customers.

This is evermore important. New Economy Customers know they hold the power, they want more than goods and services, and they are most responsive to businesses that treat them as stakeholders not just consumers, who have the ear of the owners, have a say-so in the business, and have their specific needs and interests catered to.

Since many of my clients do business at a distance, they regularly construct surveys and questionnaires to take their customers' pulse. These are not appeasement questionnaires, like the Suggestion Box on the wall covered with cobwebs. These are sincere attempts to collect detailed information from customers that may reveal opportunity. At Glazer-Kennedy Insider's Circle,™ we get a considerable amount of information from the many new Members willing to provide it, via a very detailed survey, which you'll see if you accept my free trial membership offer on pages 272–273. The questionnaire is something of an education itself! We also sometimes survey groups of our Members in advance of all our planning for one of our two annual conferences or for a special event, then we go back to them and say "See, we built what you asked for"—frankly, there's a bit of obligation there, but also a legitimate process of customer input considered and responded to. I call this "build-to-suit" product development.

A major electronics and appliance retailer took the trouble of finding out what his stores' customers liked best and least about buying televisions, stereos, and appliances. One comment was so frequent it stood out like the proverbial sore thumb: people hated having to block a whole day out of their schedules and wait around for the delivery of what they purchased. He developed a system to provide scheduled delivery times guaranteed within a two-hour range. This service became his main advertising promise, with fantastic results. At the time this little retailer reengineered his business and all of his advertising around this single idea, it was daring and new. He checked Yellow Pages ads in 200 cities and couldn't find anyone else doing it. Today it has become something of a norm, and has spread to many other product and service categories. I've noticed a radio ad campaign by a nationally franchised group of plumbing companies—Ben Franklin Plumbing—which promises $5.00 for every minute the plumbing technician is late, so, as the ad says, "if he's 20 minutes late, you get a Franklin. A $100.00 bill with my picture on it." This is powerful because it replaces typically empty advertising promises with something solid.

One of the most important changes in The New Economy is the shift of power back from sellers to customers. The recession made that clear to them. The internet has handed them a way to shop the world, to compare, to find things precisely matched to them and in some cases customized for them. Now, New Economy Customers are increasingly expectant of getting exactly what they want when and how they want it. For example, think about how viewing television programs and movies has changed. Go back. I grew up with three network channels on TV and movies in theaters. Period. Variety came with multiplex theaters vs. one-movie-at-a-time theaters, and with cable. On demand began with video rentals. As I write this, Tivo® and DVR® permits automatically recording and viewing TV programs whenever you wish, cable networks have their shows and movies available in on-demand systems, many TV programs archive shows and additional content online, and video rental has been replaced with instant access via the internet. No one is bound anymore by what the network has put together as tonight's program schedule or by what's at the theater this weekend.

Further, entertainment programming is mobile. I remember lugging a barely portable TV out into the backyard and running an extension cord through the yard and up the side of the house through a window. Today, TV programs and movies are accessible via laptops, handheld devices, cell phones. The trend is clear: entertainment will soon be entirely on demand.

This tells you what New Economy Customers will increasingly expect from all other categories of products and services: Customized. On demand.

Constantly acquiring "intelligence" about your customers' evolving and changing interests, desires, preferences, likes and dislikes, experiences with other businesses, and responding to it with constant change in your own business is The New Economy mandate.

Ask Your Counterparts and Competitors

One of the easiest, quickest research tasks you must do is examine the advertising and marketing of others in your category of business, locally, outside your geography. You'll inevitably find advertisers somewhere doing something nobody in your area is doing, and that should give you some good new ideas. As well, you may also find somebody offering a product or service that you haven't considered. It won't hurt to call them and talk to them about their experiences. You might even go visit them. It wasn't that long ago you *had to go* visit them. I recall a fresh-from-school chiropractor packing his belongings and spending a year on the road, visiting dozens of the offices of the most successful chiropractors in the country, begging to hang out at each one for a week or so, to observe. It's still a fine idea, but you could accomplish a lot of that now by visiting their websites, watching their online video presentations, downloading their free information for patients, attending their live webinars held for patients and prospective patients, and taking the virtual tours of their offices at their websites. There's no excuse not to thoroughly research successful peers in your field.

The same holds true for your direct competitors. You probably can't have a frank and direct talk with them, and pick their brains, but you can check up on them. I'm amazed at the business people who never go to their competitors' stores or buy their products, never visit their websites, never obtain their literature, never "play prospect" and have their salespeople come to call. One of my Members owns the most successful pest control company in his city. Every few months he borrows a house and has his competitors send out their salespeople and technicians and puts one after another through their paces, to see if any of them are doing something smart he isn't, to identify the weaknesses in their prices, offers, presentations that he can exploit. He is not obsessed with or worried about competition, but he is a serious student of his competitors.

Smart Direct-Mail Testing

One of my earlier books, *The Ultimate Sales Letter*, is all about how to create good direct-mail campaigns and sales letters, even if you know nothing about writing. I wrote that book because I believe direct-mail is the very best way most entrepreneurs have available for marketing their products and services, for the simple reason that it is the easiest way to test results.

Other types of advertising are much more difficult to test. How do you test a Yellow Pages ad, for example? That same ad is stuck there for 12 months; you can't change it. The most frustrating thing about producing TV infomercials is the inability to test different ideas, promises, and offers without actually putting together a show at great expense.

Direct-mail offers the unique opportunity to do cheap and very targeted testing. You can tell a lot from tests as small as a few hundred pieces mailed, depending on the market, lists used, and other factors. This means you can "split-test" one letter against another or one offer, price, or premium against another, for just a few hundred dollars. And, once you find a campaign that works, you can keep on testing other variables cheaply and easily, to try and make it better. Best of all, once you find that success formula, you will probably be able to use it to get consistent, successful results for years.

In recent years, other media offering easy and fast split-test opportunities has evolved. If you have a customer or prospect list with e-mail addresses or fax numbers, and the customers' or prospects' permission to contact them, or can joint venture with someone who does, you can conduct a decent split-test dirt cheap in one day's time. It is easy to set up two clone websites, each making an identical offer but with different prices, or each the same except for two different headlines, do an e-mail "blast" inviting people to the site, and have every other visitor directed to version #1 of the site, the alternating visitors directed to version #2. Similarly, you can build a fax, change one variable, Fax half the list version #1, half version #2.

In many instances, if I am trying to first test only the premise; *are they interested in "x" ?* I'll offer some kind of free report, CD, sample, etc. rather than try to sell an actual product. If they won't respond to get it free, they probably won't pay for it either. This allows you to "dry test." For the most part, "dry testing" i.e. offering a product for sale before it has actually been produced and inventoried for instant delivery is illegal. By giving away something free that does exist, you avoid the costs of producing product that may not be saleable and you legally "dry test."

"Steal" Already-Tested Direct-Marketing Strategies

But what if you can't test? First of all, you need to know as much as you can about what works and what doesn't in your particular business. You need to do your homework on your industry, your counterparts, your competitors, and your customers. Simply, the more you know, the better your "guess."

Let me tell you a secret. I get paid a great deal of money to "create" brilliant marketing ideas, but I doubt that I've ever honestly done that. Inventing a new idea is a lot of work. Stealing a successful idea is a lot faster, easier, and more likely to yield successful results. So, I try to legally "steal" whenever I can.

For example, I was recently hired to write a full-page magazine ad for a money-making opportunity, so I needed a "killer" headline. I found the two most successful ads I had seen for other money-making opportunities, took the best parts for each, and combined them into a new headline. Then I changed the details to match my client's offer. This ad is working like gangbusters. The headline creation process took me 20 minutes. To have thought it up from scratch could have taken 20 hours.

A friend with a specialty retail store came to me in need of an idea to stimulate a fast surge of cash flow. Fortunately, he had a mailing list of his past customers, so he could get the job done with a great sales letter. I pulled the letter out of my files, one a chiropractor had used to promote a "patient appreciation" event, and said, "Here, sit down and rewrite this letter. Don't change much except the details for your products." It took him only one hour to compose a letter that brought in over $30,000.00 in 15 days.

I am a highly paid direct-response copywriter, typically commanding upwards from $100,000.00 plus royalties to write ads, sales letters, or complete direct-mail campaigns. Over 85% of all the clients who use me once do so again. As you might guess, there's a very, very small fraternity of pro copywriters at this fee level. Most of us know each other well. I can tell you with authority, we all use these kinds of "swipe files" to efficiently recycle what we know works, rather than to invent from scratch and experiment unnecessarily.

Given the right resources, you can go a long way on 100% borrowed, already-proven strategies.

Having such a reservoir of "marketing content" relevant to your business and keeping it current with continuous research and acquisition is the key not just to effective advertising, marketing, and promotion of your business, but also the key to speed, and speed is extremely important in The New Economy. The enemy of speed is the blank sheet of paper and, as Thomas Edison termed it, "sitting for ideas."

Moving Ideas from One Business to Another

To the best of my knowledge, the drive-up service window belonged to the banking industry before anybody else latched on to it. But it sure does account for a lot of the fast-food industry's sales. It is also used by dry cleaners, beverage stores, video rental stores, and florists. In Las Vegas, one casino has a drive-up betting window for sports bettors. There are probably others using it that I haven't noticed and still others who could and should be using it.

Somebody in the fast-food business "stole" this idea. My vision is of a McDonald's executive sitting in his car in the bank drive-in line on Friday afternoon when it hits him—"Hey, I don't think we can fit the milkshakes in the little tube, but outside of that, this could work for us!"

Just about every great idea came from something already created or used. The enormously valuable Batman® franchise—made into money via blockbuster movies, cartoons, comic books, and merchandise—exists because a couple guys borrowed pieces and parts from predecessor characters, notably The Shadow and Zorro. An entire genre of highly successful TV infomercials and direct-response commercials merely moved carnival, boardwalk, and country fair pitchmen and demonstratable products to television. QVC is a Tupperware® home party conducted on TV for a million people in their own living rooms—and Tupperware® is even sold on the home shopping channel. Fractional jet ownership came from time-share real estate. On and on and on. **Somewhere, right now, outside your business and its industry and industry norms, in an apparently unrelated business, lies the moveable idea that could revolutionize your profits.**

Sometimes this can be about making the business about something different, but not actually changing the business. Dominos got its traction by focusing on delivery, not on pizza. Subway used Jared to make itself about weight loss and healthy eating rather than fast food. Apple re-made itself, from "for nerds" to "for the cool kids." And the money followed. A great business is always about something, by the way, not just a seller and provider of goods or services.

This is a time for more practical creativity than ever. Just producing or providing good products or services at good prices is nowhere near enough to justify your existence and command and keep the interest of your customers in The New Economy.

How to Be More "Creative"

I use the word "creative" with caution.

Twyla Tharp is an extremely talented woman. She has won Tony Awards for her success with Broadway theater. Over a 45-year career, she has invented 125 different dances. Unfortunately for unwary or easily influenced business people, she wrote a business book, *The Creative Habit: Learn It and Use It for Life*. I say *unfortunately* because she is all about the exact kind of creativity best kept out of business. An article in *Fast Company* about her began with these words:

Creativity starts with a blank space.

She says "The blank space can be humbling."

This kind of creativity is wonderful and awe-inspiring, and produces groundbreaking art and literature and theater. But if you're after maximum profits from minimum time and minimum agony, it has no place in business. And when it comes to your advertising and marketing, that goes double—avoid it like the plague for three reasons: one, it is horribly inefficient. As I said before, it's the mortal enemy of speed. Two, it is experimental. There's no need for experimentation with your marbles, when there's abundant opportunity to achieve your every objective without such risk. Three, it's intimidating. Most people do not think of themselves as "creative people," so being made to think business requires creativity stops them in their tracks. You just don't need "humbling."

For business purposes, focus on "practical creativity." Creative thinking guru and one-time leader in Disney's development of Disney World and Epcot, Mike Vance talks about it in terms of re-arranging the old (i.e., tested and proven) in a new way, or "plus-ing" what already works. Either way, you're not starting with a blank page. Walt Disney didn't start Disneyland with a blank page; he started with already proven, profitable amusement parks, and began subtracting things he disliked, adding things he thought could be done better, further plus-ing new ideas on top of the re-arranged old ones. Alex Osborne, a dean of creativity, filled his book with checklists to facilitate re-arranging the old in new ways. I talk about this in terms of bringing something from outside your field that is proven elsewhere into your field. Or cutting and pasting from swipe files, whether stored in file cabinets or your subconscious. But you'll never hear me talk in terms of starting with a blank slate. And catching me starting anything with a blank page is a rare event.

For purely artistic expression, raw, out-of-the-ether creativity may be an essential ingredient. But for commercial purposes, it is vastly overrated. Even if you look at the movie industry, as a "creative" business, if you examine the biggest box office successes of at least the past decade, you'll find very, very, very few to be original, birthed from the blank slate. Many have been re-makes of previously successful films. Some have featured well-established, successful, known characters, from comic books, TV shows, or sequels. Even a movie franchise like *Star Wars* is merely a classic western with a shiny new wrapping on it.

Here are a few suggestions of where to get "beginnings" so you need not begin with the blank page:

Competitors

Direct competitors occasionally have good ideas badly executed. You should keep a close eye on competitors, as well as leaders of your field outside your geographic market. You ought to keep a file on each of these, making sure you have their ads, mailings, etc. Visit their stores or showrooms, call and "play prospect" at their offices.

Comparables

This is my number-one source of good raw material. A "compara-ble" is someone selling a totally different, completely uncompetitive product or service but either selling at your price point and/or to your customers and/or using the same media you use. If you will ferret out successful "comparables" and carefully follow them, you'll often find terrific shortcuts. Just for example, I've told a cosmetic dentist eager to attract affluent patients from all over the country to fly in to him to "play prospect" and answer the full-page ads run in airline magazines by the carpal tunnel doctors in Texas, and by the Mayo Clinic for its Executive Program. These are not competitors but they are comparable in many ways: the clientele, the geographic reach, pricing, the same marketing challenge, etc. Set a goal to find, thoroughly research, and build a file on one new comparable a month. You'll thank me.

News

News events beget opportunities, based on the Collier principle of "entering the conversation already occurring in their minds." Ad man Robert Collier advised connecting your business and messages about it to the kitchen table, cocktail party, or water cooler conversation occurring at the present moment. These days, we're blessed with an arsenal of instant communications media, making this easier and cheaper than ever to implement, yet few marketers do it. Today's news can hand you tomorrow morning's marketing message.

In early 2009, when job losses were skyrocketing and the consumers were justifiably panicked about the possibility of losing theirs, Hyundai created a new kind of warranty that permitted a suddenly unemployed car buyer to get three months of his car loan forgiven, and if need be, to return the car and end the finance contract with no penalty or damage to his credit. The dealer I spoke to about this reported his busiest and best two weekends of business when these TV commercials broke. This was a great example of using news—in this case, bad news—profitably.

Old Ads

Go back 10, 20, 30 years, take big winners and recycle them. I use my swipe file of these "classics" more than I use current samples. Think about it: the direct-response advertisers from the 1930s, '40s, '50s, and even '60s had to get consumers to write out and mail in checks or go to a store or showroom; there were no websites. For most of those decades, there were no toll-free 800 numbers, no credit card ordering by phone. No fax. No FedEx. What they did then to get response and sales with such limited resources can work a thousand-fold better married to our modern ease of buying environment.

Resources, Resources, Resources!

I have a "practical creativity-to-speed" course, 8 Big Ideas, a day-long *Creative Thinking for Entrepreneurs Workshop*, and a shortcut to direct marketing for any business including a giant "swipe file" of actual examples, and *The Magnetic Marketing System for the New Economy*, all available for delivery to you, fully guaranteed. Details about these and other resources can be found at www.DanKennedy.com, with click-link to our catalog or you can request a catalog be sent to you by calling 410-825-8600. You will also see current, extraordinary examples of practical creativity transforming ordinary businesses into extraordinary, extraordinarily profitable ones every month in The No B.S. Marketing Letter; you can get two issues FREE as part of the offer on pages 272–273 or by visiting www.FreeGiftFrom.com/business.

Top Direct-Response Copywriters' Work

If you're going to crib, crib from the best. Look for direct-response ads full of copy, running repeatedly in national media, from *USA Today* to *National Enquirer* to niche magazines. Often a good ad that has nothing whatsoever to do with your business can still provide a "platform" to work on (rather than a blank slate). This is why you should scan magazines far outside your personal interests on a frequent basis.

This is just a brief, partial sampling of ways to avoid the blank page. And you must avoid it at all costs.

What If Everybody Hates Your Idea?

A lot of very smart people did nothing but discourage Walt Disney. A lot of very smart people told Wendy's founder Dave Thomas the fast food hamburger business was saturated. I'm sure we could fill a whole shelf full of books with similar examples. There's probably a product in every room of the house that was once criticized as a dumb idea.

If you really have faith in your idea, even if no one else does, and you go in with your eyes open knowing you may lose, then—charge! On the other hand, keep in mind that **the true entrepreneur marries goals and objectives, not isolated ideas.** When one of your ideas does prove itself unprofitable, don't try to raise the dead; move on to the next method of achieving your goals. The entrepreneurial graveyard is full of corpses of exhausted individuals so emotionally married to a bad idea they marched stubbornly on to starvation. Persistence in and of itself is vastly overrated. Used in proper context, a virtue. Glorified and adhered to without qualification, a deadly vice.

In 1941, 8th-grade drop-out and bakery delivery man Carl Karcher mortgaged his car for $350.00 to buy a hot dog stand. His first day's sales were an unexciting $14.75. But, by 1946, more hot dog stands followed, and then hamburgers and "Carl's special sauce" were added. Today, the Carl's Jr. chain includes over 1,100 Carls Jr. restaurants plus 1,900 Hardee's restaurants in 42 states in the United States and in 13 other countries, all based on serving a top-quality hamburger. In very recent years, the company has enjoyed considerable success by blatantly bucking the trend of low fat, low carb, low calorie, healthier eating, by creating and advertising different kinds of monster burgers bringing thousands of calories to the table in one bun. In the midst of the early 2009 slump in consumer spending, credit crunch, and store and restaurant closings, they announced new contracts with investors and operators to open 193 new restaurants in the Dallas and Houston markets. Carl and his successors have a long, strong track record of coming up with profitable ideas and executing them successfully. They obviously do a lot of right things.

But around 1983, Carl had a bright idea that didn't work out. Like all fast-food places, the bulk of the business was breakfast and lunch. Carl decided to buck that norm and go after the family dinner business. He introduced new charbroiled dinner platters—steak, chicken, and fish—at all the restaurants, and invested heavily in advertising and promoting these new items to woo customers in at dinner hour. Even the signs on all the locations were changed from Carl's Jr. Charbroiled Hamburgers to Carl's Jr. Restaurant. Millions of dollars were poured into this new approach. Instead of adding revenue, the dinner idea confused franchisees, managers, and the public. Average annual sales per location dropped. In 1985, Carl Karcher had to face up to the fact that his Big Idea was a flop. He dug in and started leading his company back to its reliable roots. The signs were changed back, menus simplified, prices cut, and the advertising spotlight returned to the famous charbroiled hamburgers. Sales almost immediately started climbing.

At the time, Carl Karcher told *Nation's Business* magazine, "The stress these last several years has probably been greater than at any time in my life. When you've put in 45 years, you think that everything's going to get easier. Nothing is easy! And

I think that's where too many people fail in business—they think they've got it made. It's fun being in business, but there's no rest for the wicked."

Carl Karcher has certainly had many good business ideas during his career, and he has backed those ideas with his faith and with action. But, as his story shows, nobody gets by without having a clinker now and again. You will too. So, go ahead, have the guts to act on those you really believe in—and the good sense to walk away from those that prove unrewarding. The New Economy demands more creativity, more new ideas, and more innovation, but the peril of pioneering remains. Business success comes from doing enough of the new but not too much, doing as much as possible by borrowing already successful ideas rather than testing entirely new ones, and from welcoming the swift sword when necessary but exhibiting Herculean persistence when called for. Easy, huh?

On (only) a few occasions in 35 years, I have stubbornly refused to listen to what the marketplace was desperately trying to tell me, and poured a lot of good money after bad, invested untold quantities of time and energy into proverbially beating the clearly dead horse. The details of these situations aren't important and are a bit painful and embarrassing to tell. No one is immune to such over-commitment. On the other hand, as I gained experience, I've gotten better at emotional distance from my own ideas, and at walking away from the overly challenging and unproductive experiments sooner rather than later.

In the direct marketing world where I mostly live, we do not even speak in terms of "success" or "failure" with regard to ads, sales letters, infomercials, marketing campaigns, or entire business projects. The word "failure" tends to inflame the stubborn streak in entrepreneurs, too often leading to the aforementioned beating of dead horses. Instead we talk only in terms of "tests." The task is to create a situation where you can put your idea to a reasonable test, to assess its actual potential, as quickly, inexpensively, and efficiently as possible.

This is the soundest approach to everything entrepreneurial. Condition yourself to think tests, not failures or successes. Then make it your priority to test fast and cheap, drop like hot potatoes ideas that test poorly, move on to the next test. Ultimately this is the only way to determine whether you have a good idea or not.

There's even danger in the terms "good" and "bad." An idea may be a good idea but still inappropriate for you to invest resources in, depending on how it fits with your major goals and objectives, your skills and talents. An idea might be "good" for one company but "bad" for another. Just because it's a great opportunity does not mean it's a great opportunity—or the best opportunity at this moment—for you. Since there is no shortage of opportunity, the entrepreneur has to be selective.

Some Quick Creativity Formulas

If you can't change the product, change the package or the delivery mechanism.

Books delivered via electronic devices like Kindle® or the iPhone.® At Glazer-Kennedy Insider's Circle,™ we have converted a number of our home study courses from packages of books, manuals, CDs, and DVDs that too often had consumers confused about where to start and what to do in what order into online delivered courses, with everything organized for the user and provided in sequential modules. Certain prescription medicines have been changed from daily doses to weekly doses to monthly doses, even to annual IV delivery— for no reason other than patient convenience and the opportunity of advertising ease and simplicity of use. The most popular "family automobile" has gone, in my lifetime, from station wagon to minivan to SUV to crossover—but its core product, seating for the whole family and room to haul stuff hasn't changed. Wine-in-a-box, laughed at by connoisseurs, is a popular product.

Make it bigger.

Big screen TVs. "Home theaters." 7-11's Big Gulp. For a time, recently, extra-big houses on small lots dubbed McMansions and extra big SUVs like the Hummer were in vogue, until gas prices, recession, and other factors created very different consumer preferences—although it's a safe bet the desire for Big in these categories will return.

Make it smaller.

How about a TV that fits in your pocket? I remember when that was a revolutionary idea! One-serving sizes of pudding, yogurt, microwavable spaghetti; 100-calorie packs of cookies and crackers are very popular at the time I'm writing this.

Add to it.

Shampoo plus conditioner in one. Cold capsules enriched with vitamin C. Vodka with added caffeine—odd but successful. The bookstore-cafe combination. Lee Iacocca told me that the first minivan was an exercise in selling $20,000.00 cup-holders. Now cars are being sold because of DVD players, GPS navigational systems, and computers—the car itself is secondary to what's been added! Combining elements of different businesses into one is a path to Addition. With the Kennedy's All-American Barber Club franchised chain I've worked on, we combined elements of a classic, traditional barber shop including expertly delivered straight razor shaves with the upscale atmosphere of a men's club (only seen by many in old movies) with the membership concept of the country club and levels of membership, borrowed from our business membership model at Glazer-Kennedy Insider's Circle™. (You can check this out online at KennedysBarberClub.com.)

Subtract from it.

The horse-less carriage gave us the first automobile. The convertible is a top-less car. Foods with no preservatives. No Appointment Hair Cutters, a successful national no-frills chain of salons. Online banking and banks—no building, branches, or tellers. Online stock broker-ages—no brokers, no commissions.

Do it faster.

The ten-minute oil change. The microwave oven—once thought only salable to restaurants, by the way. High-speed internet vs. dial-up. NetFlix instant, online access to movies vs. the DVD delivered overnight to your mailbox (too slow!). Leading hospitals' "executive physicals": an entire battery of tests, consultations with doctors, nutritionists, and even life coaches, and complete "health plans" all completed in one place, under one roof, in one day.

Do it slower.

The car wash by hand. Vacation travel by train. The spa *day*.

Do it cheaper.

Cubic Zirconia jewelry. Wal-Mart. Costco. Amazon.com.

Do it to more expensively.

The Barkley Pet Hotel, where we board The Million Dollar Dog, is a kennel given the Ritz-Carlton treatment, priced double to triple what an ordinary kennel costs. One of our Members, Diana Coutu at Diana's Gourmet Pizzeria, sailed through the rough waters of the recession undaunted, with pizza prices from $22.00 to $38.00, not in Beverly Hills or Manhatten but in Winnipeg, Canada.

Follow the Money!

Be sure to read my book, *No B.S. Guide to Marketing to the Affluent* for a comprehensive and eye-opening presentation on the myths, facts, and extraordinary opportunities in re-positioning your business to appeal to more affluent customers.

Do the opposite.

Mobile pet grooming = they come to you instead of you go to them. The Reverse Mortgage = mortgage company pays the homeowner instead of the homeowner paying the mortgage company.

CHAPTER 4

POSITIONING YOURSELF AND YOUR BUSINESS FOR MAXIMUM SUCCESS

> If you don't think advertising works,
> consider the millions of people who
> now think yogurt tastes good.
>
> —Bob Orben

Positioning is admittedly an advertising buzzword, but it's legitimately one of the most important marketing concepts you'll ever consider in your entrepreneurial career. One of the definitions of positioning is controlling how your customers and prospective customers think and feel about your business in comparison to other, similar businesses competing for their attention.

I have several specific suggestions about this process. Maybe they'll seem obvious to you, but I can tell you that I have seen many business people overlook the obvious, and cost themselves a lot of money as a result.

Positioning Strategy #1:
How to Describe What You Do to Attract
the Customers You Want

Let's start with the name of your business. I insist the best business names telegraph what the business does. This may sound elementary, but start looking at the businesses in your town and notice how many of their names, boldly displayed on their signs, do not instantly tell you what the business offers and does. I, for example, prefer Dunkin' Donuts® to Starbucks®; although to be fair, their real name is Starbucks Coffee—the public has abbreviated it themselves with familiarity. Obviously, we can point to many hugely successful, brand name companies with mystery names: Apple and Amazon.com, for example, consumers know now, but didn't know at the start. The question you have to ask is whether or not you want to invest an enormous amount of money and patience in creating awareness and understanding of what your name represents or to start with a name that clearly represents what your business is and does.

For every successful name that doesn't telegraph what the business is about, you can find hundreds that do. Outback Steakhouse® for example, tells us what we get there—steak, but also conveys its theme. *Entrepreneur* magazine, *The Wall Street Journal,* and *Investors' Business Daily* all bear names leaving no doubt about who they are for or what they are about. Our own *No B.S. Marketing Letter, No B.S. Marketing to the Affluent Letter,* and *No B.S. Info-Marketing Letter* all identify their different subject matter, and all convey the theme. Men's Wearhouse, a successful chain of many years, tells us who they are for, and, with a play on words, tells men they can get what they need to wear in an environment men (who generally don't like to shop) are comfortable in—a warehouse—and can get direct warehouse prices, implying good savings. With the same play-on-words technique, the Planters brand at Kraft Foods has a line of *NUT-rition* nut mixes; one for a healthy heart, another to improve digestion, another to boost immunity.

An old favorite of mine, a product I named for a company I had an interest in, was "Kills Weeds Dead." It was poisonous goop in an aerosol can that, when sprayed on pesky weeds, penetrated their root structure and killed them dead.

You have to consider very specific language choices in naming businesses, or in describing them. Consider these three: 9-11 Emergency Chiropractic Clinic . . . . Family Chiropractic Clinic . . . . Health & Longevity Chiropractic Clinic. In all three, fundamentally the same services are provided. But they would clearly attract different types of patients with different priorities. Do these three suggest different things to you: Hamilton & Wesley Wealth Management Advisors . . . . Hamilton & Wesley Investment Management Advisors . . . . Hamilton & Wesley, Financial Planning?

Titles matter. A lot. I have fought with all my publishers over my own book titles, except this publisher, which cheerfully accepted the long, awkward title and "No B.S." positioning of many of the books: *The No B.S., No Holds Barred, Kick Butt and Take No Prisoners Guide to . . .* (which we finally abbreviated with this one, in favor of *For the New Economy* added). That is my position; I have cultivated a reputation as a blunt, direct "no b.s." individual. Tim Ferris, author of the monster bestseller *The 4-Hour Work-Week,* revealed to Glazer-Kennedy Insider's Circle™ Diamond Members on one of their monthly tele-seminars that he had arrived at that title by testing a number of options via Google AdWords.®

Titles matter beyond the book business. Titles or names are important for products, for offers. Our Member, Dr. Nielsen, a famously successful small town chiropractor, comes up with a new name for a package of services every month, in connection with the feature story in his newsletter. One month might feature the Fast Injury Recovery, Back to Work Program; another the Golfers' Flexibility and Long-Ball Hitting Strength Program. All involve chiropractic treatment.

I have a Member in the photography business who split-tested via direct-mail a particular offer and in the test altered only the name of the offer—version #1 was "Family Portrait Mothers' Day Gift": version #2: "The Ultimate Mothers' Day Gift: The Family Portrait." Version #2 out-pulled version #1 in response by better than a 3-to-1 margin, a 300% difference.

Someone once told me about seeing a sign for an upcoming free seminar titled "12 Roadblocks to Financial Success" and concluding he had no need to attend—because he already knew more than 12! Maybe he was joking. Maybe not. But it certainly would have been improved by adding "How to Overcome" to its title.

There is the naming or titling of your "process." You can more clearly communicate and you can add value to what you do solely by its name. For example, THE 10-MINUTE OIL CHANGE is perceived differently if it's THE 9-MINUTE OIL CHANGE or if it is the GUARANTEED 10-MINUTE OIL CHANGE or the INDY 500-STYLE 10-MINUTE OIL CHANGE. Little words can make a big difference. For my client HealthSource's® weight loss programs' marketing I coined the term Weight Loss Resistance Syndrome® to describe the collection of weight problems and both physical and psychological barriers to weight loss that their program counters. In my book, *No B.S. Guide to Marketing to the Affluent*, I also show how you can illustrate your process, to make it appear valuable and unique.

Positioning Strategy #2: How to Price

You'll hear a lot of different opinions about pricing strategy. Personally, I don't think I'd ever want to be in a business that procured its customers with the lure of "lowest prices." You cannot build long-term customer retention via the cheapest price. The way you get a customer has great impact on how you will sell to that customer again. There will always be someone willing to offer a cheaper price. If the only thing binding your customers to your company is the lowest price, your business will be as fragile in its tenth year as in its tenth week.

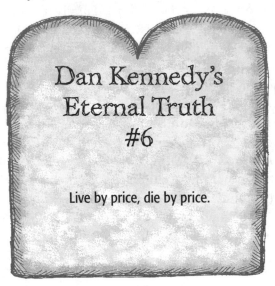

Dan Kennedy's Eternal Truth #6

Live by price, die by price.

In every business I'm involved in, we sell quality, value, service, and unique benefits. We do not sell price. I'm very pleased that I've become very well known for guiding countless business owners among Glazer-Kennedy Insider's Circle™ Membership to creating premium versions of their goods and services and to selling at substantially higher prices or fees than they or their competitors ever imagined possible. At my urging, business owners and professionals discover what I call Price Elasticity. Usually, businesspeople underestimate the elasticity available to them and afforded by their customers.

I have vivid and permanent memory of such a lesson delivered to one client. He was one of fifteen business owners in a group I coached. I and every other member of the group insisted he was underpricing a particular service he sold for $1,000.00, with the number of customers accommodated each time limited to 100. Finally, exasperated with the debate, I left my conference room where the group was meeting, returned with my checkbook, and offered to buy all 100 positions in the next group for $1,000.00 each with the intent of re-selling them at $3,000.00 each and keeping the profit, letting them deliver their service as usual. They went home and—with fear and trepidation—doubled their price, with no ill effects. My best calculation is that they've pocketed over $2 million a year extra every year since, having discovered their price a lot more elastic than they believed.

The worst thing for any business, for any provider is "commoditization," being perceived as interchangeable commodity. When you sell emphasizing cheap price, you invite that perception.

Another interesting thing about price is how fearful most business owners are of raising prices or offering premium priced options. **Here's a scary thought**: you are selling everything you sell for less than you need to. **Scarier thought**: you're selling less of it at lower prices than you would at higher prices.

One of the most interesting things about price is not its impact on profit and income, but its impact on positioning. Often, under-pricing sends the wrong message. The business owner thinks he's optimizing sales by offering the lowest price possible when he's actually creating skepticism and causing discerning customers to look elsewhere. One ad I have in my files even includes the line "Reassuringly Expensive." For years, I have cheerfully told everybody I can that I am the highest paid direct-response copywriter on the planet, and that most have chest pains when they first hear my fees. Taking this position has gotten me a lot more interest and, as a result, clients than it has cost me, and it has definitely saved me from a lot of time wasted with clients I wouldn't have wanted under any circumstances.

Price, Profit, and Power

Price strategy, price confidence, and presentation of price is so important that I developed and conducted an entire day-long workshop about it, now converted to an online learning program you can go through at home, at your convenience. You can find more information about this via click-link at DanKennedy.com.

In most categories, as few as 10% to no more than 20% of consumers make their choices based on lowest price or fee. The other 80% to 90% look for more information and strive to make their decisions based on more complex criteria, factoring in quality, value, reliability, service, reputation, pride of ownership, and overall confidence they feel for the seller. The New Economy Customer is even more thoughtful about complex value vs. simple price. You'll find a more detailed discussion of The New Economy Customer in my book *No B.S. Sales Success for The New Economy*. The final piece of advice on price I'll give you here is that successful businesses based on factors other than low or aggressively competitive pricing outnumber successful businesses that feature low or lowest price promises by at least 500 to 1. Play the odds.

Positioning Strategy #3:
How to Make Your Image Work for You

As long as I live, I will never forget a bank manager looking me straight in the eye, and in a genuinely sincere, shocked voice saying, "You can't be president of a company—you're not wearing a tie." To be perceived, without risk of exception, as a successful entrepreneur, you must match the image of a successful entrepreneur. To be perceived, without risk of exception, as successful and trustworthy in your field, you must match the image of a successful person in your field.

Places of business, product packaging, literature, and advertising, all are subject to the same image concerns as are individuals' appearances. Whether I walk on stage in a suit or in jeans has nothing to do with the quality or value of the speech I'll deliver, but it will have everything to do with how that speech is received. If I come on in the jeans, I instantly create psychological obstacles to acceptance. I've proven to myself that the most authoritative look makes a difference. At most of my speaking engagements, I sell my books and audio learning programs. I've tested, with identical types of audiences, tie, sport coat, and slacks vs. light-colored suit vs. dark, navy, or black pinstriped suit, and I always enjoyed greater sales with the last "look."

Is this fair? Of course not. It, unfortunately, allows racist, sexist, and other prejudices to live on. And you can certainly have a lot of moral outrage over it if you want to. But I'm going to ask you **a defining question: would you rather be right or rich?** I call this a defining question for entrepreneurs because it challenges

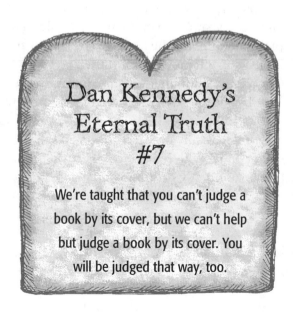

Dan Kennedy's Eternal Truth #7

We're taught that you can't judge a book by its cover, but we can't help but judge a book by its cover. You will be judged that way, too.

you to be totally realistic and pragmatic, give up your excuses, and succeed. A lot of people would rather live mediocre lives under the protection of the "it's not fair" excuse umbrella than to face the world as it really is and do what is necessary to win. A lot of people will cling to certain beliefs and behaviors even at the expense of desirable results. The most successful entrepreneurs I know are willing to change their beliefs and behaviors whenever that change can facilitate the most desirable results.

Now, don't misunderstand; I'm not suggesting the politicians' chameleon game, changing minute by minute, audience by audience, dressing up for one group, down for the next, telling anybody and everybody what they want to hear with no regard for truth or contradiction, having no core philosophy other than desired results. There has to be a "you" in there somewhere. There has to be a collection of core values not subject to easy change. But there are many things not nearly as important as core values that can be easily modified to permit success.

I once counseled a struggling attorney who couldn't understand why he wasn't attracting or keeping solid business clients. The day he drove me from his office to a lunch meeting in his canary-yellow, four-year-old pickup truck, I told him why. Of course, he protested mightily; he loved his truck, it was paid for, it shouldn't matter, etc. but his practice started picking up when he started driving a Cadillac. Individuals and businesses have images and are judged by them, usually long before the customer has an opportunity to fairly judge the actual competence or expertise of the individual or the quality of the products and services.

On the other hand, with regard to advertising or literature or direct mail, I must strongly caution you against image over substance. All too often, marketing material is pretty (and expensive) but fails to deliver a compelling direct-response message. Most businesses are better served by thinking about their marketing tools as "salesmanship in media" rather than as "advertising." In simple terms, copy is king. Message matters most. Yes, the wrong presentation for a given market can sabotage even the best message. But the more common error is a beautiful presentation of—nothing.

Ultimately, there must be an appropriate marriage of substance and style. Customers' expectations must be met and exceeded, anxiety avoided, reassurance given by the image presented by you, your staff, your physical location, your marketing material.

Positioning Strategy #4: Self-Appointment

When we are kids, our parents "appoint us" old enough to stay home alone, old enough to babysit our younger brothers or sisters, old enough to date, and so on. At work, employers or supervisors "promote us." In all these experiences, there is someone else, some authority figure determining that you are qualified to do a certain thing or handle a certain responsibility. This conditioning is not particularly useful when you step into the entrepreneurial world.

People often ask me: "How do you become a professional speaker?" They're looking for some kind of organized path such as going to a school, passing tests, and, finally, getting appointed as a professional by some kind of group. They're disappointed when I say, "Be one." I give the same answer regarding "business coach" or "consultant." Of course, there are alphabet soup designations you can go and get from groups that have set themselves up to sell them—themselves masters at manipulating perception, but clients care nothing about these things. Only peers do and peers do not make deposits to your bank account.

Early in my career, I read Robert Ringer's book *Winning Through Intimidation*, which made me understand that the biggest problem with getting to the top is getting through the crowd at the bottom. Ringer suggested simply "leap-frogging" over them. I've done that all my life. But I notice most people waiting around for someone else to recognize them, to give them permission to be successful.

Please understand, you do not need anybody's permission to be successful. And, if you wait for "the establishment" in any given field to grant you that permission, you'll wait a long, long time. And remember, success is never an accident, no matter how it appears to outsiders.

Jay Leno got Johnny Carson's job, arguably the best job in show business. At one time, comedian Gary Shandling was considered the front-runner for that job, and David Letterman was after it, too. But only Leno quietly went out and appointed himself to the job. In his travels, he went to the local NBC affiliates in different cities and towns, befriended the station managers, did promotional spots for them for free, and operated as the self-appointed ambassador of goodwill for the network and the show. By the time Carson retired, Leno was the only candidate with the solid support of all the NBC affiliates. Who told him he could do this? Nobody. He just did it. How dare he? That's the point.

Business success just isn't conferred upon you.

Power and influence is not granted—it's taken.

"Expert positioning" is all about self-appointment, self-promotion, and self-aggrandizement. Years ago, a client of mine, Dr.

Free!

Hear my personal interview with Robert Ringer at www.NoBSBooks.com. This is a good example of the exclusive interview audio programs Glazer-Kennedy Insider's Circle™ Members receive every month—which you can receive, too; refer to the Free Gift Offer on pages 272–273.

Robert Kotler, a Beverly Hills cosmetic surgeon, wrote and self-published a book titled *The Consumer's Guide to Cosmetic Surgery*. He was then able to promote himself as the doctor who wrote the book. You may have seen him on the TV program, Dr. 90210. Easy for a doctor, you might think, but not so easy for me—I own a shoe repair shop or

> "There are no wishy-washy rock stars, no wishy-washy astronauts, no wishy-washy CEOs . . ."
>
> —KAREN SALAMSOHN, AUTHOR OF
> *BALLSY: 99 WAYS TO GROW A
> BIGGER PAIR*

my company installs windows or I own a landscaping company. Actually, every business, every business can benefit from its owner or its "face" being promoted and then recognized as an expert. Examples abound if you'll look for them.

Make this note: you become a promotable expert by decision, acquisition, and organization of information, pronouncement, and promotion. Not by anointment by some authority on high.

A Story of Positioning Success

A long-time Member as well as a private client of mine, Darrin Garman, was once a commercial real estate broker in Cedar Rapids, Iowa, handling apartment building, shopping center, and office building transactions in that area, by soliciting and securing listings, then hunting for investor-buyers. His business was local. It was helped enormously with my kind of marketing, so that he became the dominant leader in his field there, with over 80% of all such transactions going through his office. But his transformation from having a very good local business to a truly exceptional international business came by positioning himself as the expert in "heartland-of-America commercial real estate investing," and reaching out to investors outside the area. Today, 90% of his investors buying all these properties are from states

An Example of Darin's Marketing

An example of Darin's marketing can be found in my book *The Ultimate Sales Letter*. You can also see Darin's business at www.commercial-investments.com.

other than Iowa and even overseas, most invest in or buy the Iowa properties sight unseen, all pay membership fees to be clients just for the privilege of having access to Darin's expertise, property owners listing properties with him pay client fees above and in advance of customary commissions, and he's never pressured to discount commissions. His business held up just fine during the recent recession years, too. In fact, there was flight of investment funds to him from clients taking their money away from the stock market and other places.

In just a few short years, Darin has gone from a "salesman" with a nice six-figure income to a nationally respected expert and sought after advisor with a very nice seven-figure income and a multi-millionaire investor partnering in many projects with clients.

There's a lot to this business story. Darin transcended traditional geographic boundaries of his business. He created unique concepts. He wrote books, gave teleseminars, built a list of interested investors-in-waiting for good opportunities, through advertising in national publications like *Forbes* and *The Wall Street Journal*. But all that hinged on a positioning decision.

What does this have to do with your shoe store, restaurant, insurance agency, or widget distribution business? Everything! Darin's "trick" shows the income-multiplying power of positioning.

Who Do You Think You Are?

There's an old story that many speakers have appropriated and told as their own: the featured guest speaker seated at the head table says to the waiter, "Bring me some more butter."

The waiter says, "Can't. One pat of butter per person."

"Do you know who I am?" asks the frustrated speaker.

"Nope," says the waiter. "Who are you?"

"I am a famous author, here tonight as the featured guest speaker. After dinner, I'm going to share my wisdom with all these people. This group has brought me in at great expense. That's who I am. And I want another pat of butter."

"Well," says the waiter, "do you know who I am?"

"No," admits the speaker.

The waiter smiles triumphantly. "I am the man in charge of the butter."

The point of the story is that we all need to maintain some modesty and some appreciation for everybody else's right to be important. But in positioning yourself and your business for success, you have to clearly determine who you are, then drive that message home to your marketplace. And it's important to make the right decision. The marketplace will usually accept the positioning you choose for yourself and present to others. You really are in control.

CHAPTER 5

HOW ENTREPRENEURS *REALLY* MAKE MONEY— BIG MONEY!

Humorous writer Robert Benchley admitted that, after 15 years,
he had concluded he had no real talent for writing.
"But then it was too late," he said. "I can't quit
because I'm too famous."

P aul Hawken, *the extraordinarily insightful expert* on the entrepreneurial experience, founder of the Smith & Hawken gardening products company, wrote in his book, *Growing a Business*, "The more exposure I gained to the 'official' world of business, the more I began to doubt that I was in business at all. I seemed to be doing something entirely different. I get that same feeling today when I read most of the standard literature."

When I read that, I said, "Me too!" And I suspect that many readers of this book may feel that way anytime they read a business book put out by a big corporation executive-type or a college professor. In truth, there are a number of different business worlds, each barely touching the other, with very little overlap of their inhabitants' experiences.

There is that world where the really big corporations and their employees live. There, leaders' agendas are very complex and often, ironically, have profit subordinated to image, to pacifying Wall Street or investors or bankers, to directors' other interests. In my consulting work I've mostly avoided visiting this world. On one such visit, I created a marketing program for a fraternal insurance company that featured a direct-mail campaign soliciting appointments for their agents which proved itself 500% more productive than anything else they were using or had previously used. Yet after testing it, the CEO informed me it could not be used. Why? Because it positioned the company's financial products against banks and made sarcastic fun of bankers, and two members of the insurance company also sat on boards of and had significant ownership in banks. Their sensitivity took precedence over optimum results. I have five other very similar stories I won't bore you with. They illustrate a belief I hold about corporations: the bigger they are, the dumber they are.

Then there is the world populated by small business owners. And a completely different world populated by entrepreneurs. The terms "business owner" and "entrepreneur" are commonly used as interchangeable synonyms, but they are different people. A business owner can become an entrepreneur. But they are different people. Here, I want to talk about how entrepreneurs make really big money, but first we need to get clear about what defines an entrepreneur in the first place.

The typical small business owner marries a specific, narrowly defined business, manages it, and, essentially, employs himself or herself as a general manager. When he starts a business, buys a business, or buys a franchise, he really buys himself a job, hopefully a very good job. He makes money by taking a salary, benefits, and perks. In the long term, he may make a significant sum that he can retire on when he sells his business. If he gets rich, it will probably be by stabilizing his first store, then opening a second, then a third, and eventually developing a chain. His first business may only give him $50,000.00 to

$100,000.00 a year in income—the equivalent of a good job. Six such businesses, though, may give him $300,000.00 to $600,000.00 a year and allow him to become quietly, slowly rich.

There's nothing wrong with this model. In fact, there's a lot that's right about it. There are a lot of millionaires made slowly by very "ordinary" small businesses. According to Thomas Stanley, professor of marketing from Georgia State University, a serious student of the affluent in America, and author of the bestseller *The Millionaire Next Door*, most millionaires make their money "the old-fashioned ways: hard work for 30 years, 6 days a week . . . . in businesses that cater to the needs of ordinary people." His and other research shows that a lot of owners of small businesses get rich slowly and steadily over 30, 40, or even 50 years. This serves to demonstrate that you certainly don't need a revolutionary new mousetrap to get rich; there are still plenty of unexploited opportunities in already-established, proven fields of business, and you can build wealth in any number of these fields just by doing things a hair better than the average.

In The New Economy, this path is a bit more problematic than it was during the Reagan-Clinton-Bush boom, when consumer spending in every category was so rapidly expanding and the market was willing and able to support a huge number of duplicative, me-too businesses. A slight different or slight quality, service, or marketing advantage was sufficient for a satisfactory level of success. The New Economy's demands favor the entrepreneur more than the business owner.

True entrepreneurs do things a little differently. Looking carefully at how they really make big money should open your eyes to new and different opportunities, too.

How to Tell If You Are an Entrepreneur (or Not)

Distinction #1: The true entrepreneur is *not* married to a specific business. If you ask the typical small-business owner what he or she does, you'll get a narrow, easily understood answer: I own a restaurant. I'm a jeweler. I own a gift shop. The entrepreneur's answer is never that simple. I imagine both my parents died still wondering exactly what I was going to be when I grew up. Business owners place themselves within narrowly defined, strict limits. Entrepreneurs think expansively.

This is particularly relevant to The New Economy, because change is more constant and faster than ever, so flexibility and agility in business is critical. I have long taught: if you're trying to be in the same business five years from now that you're in now, you'll be out of business in three. I would now shorten that grace period.

Distinction #2: Entrepreneurs, first and foremost, make their money with innovative *ideas*. They are creators much more than they are managers. For this reason, they often start, develop, and sell a business only to move on and do it all over again. Some entrepreneurs who try to stay get forced out by their investors, who correctly recognize that being very successful at creating businesses does not necessarily mean that you are ideally suited to managing a maturing business.

Distinction #3: Usually, entrepreneurs are in many businesses, not one, even when it looks like one. This is the case with my long-time clients, Bill Guthy and Greg Renker. Guthy's initial business was an audiocassette duplicating business for speakers and conventions. Then he got interested in using his production capability for proprietary products he could market, not just as a contract manufacturer for others, and that led to a licensing agreement with the Napoleon Hill Foundation for an audio product based on the book, *Think and Grow Rich*. Next, as Bill saw several of the people he was duplicating cassettes for doing well with television infomercials, he decided to produce a TV show to sell *Think and Grow Rich* tapes. Today, the Guthy-Renker

Corporation is a $1.5-billion-a-year collection of unique vertical businesses all fueled in part by TV infomercials: as of this writing, Pro-Activ acne treatments products, Victoria Principal skin care, Susan Lucci skin care, and Comprehensive Nutrition— each with its own clientele receiving automatic shipments of product every 30 or 60 days. They still occasionally market nonconsumable products too; they brought Tony Robbins, the personal growth guru, to the market. There's no simple answer to "what do you do?" for Bill and Greg. And, they are in eager search of their next great idea, their next new business within their business. The money made managing the business is mostly made for them by other, hired managers. They make their money with ideas.

On a couple of occasions, I was on programs as a speaker with Jim McCann, the CEO of 1-800-Flowers, which he built from a single brick-and-mortar small business into a giant business encompassing retail locations, a large e-commerce operation, a direct marketer using radio and direct mail, and owner of several candy and gift companies as well as the original flower business. It's a long way from a corner flower shop. A business owner would have concentrated on opening a second store, then a third, not developing a multi-media direct marketing enterprise.

Distinction #4: Entrepreneurs develop equity differently. Small business owners are very traditional in their thinking about value. They think in terms of buildings, real estate, location, inventory, equipment, and income. Entrepreneurs realize that the most valuable asset is the customer. All other assets look solid but are actually quite fragile, because they are subject to severe interference by others and by external circumstances. Anything from a road torn up and under construction for months to entry of a new, tough competitor to the market to economic trauma can erase the value of all assets unless the customer list is in good order and the direct relationship with those customers is strong.

The Fortune-Building Secret of Total Customer Value

I am amazed at business owners who do not have mailing lists and e-mail lists of their customers. I am amazed at the businesses that never do anything when they lose customers. And I am amazed at the businesses that do nothing to maximize their *total customer value*—TCV.

The customer who is satisfied with you and trusts you is an enormous, enormously exploitable asset. Let's say you have a neighborhood dry cleaning business. Most dry cleaners take whatever business comes their way, live on their repeat business, and never think much more about it. But let's think about the entrepreneurial dry cleaner who understands TCV. Here are some of the things you'll see that dry cleaner doing:

- *Aggressively expanding usage of core services by repeat customers.* With in-store displays, bag stuffers, handouts, coupons, and mailings, the entrepreneurial dry cleaner encourages customers to use leather and suede cleaning services, spot removal, fur storage, necktie cleaning, etc. By continually reminding these customers of all the different services offered, the total purchase average per customer, per year will increase. If the dry cleaner increases the total purchases of a customer by just $4.00 per month, or $48.00 per year, and keeps that customer for ten years, that's a $480.00 swing in the plus direction. With just 500 customers, that's $240,000.00, and if the dry cleaner does that to four outlets, that's a creation of an extra $1 million!

- *Diversifying into joint ventures or "hosting" other businesses with some logical relationship to his own.* The dry cleaner rearranges the location's layout to free up a corner for a shoe repair shop, and arranges with a local shoe repair shop owner for the repair person to be on premises two afternoons a week. The rest of the time, repair work is dropped off at the cleaners one day, back and ready for the customers the next. Of course, the shoe repair corner also stocks and sells quality lines of shoe polishes, brushes, laces, etc. The dry cleaner and two friends get in the carpet and drapery cleaning business and promote that business to the dry cleaning customers. Several times a year (e.g., Christmas, Father's Day, etc.), the dry cleaner brings in displays of high-quality men's neckties and offers them at very good prices, as "impulse buys" to customers.

- *Exploiting the testimonial and referral potential of the customer list.* Using a criss-cross street directory, the dry cleaner builds a list of all the people who live next door to or across the street from satisfied customers. Then, on a Saturday, using a small army of staff and neighborhood kids, they go out and personally call on these prospects, letting them know that their neighbors are customers, inviting them to try the services, and giving out coupons. Follow-up is accomplished by using a series of postcards sent through the mail. With such a targeted, personalized approach, a large number of new customers are added to the base with nominal expense.

This is a very different way of thinking about business.

While most business owners think that the purpose of getting a customer is to make a sale, my clients and I do the reverse; we make a sale to get a customer.

When I go out on a speaking engagement or to conduct a seminar, I'm viewed as a professional speaker, and I'm paid a substantial fee for my services ($18,800.00, as of this writing). But I'm a very entrepreneurial speaker. When I'm speaking, I'm also acquiring customers with great, long-term potential value. First of all, at every speech, I'll offer and sell appropriate, relevant books and home-study courses. Second, those buyers will subsequently get our catalogues, one of our newsletters, and a series of offers by direct mail and e-mail to create additional purchases. Third, they'll become Members of Glazer-Kennedy Insider's Circle™, many at the Gold level, many ascending to the Diamond level—and about one in five become "lifers"; those acquired two decades ago are still with me. Fourth, they'll be encouraged to attend other, future seminars. Fifth, some will become private clients for my consulting services, or my direct-response copywriting services.

The point is, I'm thinking of the customer as a very important asset with continuous, expandable lifetime value. There are customers who have given me income as recently as this month who were acquired when they first saw me speak 30 years ago. I actually have individual customers who have been worth a million dollars, total.

Another way to say this is that ordinary business owners think in terms of growing sales and businesses, while the entrepreneur thinks in terms of creating value, predominately by creating customer value.

The key to profits is rarely more customers—it's better found through more valuable customers.

If we return to our mythical dry cleaner for a moment, because he is focused on developing maximum value in his customers, his business will be infinitely stronger, more stable, and more profitable than ordinary dry cleaners. This may enable him to expand by opening more locations or buying others' existing stores, or lead to franchising, or to a second business consulting within the dry cleaning industry.

Networking, Strategic Alliances, and Joint Ventures

Today's successful, innovative entrepreneur is very much in tune with the idea of cooperative marketing and with networking with other entrepreneurs for mutual benefit and profit. This concept is so important that we facilitate this in many ways for our Glazer-Kennedy Insider's Circle™ Members including via local Chapters in over 150 cities.

Most business owners limit their thinking to their own business and their own resources. If they go beyond that, they think about OPM—Other People's Money—in the form of credit or investment capital. Entrepreneurs often leverage OPR (Other People's Resources) and OPC (Other People's Customers) far more than OPM or just their own resources.

For example, I have a client who went from zero to over 200 franchises sold in his first 18 months—speed of growth just unimaginable in his or most categories of franchising, and probably unattainable through normal means regardless of the amount of capital that might be available to invest in the marketing. Through an alliance with another client of mine, he was able to market to that client's following—several thousand doctors across the country ideally suited as prospective owners of the franchise. OPC. And he was able to reach out to them initially by speaking at that client's conferences, appearing and being interviewed on that client's tele-seminars, and utilizing the client's e-mail list. OPR. The entire situation a win-win-win. My franchisor client got a fast start without significant out-of-pocket investment; my other client earned a very substantial income from his "toll booth position"—his control of and quality relationship with the doctors; and the doctors were brought an exclusive opportunity ahead of anyone else in their areas. This is a national situation, but the same strategy applies locally.

Ideally, you find opportunities to participate in groups of progressive entrepreneurs where you can explore potential alliances like this openly, and everybody is pre-disposed to engaging in them. But you can go in "over the transom" and approach another business owner or entrepreneur with this kind of idea and, while not easy, a connection is possible. I have one client who regularly identifies companies that should have customer lists well suited to his product and his complete marketing campaign, sends them his letter of introduction headlined "Free Money for Your Company"—and creates one good working relationship per ten companies approached.

The Language of Leverage

OPM: Other People's Money

OPR: Other People's Resources

OPC: Other People's Customers

STRATEGIC ALLIANCE: A working relationship typically between two companies or entrepreneurs in which each brings something to the other and there is cooperation without monetary consideration. For example, a chiropractor might endorse a dentist and send information about the dentist to his patients; vice versa, the dentist might endorse the chiropractor and send information about the chiropractor to his patients.

JOINT VENTURE: A working relationship between companies or entrepreneurs, typically involving a particular moneymaking project, in which each may contribute different resources and share revenues or profits.

HOST/PARASITE RELATIONSHIPS: A relationship where a Host controls customers and/or media and a Parasite utilizes those resources.

HOST: The owner of a customer list, of retail locations, of a conference or trade show, etc.—in one way or another, the person providing access to established customers. Strategic Alliances and/or Joint Ventures and/or Host-Parasite Relationships provide extra income opportunities to Hosts, which can equate to increased customer value without increased overhead, infrastructure, or fulfillment responsibilities.

PARASITE: Not, I suppose, a flattering term, but I've been very happy to make a great deal of money as one many times. The Parasite has products, services, opportunities that can be promoted to a Host's customers, with revenue or profits shared. These arrangements are most easily arranged when a) the Parasite has an entire marketing campaign prepared and proven elsewhere, and requires no work from the Host; b) the Parasite's offer is in no way competing with the Host's products and services; c) the Parasite has an excellent reputation, so the Host is free of anxiety about how his customers will be treated. A savvy Parasite makes the arrangement exceptionally attractive financially to the Host for reasons discussed in this chapter.

NETWORKING: The process of making your business, your resources, and your interest in cooperative relationships known to potential allies, through active membership in organizations, attending meetings and conferences, and participating in online communities.

The Remarkable Value of a Duplicatable Model

My former client and friend Len Shykind had a collection of a few dozen different business cards framed, hanging on his office wall. All the cards were his own from the various businesses he had struggled with prior to hitting his home run with Gold By The Inch. Len invented the idea of taking gold chain on spools to high-traffic locations like swap meets and making bracelets to size, on the spot, for customers, rather than displaying and selling pre-sized bracelets. The public loved this concept. Whenever he set up his display, people flocked around—and bought jewelry.

Len was smart enough to realize he'd invented a business that just about anybody could do. He had a duplicatable model.

He quickly recruited tens of thousands of Gold By The Inch distributors throughout the United States, Canada, and elsewhere, some full time, most part time, setting up their portable businesses at swap meets, bazaars, in stores, and in kiosks.

Together they sold tens of millions of dollars worth of Gold By The Inch every year. In fact, the market was so big and the need for more distributors so great, I produced a TV infomercial for Len to interest people in getting into this business. That program ran on national cable networks for eight years and made Len so wealthy that he was able to take a very early retirement.

Creating a direct sales opportunity like Len did is but one of many ways of leveraging a duplicatable model to a fortune. My client Michael Gravette has done exactly the same thing with personal and home safety products, but also added an online marketing component equipping distributors with their own catalog-style websites. His company, Safety Technology.com, generates tens of millions of dollars in revenue predominately by supplying independent "mom 'n pop" distributors.

Another fairly common although slightly more complex model appropriate for many businesses is franchising. I have worked closely with several clients in developing, launching, and growing national franchise organizations based on their own successful business. One type of franchise that lends itself to speed is conversion franchising—converting existing, independently owned businesses into franchisees. Century 21® did this in real estate, beginning a transformation of a previously fragmented industry absent any national brands. My client, HealthSource®, has done this with chiropractic practices. A regular franchise sold to anyone interested in being a small business owner is more common—you patronize some at least every week of your life, and they dominate the fast food industry, although they can be found in just about every product or service category. As you drive down the street and pass a Midas Muffler® shop, a 7-11® convenience store, an Ace Hardware® store; if you have your carpets cleaned by Stanley Steemer® or Dura-Clean®; if your house is protected from bugs by Terminix®—you're a customer of a franchised business. The important thing to remember is that every one was first put together by somebody with one successful shop and good systems for marketing and selling, and operations that could be duplicated with consistency thousands of times. Sometimes, franchising occurs when an entrepreneur spots such a small business ideal for duplication and acquires the franchising rights or partners with its owners to market it. Milkshake salesman Ray Kroc created McDonalds© based on the McDonald brothers' hamburger stand; they did not initiate franchising. Similarly, a group of entrepreneurs I advise bought a small, local chain of successful upscale men's barber shops, converted them to an improved, dulicatable business model, re-branded them, and franchised as Kennedy's All-American Barber Clubs™.

Incidentally, many franchise organizations have three types of franchise opportunities: individual unit or territory owner; multi-unit or multi-territory owner; and master or regional developer. The third may or may not actually operate a franchise himself, but acts as "lord and master" over all the franchises in a relatively large region, and provides support services, co-ordinates advertising, conducts training, and works with the franchise owners in his region in exchange for a share of the franchisor's royalties of all their gross sales. Owning a master franchise is very much like being a franchisor, but with the actual franchise business model built for you, the national brand created for you, and a home office behind you. Master franchise owners frequently enjoy seven-figure yearly incomes and create substantial equity in their businesses for later sale. There are even professional master franchise owners who take on one promising new one after another, build it up in their region, sell their position, and do it all over again with the next one. In the Kennedy's All-American Barber Clubs™ business we do have master franchise owners.

A third model is a "nonfranchise model," still, typically, assigning area exclusivity to the person in the business, and having them using a furnished, turnkey marketing and/or management system and, in many cases, distributing proprietary products or delivering proprietary services. This is often done within a niche.

Someone will develop a very successful means of marketing an optical store, for example, with original ads, direct-mail campaigns, TV commercials, a powerful website, etc., and then package all that up with ongoing coaching and support and sell it to one optical store owner per area, for an initial fee plus an annual or monthly fee. I have helped over 200 entrepreneurs develop this kind of business—most providing seven-figure yearly incomes. This is the approach used for a program I helped create called Dentistry For Diabetics®, which is provided to and used by only one dentist per geographic area.

Finally, there is wealth created through duplication via information marketing, and most entrepreneurs with successful strategies and methods proven in a particular category of business at least have this opportunity. As example, there's the President of Glazer-Kennedy Insider's Circle,™ Bill Glazer. In what we like to call his former life, Bill owned and operated extraordinarily successful menswear stores which he made even stronger with discovery of my kind of direct marketing strategies—we met as a result of his attending an event where I spoke, buying one of my marketing resource kits, using it very profitably in his businesses, sending me examples, and inviting me to lunch the next time I was in Baltimore. At that lunch, I educated Bill about opportunities to profit from his successful ads, direct-mail campaigns, sales strategies, and other elements of his own duplicatable model, in a simple and streamlined way, as an information marketer to his industry. He then packaged up all the examples of everything he was using, wrote how-to manuals, and recorded audio learning programs to accompany the examples, and began marketing his first marketing kit for menswear retailers to his industry peers. This quickly established a thriving business, with multiple info-products and a newsletter. In only a few years, Bill expanded to other retail niches including ladies wear, sporting goods, jewelry, and home furnishings, peaking with over 5,000 retailers buying and using his advertising-marketing-sales system, subscribing to

Curious About Your Opportunities in Information Marketing?

Check out the Information Marketing Association at www.info-marketing.org and/or obtain a copy of *The Get Rich Guide to Information Marketing* put together by the Association, and its Executive Director, Robert Skrob, published by Entrepreneur Press, available at all booksellers.

his newsletter, paying monthly membership fees, and purchasing other services. A multi-million dollar info-marketing business.

What I've just described, simplistically, of course, is a path I've personally guided hundreds and hundreds of entrepreneurs in different fields down—including successful carpet cleaners, restaurant owners, hair salon owners, chiropractors, dentists, real estate agents, and on and on. And, indirectly, thousands of business owners have used my approach to convert the successful methods used in their own business into information products, seminars, coaching, and services sold to others in their industries.

One way or another, the astute entrepreneur works at reducing the driving forces of his business to replicatable systems so his business can run profitably without him, and then often finds ways to leverage the work he's done in perfecting those systems for himself into yet another business, selling the systems to others.

Mastering the Six Entrepreneurial Competencies

Figure 5.1 shown on the next page illustrates the Six Competencies the entrepreneur must master. One big difference between a small business owner and an entrepreneur is the

FIGURE 5.1: Core Entrepreneurial Competencies

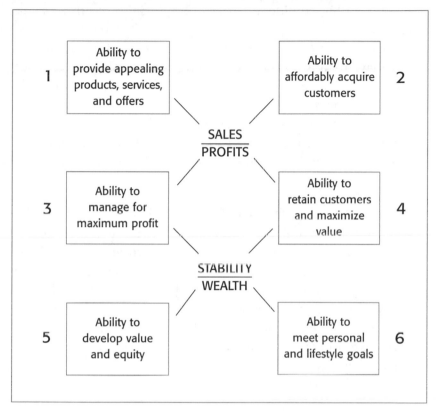

emphasis given each of these competencies, and whether approached sequentially or simultaneously.

The business owner typically gives 70% of his attention to Competency #1, 20% to #2, 9% to #3, and 1% to #4. Ever so gradually, over time, if he gets smarter, and if he's making money, the ratios shift. Late in the game, he tackles #5. He hardly ever thinks about #6. If he does, it's in context of retirement. The business owner is often comfortable only with #1, having gotten into business in the first place to do the thing (not to market it). A more accurate visual depiction of the business owner's relationship to these competencies would be #2 through #6 as small boxes inside one big box identified as "The Business" with #1 as its function.

For the entrepreneur, the Six Competencies illustration is an "overlay" for any business, moved from one business to another. He feels he can move his attention fluidly from one box to another as warranted.

While the business owner may work to implement these competencies inside a particular business, the entrepreneur works to master these competencies, *period*. (See Figure 5.2.)

Live Outside the Lines

If given a shoe store, the small-business owner will manage and promote that shoe store well. But ten years from now, it will still be a shoe store. Give that same shoe store to a true entrepreneur and, ten years from now you probably won't recognize it!

Maybe, as a child, you were urged to "color inside the lines." This was not great training for entrepreneurial success. As you can see, most entrepreneurs make most of their money "outside the lines."

FIGURE 5.2: Portable Entrepreneurial Overlay

	1		2		3		4		5		6	
	Ability to provide appealing products, services, and offers		Ability to affordably acquire customers		Ability to manage for maximum profit		Ability to retain customers and maximize value		Ability to develop value and equity		Ability to meet personal and lifestyle goals	
	Strengths	Need to Improve	Strengths	Need to Improve	Strengths	Need to improve	Strengths	Need to Improve	Strengths	Need to Improve	Strengths	Need to Improve

CHAPTER 6

HOW TO CREATE EXCITING SALES AND MARKETING BREAKTHROUGHS

People love to buy.

—BILL GOVE

O K, here it is—what you probably bought this book for: a no-holds-barred, no-B.S. collection of break-through strategies, to get rich, preferably quick.

By the way, nothing wrong with quick, and no special virtue in slow. I know you've been told that "get-rich-quick schemes" are bad news. But the word "scheme" has simply been tarred with a broad black brush. A good, sound scheme is a perfectly fine thing. And when you deposit money at the bank, you don't get penalized for having made it quickly or easily.

And contrary to popular myth, a lot of fortunes *are* made fast.

Once Dave Thomas got really cooking, pardon the pun, he opened 1,000 Wendy's restaurants in one year. While not that many that fast, a client of mine went from zero to over 150 franchised locations operating in one year, in a service category where franchising had never been successfully done at all. Ever. It's actually quite common for me to spend a day consulting with a client for the first time and find the hidden or neglected opportunity in his business that is better than the core business, and that lends itself to speed to market and speed to wealth because of the platform provided by the first business. One that is quite memorable involved a small business owner with a nice, successful, local small business from which he earned a perfectly respectable $150,000.00 a year—but worked much too hard doing so. Midway through our day he mentioned, as an "oh, by the way," a little sideline enterprise run out of the business during its down time that brought in nearly as much as the full-time earnings but required virtually no work on his part. We hatched a plan to ten times it before he left, and in the next 24 months, it produced over $2-million.

The first breakthrough is in thinking bigger and bolder rather than small and incremental. You won't experience a big, fast financial breakthrough if you aren't looking for one.

Then you need to know where to look. These kind of gigantic, fast leaps come from only one place: sales and marketing breakthroughs.

The big money in the world is made in sales and marketing. Nobody gets rich dusting shelves, changing light bulbs, keeping books, or managing employees. Yet, I'm amazed at how many entrepreneurs let such things suck up all their time, focused on everything and anything but sales and marketing.

So let's get this straight from the start: the place for you to direct your time, energy, creativity, common sense, hard work, and resources is marketing.

In fact, the first quantum leap from ordinary good-job-type income to big entrepreneur-type income occurs very rapidly after the business owner makes the intellectual, emotional, and actual switch from "doer" of his "thing" to "marketer" of his "thing."

The fact that marketing's where the money is can be seen at play in small or big business.

Some years ago, I was doing a lot of consulting and advertising copywriting work for a big company owned by an even bigger Fortune 500 company. Its president, a nice, pleasant fellow, called me in to his private office, closed the door, sat across from me, and said: "I've done some calculations and realized we are actually paying you more per hour than we are paying me."

Imagine being a consultant confronted with this one!

I answered, "There is a very good reason for that. You see, you know how to do everything in this company better than I do by a big margin except for one thing, and it is essential and vital that one thing gets done the best way it can, because nothing you know how to do matters if it doesn't. That one thing is getting customers. That's the one thing I know how to do that you don't, and that's why I get paid more. But look, " I said, "we'll just keep this as our little secret."

That is a true story and it makes more than one important point. One is, as I've said, any rapid and dramatic value improvement in a business is going to come from the sales and marketing side, and usually the only indispensably valuable people are the ones who know how to create sales and marketing breakthroughs. Two, you do not want to be in the position that corporate CEO was. You do not want a guy like me holding you and your success hostage. The only way to prevent that is to personally master the sales and marketing aspects of your business.

At Least Avoid the Ultimate Marketing Sin

I've created more marketing breakthroughs by being exciting, different, and outrageous than by any other means. Many have emulated me.

Bill Glazer became famous for the "Outrageous Advertising" he created for his own wildly successful menswear stores, and then provided to other store owners nationwide. He has sent out direct-mail pieces that look like hand-scrawled notes on a diner's placemat, complete with coffee cup stains; handwritten notes on torn legal pad paper; and notes on lunch bags.

One of my long-time followers in the business of advising leaders of mid-sized family owned companies on investments, asset protection, succession planning, and other financial matters solicits appointments with new prospective clients by having his very-oversized sales letter delivered to the prospect's office in a full-size aluminum trashcan, brought there by a uniformed messenger. The letter cautions against "permitting the legacy you've built to be trashed or throwing away any of the wealth you've worked so hard to earn." He secures appointments with better than 50% of the prospects he hand selects every month for such a delivery. I have been telling this story for many years but as far as I know, no other financial advisor has copied the tactic—but many have told me they never would because it's just too unprofessional. They say they would be embarrassed. Being privy to this advisor's income, I can assure everybody he has nothing to be embarrassed about.

Incidentally, ad-man-turned-CNBC-TV-commentator, Donny Deutsch, recounts a story of deciding to go after a $3-million a year account, a tri-state area auto dealers' association. If they got it, it would have then been their largest account. They had no auto industry experience. The client used TV extensively and, at the time, Donny's agency had no TV experience. Donny wanted to do something "different" to get the key man's attention and get him to decide "We've got to at least give these guys a chance."

Donny and a couple of his associates got a bunch of used car parts from a junkyard and had one after another delivered to the prospect, every half hour. A headlight came with a note promising bright ideas. A steering wheel with a note promising to steer them in the right direction. Etc. Donny admits it could have backfired. But it didn't. And I can promise you from extensive experience

Donny Deutsch

Read Donny Deutsch's book *Often Wrong, Never In Doubt—Unleash The Business Rebel Within*. And look for current Outrageous Advertising examples from Bill Glazer in every issue of my *No B.S. Marketing Letter*. See pages 272–273 for a free trial subscription gift.

with countless of our Members using this kind of approach multiplied to many prospects not just one, it works more often than not.

One of my long-time Members, who has been studying me for over 20 years, Dr. Gregg Nielsen, does the most outrageous advertising and marketing in the entire chiropractic profession. I've reprinted one of his direct-mail pieces, a funny letter from his staff, at the end of this chapter, so you can get a feel for what I'm talking about. Believe me, his doctor peers and even his wife cringe at mailings like this. But his patients love it and refer like crazy—at a rate five times better than his profession's average.

I could show you hundreds more examples from the ever-growing tribe of like-minded marketers I've inspired.

Their output is the antithesis of dull, boring, institutional, stuffy professional marketing.

The worst marketing sin you can commit is to be boring. People love to buy when it's a pleasure to buy. When it's interesting to buy. When the experience of buying itself is involving and rewarding.

This crosses all demographic boundaries and applies whether you market to consumers or B2B. Boring is boring. Leap-out-at-you, outrageous, fun, and interesting is what it is. People are people, in the boardroom on the 50th floor or in the living room, on the floor.

The entrepreneur's responsibility and opportunity is to create breakthrough ideas that foster exciting, positive relationships between the company and its customers. This chapter gives you the very best ways I know to create those kinds of breakthrough ideas.

Breakthrough Strategy #1:
Find a Market Niche and Exploit It

In niches, there are riches! A market niche is a crack, a crevice, an opportunity gap, sometimes a tiny segment of a market being overlooked, ignored, abused, or very poorly serviced.

It might be a story not being told with special appeal to a segment of a market. Subway's clever reinvention of itself as a weight-loss program with Jared's diet gave the company great differentiation from all other fast food restaurant chains. Our Member Diana Coutu, owner of Diana's Gourmet Pizzeria, has dieter-friendly and even diabetic-friendly pizzas that still taste terrific.

It might be a way to be of service to a special segment of a market. Consider the printing company specializing in medical forms for hospitals. They (and their competitors) packaged and sold their various forms in cartons of 1,000, 5,000, and 10,000. Many small hospitals and nursing homes refused to buy from them because they didn't need 1,000 copies of any one form. The president of this printing company took the time to ask how many forms they would buy. (Asking your customers what *they* want—now there is a radical concept!) He then put out a new catalog with all their forms priced in packages of 150 for smaller hospitals and institutions and, in short order, they captured the niche market of small institutions.

It might be making ordinary goods and services proprietary. I watched Jim and Naomi Rhode build a small company originally called Semantodontics into a very large company now called Smart Practice, based on marketing imprinted advertising

"If you had a Shih Tzu dog, wouldn't you pay more for doggie bis-
cuits created just for the dietary needs of Shih Tzus? If you were an
attorney, wouldn't you pay more for a software program that was
designed specifically for lawyers? If you were a woman over 50,
wouldn't you pay more for a face cream that claimed it had ingredients that would diminish the appearance of fine lines and wrin-
kles? **Everyday people spend more for products and services
that they believe have been created or designed specifically for
their particular needs or situations.** Could you create a version of
the product or service you sell for a niche within your market? The
product or service can be identical to, or a slightly tweaked version
of, one you offer to all other customers. But if the niche customer
believes there is something special and different about it, if it
sends the message 'this is for ME!', that is the one they'll buy."

—SYDNEY BIDDLE BARROWS, AUTHOR, *UNCENSORED SALES STRATEGIES: A RADICAL
NEW APPROACH TO SELLING YOUR CUSTOMERS WHAT THEY REALLY
WANT—NO MATTER WHAT BUSINESS YOU'RE IN*

specialties, freemiums, premiums, gift items, office supplies, and
imprinted forms exclusively to dentists. Much of what they sell
to dentists can be purchased from any number of other, generic
vendors to any and all, but the Rhodes were smart enough to
organize it, "tweak" some of it to dentistry, and present their
company as the source of it all *just for dentists.*

In a very similar way, another long-time Member built a
hugely profitable business virtually invisible to anyone not in
leadership in a fraternal organization, like the Shriners or
Kiwanis—but those folks know him well, because he is the dominant provider of awards, promotional items, glassware, apparel,
and other products emblazoned with these organizations' logos.
He also publishes a newsletter about group leadership for the
clients who buy these goods from him. Almost all the merchandise

The Power of the Price Gap In a Niche

Way back in 1983, I was doing some speaking for a practice management company in the chiropractic profession, another in the dental profession. As I analyzed the professions, I identified an enormous "gap" in what was being offered to help doctors market, promote, and grow their practices. There were a number of management companies offering multi-year programs requiring fees upwards from $30,000.00 per doctor. There were books and how-to manuals in the trade journals, for $10.00 to $50.00. But there was nothing in between. It also was true that almost all the management companies acquired their clients by inviting doctors to free seminars, then delivering sales presentations, ultimately asking for $30,000.00 or more. I devised a company that would copycat the entire seminar method, but offer do-it-yourselfer-type "marketing kits" and complete courses for $100.00 to $1,000.00.

We hit the "price gap" perfectly. Within the first 12 months the company I created became THE largest seminar and publishing company exclusively serving chiropractors and dentists. Actually, we became that our first day because we were the only company mixing chiropractors and dentists into the same seminars; I defined my own niche, so I could trumpet being the biggest instantly. Some call that creating a "category of one," and it is a terrific positioning strategy. Beyond that, we did quickly grow to millions of dollars. We trained well over 15,000 doctors.

In recent years, a number of companies have created fabulously successful businesses by finding a price position far above all others' in their category. There is, for example, a $25,000.00 mattress, typically sold by private invitation demonstration parties with fine wine and appetizers served, in upscale department stores. Very pricey time-share programs have appeared and prospered with invitation fees in the $500,000.00 neighborhood. On the other hand, some luxury manufacturers identified price gaps they were not responsive to, where customers eager for their brands were available in significant numbers. Mercedes-Benz, as example, created a new "S class" of smaller, more modestly priced Mercedes automobiles for this reason and has done well with them.

his company sold can be provided by any of the thousands of "generic" ad specialty companies, but Shawn has created a niche business and dominated a target market.

It's important to understand that all of America—the world, really—divides into niches and sub-cultures, and just about everybody belongs to one to several of each, and close-ly identifies with them. For example, for years I made a lion's share of my living as a professional speaker, and another big portion as a direct-response advertising strategist and copy-writer. Those are professional niches not even known to many outside of them. For many years I also traveled constantly on business, a "road warrior"; that's a subculture. Road warriors describe themselves that way and have profound interest in many things that are of little interest to anyone but a road war-rior—from the OAG Guide to any good tricks for getting to sleep quickly even in a noisy airport hotel, with planes flying overhead and your room next to the elevator shaft. I travel little now for business, and I fly by private jet, so I no longer consider myself a road warrior. But those of us who fly private are also a subculture.

This is all very important from a marketing standpoint because people want and respond best to whatever they perceive is for them, preferably *exclusively* for them, relevant *specifically* to them, and offered by somebody who really understands, respects, and appreciates them. The further you drill down, to make whatever you offer feel customized for and unique to a very well-defined niche or, better, niche within a niche, or subculture or, better, subculture within a subculture, the better your results may be and the better able you are to command premium prices or fees and above-par profits without resistance.

Breakthrough Strategy #2:
Find a New Sales Media and Let It Make You Rich

In Arizona, there is an industrial cleaning products manufacturer with a very successful line of citrus-peel-based cleaners and stain removers. For years, they bottled these chemicals in giant drums and sold them to factories, restaurants, hospitals, hotels, and other large institutional buyers. Like every other industrial chemical company, the only sales media they used were industrial sales representatives and catalogues distributed to their customers.

They made the leap to marketing directly to consumers through a sales medium far, far outside their norms—a shopping channel on cable TV. It works for them because their products demonstrate like magic tricks. They're perfect for television. After their first on-the-air test, they couldn't bottle product fast enough. They were instant "TV bestsellers," and this very different sales media made these entrepreneurs rich, quick, and has continued to add to their wealth year after year.

The internet has come into its own as provider of media many find ways to use profitably. As I write this, social networking media like MySpace, Facebook, Twitter, and the countless niche/subculture versions are being used by everyone from comedians on the rise to entrepreneurs promoting their products . . . .

YouTube used by companies like the venerable direct-selling company Vita-Mix as a means of reaching a new, different audience for its product demonstrations . . . Google AdWords® a means of purchasing "eyeballs" i.e., website visitors who are actually searching for the exact expertise, information, products, or services a particular company provides . . . . and the list goes on and on. Websites, of course, grow increasingly complex and sophisticated, and many companies have reason for more than one kind, including catalog-type sites, sales letters and video-assisted sales letters, and customer service and support.

Much of this is now a necessary part of business. Within it all may be the combination of media you need to create a dynamic sales breakthrough. None of it, however, is any sort of magic bean or panacea. No media is inherently good or bad; it's all in appropriate application. With online media, it's important not to be fooled by its appearance of "free"—there is time, manual labor, and distraction cost. It's also important to carefully and critically analyze the quality of the customer it brings you, not just the quantity. And my final caution: over-reliance on any one media for new customer acquisition or for communication with established customers is a huge, costly, dangerous mistake. That goes double for e-mail.

My own preference is for multi-channel marketing. A made-for-the-internet company like LegalZoom.com makes its sales of do-it-yourself legal filings, forms, and kits online, but it drives traffic there with television, radio, and print advertising. Similarly, the overwhelming majority of new Glazer-Kennedy Insider's Circle™ Members may learn about and opt in to a free trial membership online at any one of many websites like FreeGiftFrom.com/business, but they are sent there from books like this, advertisements in print magazines, articles in magazines and newsletters, and direct mail; and our Members get many deliverables online including webinars, archives of information, directories, blogs, and community, and receive e-mail from us at least twice a week. But they also receive from one to three monthly print newsletters, audio learning programs (presently on CDs), other direct mail, and telephone support.

The company 1-800-Flowers is a full-scale multi-channel merchant. It began with a brick-and-mortar flower shop, expanded via toll-free number and mail-order, then online, and with additional stores and licensed retailers. Today, its online marketing and sales operation is the centerpiece of the business and while a lion's share of its marketing to existing customers is done by e-mail, it continues advertising on radio, TV, and by direct mail, as well as continues brick-and-mortar retail operations. Each channel feeds the other and feeds into the center. Many retailers also have e-commerce sites and owners of e-commerce businesses sometimes open retail stores, but few become truly sophisticated multi-channel merchants with smart synergy interconnecting every channel.

Many sales breakthroughs don't require a new media to become available; instead they come from fitting a product together with an existing media not previously used for that type of product.

My friend Joe Sugarman, a bona fide direct marketing legend, has had mammoth success with his product "Blu-Blockers" sunglasses. Today, you can buy them in retail stores and in catalogs, but their launch was via a 30-minute TV infomercial, and that success in turn led to QVC, the home shopping channel, where millions of pairs have been sold. To my knowledge, sunglasses had never been sold via infomercial before Joe.

In a short time, it went from radical to common for doctors to promote Botox® injections via Tupperware®-style party plan selling. The in-home sales party is certainly not a new media. But doctors using it—that was new. The in-home party is a distribution channel using human media that is at least 100 years old, is always with us, is viable, and enjoys repeated renaissance and new popularity with each new generation. It is often fueled by recession, when more people become interested in extra income opportunities in direct-selling, and more consumers are receptive to a "night out" with friends and neighbors in someone's home. Today, the diversity of products and services sold via home parties includes sex toys and lingerie, cruises and vacation tours, investment real estate, children's toys and games, personal and home security products, and, still, Tupperware® Far, far, far from a new distribution channel or media, and certainly not high tech, yet used by an ever-increasing number of diverse companies to profitably promote their products. It is case in point that the old used in a new way can be just as powerful as the entirely new, and that no means of marketing should be ignored or too easily rejected.

E. Joseph Cossman's Million-Dollar Secret

Years back, I did a lot of work over several years with E. Joseph Cossman, who has written several books about mail order, which I urge you to read. Joe made a million dollars or more from scratch at least 20 times, using the very same formula each time: he found a company with a good, salable product that marketed it via only one or two distribution channels. Often it was a manufacturer omitting direct-to-consumer marketing, such as mail order. He acquired exclusive rights to the product only for one or all of the neglected distribution channels. In one instance, it was an insect-killing product called Fly Cake, being manufactured and sold to the military; Joe turned it into a consumer product and began selling it through classified ads. In another case it was a children's bathtub toy that could be powered by a little chemical pellet and would move about for a long period of time underwater; Joe popularized it, in several forms including a scuba diver, as an underwater aquarium ornament and sold it through pet stores and tropical fish stores and by mail order, direct to consumers. Joe is best remembered, though, for popularizing the famous Ant Farm. At the time he found it, it was being sold only to schools for use in science and biology classes. Joe saw its potential as a toy/novelty, and controlled its sales through toy stores and other retail stores, mail-order catalogs, ads in comic books, and other print advertising. Joe made his fortunes quite a bit before the existence of the internet; and I can only imagine what a field day he might have had with so many more media options at his disposal.

Of course, what Joe did any manufacturer, marketer, retailer, or service provider can do for himself. The lesson of Joe Cossman's entire business life is: most think too narrowly and provincially about their product, service, or business and therefore leave many sales and distribution channels unexploited.

Breakthrough Strategy #3: Create a New Type of Guarantee and Confound Your Competition

I love marketing on the strength of guarantees. For me, nothing's better than finding a way to offer the very best guarantee any given field.

I've been told that guarantees are outdated, overdone, and no longer effective, but my experience proves this to be nonsense. Good guarantees work just as well today as they did 25 years ago, and they may be more necessary than ever.

Lee Iacocca used this idea to save Chrysler many years back, with its 7-year/70,000-Mile Warranty along with the argument: if you want to know who builds them better, take a look at who guarantees them longer. At the time, this was a ground-breaking guarantee. It left the competition gasping and galloping backwards. It got the public's attention, and it sold a lot of cars. (Eventually, of course, the competition caught up. That's to be expected.) Much more recently in that industry, Hyundai responded to recession by promoting the most unusual auto warranty ever—if you lost your job, they would make three consecutive months of car loan payments for you; if you still were in trouble, you could return the car, have your loan voided, owe nothing, and your credit would not be negatively affected. I'm told by one of the biggest dealers that when those TV commercials began, his showroom had a huge surge in traffic and he sold more cars in the ensuing two weeks than in any two months before.

More than 35 years ago, my ad agency had a small chain of eyeglass stores as a client, and we created, I believe before anyone else in the country, the "free eyeglass replacement guarantee." My client ran large newspaper ads featuring this remarkable guarantee—and he brought in a flood of customers. He sucked customers right out of his competitors' stores. His stores kicked butt for nearly a year with this promotion. In one store, sales increased by 800%. Today, big chains use the same strategy and it has long ago lost its unique magic. But the business built with this breakthrough guarantee matured successfully and was sold for millions of dollars.

I have clients who use what we call "penalty guarantees." Financial advisors who guarantee they will uncover and present hidden opportunities to a new client in the first one hour meeting or pay the client $100.00 to $1,000.00 for wasting his time. Marketers who guarantee reading their lengthy sales letters will be worthwhile or the reader can say his time was wasted and be paid $25.00, $50.00, $100.00. An appliance company that guarantees service on time or they do the repair work free. There is a franchise company, Ben Franklin Plumbing, that has Ben in its commercials promising to pay $5.00 for every minute a technician is late in arriving, so that, if he should be 20 minutes late, you, the customer, would get a Franklin (slang, of course, for a $100.00 bill). This goes back to a guarantee that built a David into a Goliath almost overnight: Dominos' original ". . . delivered in 30 minutes or less, guaranteed."

You should also think about the way you describe and present your guarantees. My client, Guthy-Renker Corporation, has, for many years, had Victoria Principal delivering her Bottom-of-the-Jar Guarantee, i.e., use the whole jar, return it empty if dissatisfied for refund. Still the best worded guarantee in skin care that I've ever seen came from my friend, copywriting genius Gary Halbert, for Nancy Kwan's Pearl Cream: "If your friends don't actually accuse you of having had a face-lift, return the empty jar . . ." I swiped it for a weight loss product: "If your friends don't accuse you of having had liposuction . . ." These are nothing more than ordinary satisfaction guarantees presented in more interesting ways.

It may be marketing consultant Jay Abraham who coined the term "risk reversal selling" for the use of strong, creatively worded guarantees. Whether he originated it or not, he and I share position as committed advocates of risk reversal. Every time I have convinced a client to take a particularly daring risk reversal position, his increased sales have far exceeded the cost of honoring the guarantees.

Breakthrough Strategy #4: Deliver Exceptional Service and Earn Word-of-Mouth Advertising

As a customer these days, aren't you frustrated more often than not? I find spending money as tough as making it! Think about all the aggravations you have had as a customer and the number of times you've turned away from a business because of poor service. In the New Economy, unsatisfactory service is deadly. Now that all the power is in the hands of the consumers and their spending has become more thoughtful and deliberate, no business can afford to disappoint.

What is exceptional service? It means different things to different people in different businesses at different times, so I can't define it for you in your business with a general statement. But I can tell you where to look and who to study to get close to it.

Walt Disney preached that customers should be viewed and treated like guests. That's why at Disney World and Disneyland all the employees, from the broom pushers to the managers, learn how to direct guests to any attraction and how to answer the most common questions. They are taught that they are important to the success of each guest's visit. The next time you're at a Disney Park, stand near a broom pusher for a few minutes. Watch how people go up to him or her and ask questions. Watch how well that employee responds. You'll witness exceptional customer service in action.

My favorite Disney marketing principle is *do what you do so well that people can't resist telling others about you.* Following this principle gives you marketing leverage. A lot of leverage. If you get one customer from an advertisement, that's one thing, but if you get that customer plus three referrals, who in turn each refer two people, that's nine new customers from leverage rather than direct monetary investment.

As service overall has worsened and customers grown more demanding, your opportunity to stand out through service superiority gets more and more significant. I delve into this in exhaustive detail in my book *No B.S. Ruthless Management of People and Profits.*

Breakthrough Strategy #5:
Get Professional Prowess on a Percentage

I'm about to suggest hiring an expert or two to help you with your marketing. But, first, a few words about expert advice in general.

There are a lot of "experts" out there very eager to get their hands into your entrepreneurial pockets. Most of them aren't worth the powder it would take to blow them up. Most couldn't run your business or any other for a week. Most couldn't sell their way out of a closet. They may be good song 'n' dance people, but that doesn't mean they can conceptualize a great song, write a musical, or attract crowds to the theater. When you peel away the top layer of veneer, you'll find another layer of veneer.

So, the expert advice I have for you about expert advice is to proceed with great caution. And I'm an expert!

Never let yourself be intimidated. Ask a lot of questions. Check references. Ultimately, trust your judgment and retain control. And, in the case of getting marketing assistance, get it from people willing, even eager, to be paid based on performance, not just on task completion.

You'll be hard-pressed to find a Madison Avenue ad agency that will play this way. If they did, they'd starve. The hard, tough truth is that most of what they do fails to work. It wins awards, it gets talked about, it jazzes up half time at the Super Bowl, but it doesn't sell. That's why most agencies that win the industry's Clio Awards quickly lose the clients for which they created all that award-winning, expensive, but ineffective advertising. That's why in my seminars, when I've asked everybody to jot down the brand name of the battery advertised by the famous pink bunny banging his drum, one-third to one-half of all people write down the wrong brand name.

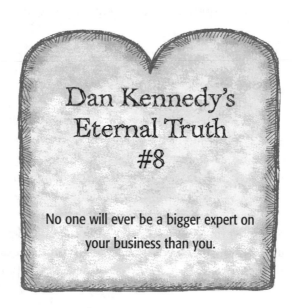

Dan Kennedy's
Eternal Truth
#8

No one will ever be a bigger expert on
your business than you.

But every top marketing consultant and every top copywriter I know eagerly looks for clients they can really help, then get most of their compensation from a small percentage of the sales created and measured. For example, when I develop direct-marketing and direct-mail campaigns for a client, I charge a hefty fee, but as my main compensation, I take 2% to 5% of the resulting sales. My personal objective is to choose projects right and do the work so well that each client winds up paying me $100,000.00, or much more over time.

Also, keep in mind that the best marketing experts do not tell you what to do. They try to create a partnership with you to combine your unique understanding of your business with their special expertise. Then they do the mechanics.

We realize no one's more of an expert on your business and your customers than you are, although you may benefit from help in extracting what you know and putting it into useable form.

A good marketing professional can save you a lot of time and trial-and-error experimentation, bring you already-proven ideas from their broader experience, and help you clarify your own thinking.

Breakthrough Strategy #6:
Reasonable Investment

This relates to several of the above strategies. While throwing money at marketing is never assurance of success, the opposite extreme, being unreasonably Scroogish about it, being unwilling to invest in acquiring and developing customers, and having wholly unrealistic expectations about what can be achieved pinching pennies is just as destructive as is wholesale waste.

One of the most important numbers you need to determine is your "maximum allowable"; what will you invest to acquire a customer? That number may entirely rule out certain opportunities, media, and methods. It may prohibit your even walking on to certain playing fields. Or it may make every media viable.

You must view this as managed investment. The customer as asset, into which you place investment capital, from which you extract a reasonable return. I encounter business owners all the time who are perfectly willing to accept some small percentage of interest on money parked in CDs at the bank or even put their money at risk in the stock market or elsewhere for single digit percentage yield year to year but balk at investing $500.00 to buy a customer with a $5,000.00 five-year value—or dumber yet, want to acquire such customers for no more than $50.00 each. Val-Pak® and similar merge mail media happens to be one that sparks this discussion a lot. In the years I did a great deal of work with chiropractors and dentists, they would often complain to me about the poor performance of this coupon media—"In two months, all I got was one good patient and, geez, it goes to 10,000 homes every time." The money invested, I would point out, was about $450.00 a month, $900.00 total, and the minimum value of the patient $5,000.00 or $2,500.00 net if operating the practice with no more than 50% overhead. So, if you could trade $900.00 for $2,500.00 at your bank today, how many times would you like to do so?

Of course, if you are to aggressively and confidently invest in acquiring new customers and further in nurturing and developing them, you need to have your act together in serving, satisfying, and retaining them, obtaining maximum purchasing from them, and multiplying them through referrals.

In a meeting with two financial advisors from the same firm, both enunciated roughly the same goal: adding about 50 top clients over the next two years to arrive at a doubling of their present $500,000.00 yearly income. I asked what they would invest to acquire each client. The first said his average first-year value was $5,000.00, lifetime value over $100,000.00, and said he would gladly invest up to $5,000.00 in marketing to acquire each client. The other advisor said he didn't *think* his first-year value was that high, wasn't sure about lifetime value, definitely was not prepared to invest thousands in each new client, but didn't know what would be a good acquisition cost that he'd be comfortable with. I told the first one I could help him achieve his goal; I told the other one to leave the room and hit the road.

There is a "dirty little secret" about marketing that can grow a business substantially and rapidly while successfully targeting and attracting ideal customers or clients. The more you can and will invest to acquire each customer, the more likely you are to succeed, the bigger and more crushing is your competitive advantage, the faster you can get from point A to point B. Again, the money itself isn't magic. It can't be wasted or carelessly thrown about. But to think you can compete in the Indy 500 with a soapbox-derby car you cobbled together with spare parts and items from the bargain bin at Home Depot is downright foolish.

FIGURE 6.1: Nielsen Exhibit

STAFF MEMO

FROM: Dr. Nielsen's Staff (Mostly Marie)
505 Aber Drive
Waterford, WI 53185
Ph: (262) 534-3767

Thursday 2:37 P.M.

"I Want To Give You A FREE Office Visit...Because...
I'm Taking Full Responsibility For This Traffic Jam"

Dear Dan:

Hi again!!! As you can see, I've attached a little note to this letter. I'm doing this because I feel responsible for the traffic jam that happened in our office last Wednesday morning. And I want you to hear my side of the story first...before Dr. Nielsen tells you about it on your next office visit.

You see, last Wednesday morning our Yellow Pages ad representative stopped by to pick up our ad for the new Waterford phone book. He's a little old guy who always struts around in a cute, blue three-piece suit...and... he sports a white handlebar mustache. I think he looks like the guy from the Monopoly Game. And Wednesday morning he also finally decided to get treated for his headaches.

Anyway, Dr. Nielsen decided to change this year's Yellow Pages ad at the last minute. Mostly because Dr. Nielsen just added his FREE e-book, **"Wisconsin Fold Medicine"** (a collection of simple and easy home remedies) to his web site at www.doc nielsen.com... and... he also wanted to add this info to his new Yellow Pages ad just before the deadline Wednesday morning at noon.

Dr. Nielsen told me to have Stefi x-ray the ad rep, and throw out the old ad...because... he had a new ad. And he then gave the new ad to me to proofread. Maybe it was the full moon. Maybe it was all three phone lines ringing at the same time. Maybe it was all those people standing at the front desk staring at me. Maybe it was that 9 month old baby screaming nonstop while his mother jabbered on her cell phone in our lobby. And maybe it was just the combination of everything that day. Who knows?

In any event, I got slightly distracted. And I yelled to Stefi: *"Go ahead and x ray the ad ...and... throw out the old rep."* You know, Stefi is so cool. She snagged Monopoly Man by the collar and muscled him out the front door. Then Stefi snatched Dr. Nielsen's new ad from me and x-rayed it. I've attached her x-ray of Dr. Nielsen's Yellow Pages ad as proof. For the record, she did a great job x-raying the ad.

Oh, the best part was when Dr. Nielsen asked Stefi why she was x-raying his Yellow Pages ad. I could not hear her response, because the lady with the cell phone was now standing in front of me yakking away...and her kid decided it was a good time to start screaming in my face. But, I bet Stefi's response was something like... *"I'm x-raying your Yellow Pages ad because it's my job, Sir."* Again, Stefi is so cool. She never questions anything around here. I guess that's a good thing.

Now, I want to thank you for listening to my side of this story. And, please use the attached **"FREE OFFICE VISIT"** prescription on your next visit (before the expiration date.) Also, please make sure you call ahead. Just call Stefi or me today at (262) 534-3767 to schedule your **FREE** office visit.

Thanks! *Marie*

P.S. I printed this letter on yellow paper because I'm telling you my story about our Yellow Pages ad. Pretty cool, eh? By the way, Monopoly Man came back after lunch. He's doing great now. Bye!!!

FIGURE 6.1: Nielsen Exhibit, continued

WATERFORD CHIROPRACTIC OFFICE
DR. G.E. NIELSEN • DOCNIELSEN@AOL.COM
505 ABER DRIVE, P.O. BOX 86
WATERFORD, WI 53185-0086

PHONE: (262) 534-3767 FAX: (262) 534-2363

(PATIENT'S NAME) (DATE)

Rx: *One Free Office Visit*

G.E. Nielsen D.C.

(DOCTOR'S SIGNATURE) EXPIRES: 30 AUG 2003

FIGURE 6.1: Nielsen Exhibit, continued

CHAPTER 7

WHY AND HOW
TO SELL YOUR WAY
THROUGH LIFE

You can succeed if others do not believe in you.
But you cannot succeed if you do not
believe in yourself.

—Dr. Sidney Newton Bremer, *Successful Achievement*

I n this chapter, I'm not going to attempt to teach you how to sell—that deserves an entire book and then some—but I am going to make a case for your becoming a master salesperson.

Good News

Good news: there is an entire book on this! *My NO B.S. Sales Success in the New Economy*. At your favorite bookseller. I also strongly recommend Sydney Barrows' book, *Uncensored Sales Strategies*, to which I contributed.

You probably don't like the idea of being a salesperson. If you're like many people, you may think of salespeople as fast talkers—people who talk you into things. You may look at sales as combative: somebody has to lose for the salesperson to win. And you may believe that you can't learn to sell, that there really are such things as "born" salespeople. (And people born absent some gene necessary to succeed in selling.) Finally, like many people, you might think that selling is unimportant in your chosen business.

I am here to tell you that these ideas are all false and must be corrected. If you expect to make any money as an entrepreneur, the mastery of selling is absolutely necessary. In The New Economy, everybody who seeks success in business, for their business, must be passionately committed to mastery of salesmanship and actively, happily engaged in selling. Why? Because consumers are no longer just buying as they did during the long boom that preceded the 2008–2009 crash. It'll be a long time before such indiscriminate, profligate buying returns, if it ever does. People must now be convinced to part with their money. Convinced of many things, discussed throughout this book and the *No B.S. Sales Success* book. That convincing is selling at its highest level. It is more critical than ever for you to adopt productive attitudes about selling.

Changing Your Attitudes About Selling
Myth #1: Selling Is Just Fast Talking.

Selling has more to do with listening than talking. Tests done with telemarketers have demonstrated that those who listened twice as much as they talked wound up booking five times as many appointments. Selling is empathy in action. "Push" selling . . . . the pushing of products by brute force . . . can still work, typically for relatively simple products and propositions, deployed by extremely skilled "pushers." But even if it can work in your business, it's ill-advised, if you grasp the importance of a point made earlier in this book: the wisdom of making a sale to get a customer, not getting a customer just to make a sale. Selling at the highest level is all about relationship, not rape. So it is about the discovery of needs, problems, interests, priorities, values, and desires then about crafting the right combination of products and services, expertise, and customer care to meet those needs and desires. Every entrepreneur should want to do this and do it as effectively as possible with each customer and with his business' customers as a group.

Myth #2: Selling Sets Up a Win/Lose Situation.

Selling can have winners and losers, but it doesn't have to be that way. Personally, my type of selling is win/win; the person buying my ideas, products, or services benefits at least as much as I do. The most successful salespeople uncover, clarify, and fulfill people's strongest needs and desires. My speaking colleague Zig Ziglar's most famous quotation is "You can get anything in life you want by helping enough other people get what they want." Actually, you can get not only anything you want, you can get *everything* you want that way.

In my *No B.S. Wealth Attraction for Entrepreneurs* book, I talk about people's negative feelings about selling as a transfer of money from buyer to seller, leaving the buyer with less than he had before. Whenever that negative feeling represents reality, no one with a conscience can long succeed selling those products or services, and the business itself cannot sustain itself in the marketplace. However, it's rarely the case. Usually, the money that changes hands would have disappeared from the buyer's life one way or another regardless of his purchase of your goods or services, but the benefits derived from ownership and use of what you sell may last for years. It's important for both sales professionals and business owners to do two things, strategically: one, identify the most appropriate people to sell to, who have the most to gain from the products and services being sold; two, fully understand and be able to present the full value of those benefits to those people.

Many business owners err mightily in thinking about anybody or everybody with a pulse and a purse as a potential customer. In my consulting work, my clients are often eager to discuss the "how" they will acquire customers most efficiently, sell their wares or services to them most successfully, and reach their business growth and income goals as quickly as possible—and that is what I'm paid to figure out for each client, each time I help them build a comprehensive marketing system unique to their particular business. But in front of all that must be the discussion of the "who."

Some years back, I had a client in the unusual business of helping American men find foreign brides. While there are many scams in this field, my client ran a legitimate business and provided a complete, very professional service, at a significant fee. Initially, he described his clients as middle-aged men, divorced one or more times, frustrated with American women, and seeking a wife with old-fashioned, traditional values; he said his clients came from every imaginable occupational group—from pastors to painters to professional athletes. With deeper investigation, it turned out that over one-third of his clients were, in fact, long-haul truck drivers. They had work schedules and lifestyles that made it difficult to meet and date women, and that often made wives unhappy as well. Once we knew this, we could focus most of his marketing efforts on media that directly reached only this occupational group and slightly recraft his generic marketing message and his services to more precisely match this group. And we delivered a better-than-ever win for this client. This was a million dollar breakthrough in his business, and it is actually typical of what is accomplished over and over and over again, by first figuring out who is *the* most ideal Who for a business.

The better matched the business' deliverables and the customer, the greater a win it is for the customer—so the business owner can feel very good about selling.

Myth #3: Sales Ability Is Hereditary.

Selling is a combination of scientific and mechanical processes that can be learned by anybody, combined with the human qualities of compassion, empathy, and enthusiasm that exist—or at least potentially exist—in everybody.

The late Mark McCormack, super sports agent and author of *What They Don't Teach You at Harvard Business School,* looked at it from a different angle. He said that most people are born salespeople, but that we "unlearn" it as we grow up. If you stop to think about it, most kids do have good sales instincts. They're not afraid to ask for what they want, persistently. They're big on asking "Why?"

I suggest that you, too, are a born salesperson; that you already possess great sales instincts, even if you are suppressing them, and that you have the ability to release those instincts and to add new sales skills. With the combination of what you have inside naturally, and what you can learn, you can become a master salesperson.

Myth #4: Selling Isn't Important to Every Business.

Many books on business would have you believe that companies fail because of poorly selected locations, ill-prepared management, even bad bookkeeping. I think this is all B.S. *Businesses fail, more often than not, because the owners sit on their butts waiting for something to happen rather than going out and selling.* You can sell your way out of a lot of the trouble entrepreneurs typically stumble into if you have confidence and competence to sell.

Furthermore, the real business of every business is marketing—and by extension, selling. This is true even if there is never face-to-face, human-to-human contact with a business' customers. If you use any media—print, direct mail, websites, e-mail, TV, radio—it is (hopefully) delivering sales messages.

But When Can I Stop Selling?

I used to look forward to the time that I might be able to take a break from selling. But that's the wrong attitude. As entrepreneurs, we have to be in the selling mode 100% of the time, so we might as well enjoy it.

Entrepreneurs actually need to do more selling them many salespeople. We have to sell and re-sell ourselves on our ideas, goals, plans, and decisions each and every day. We have to sell our associates and our employees on doing the things we want done, the way we want them done, when we want them done. We have to sell our salespeople on our products, our services, our ideas, our leadership, themselves, their futures, on selling. We have to sell our vendors and suppliers that what we want done can be done, can be done by them, should be done by them, can be done when we need it done, and can be done at reasonable costs, under favorable terms. We have to sell our accountants and lawyers on our strategies. We have to sell to our bankers, our lenders, and investors.

The decision is <u>not</u> whether to sell. The decision is whether to do it masterfully and whether to enjoy it.

I am not just talking about face-to-face selling either. Most advertising is better done as selling in print, most of what we call marketing better viewed as selling in media. Everything in business should be critically analyzed through the prism of: *Does it sell?*

Consider "environment," just as example. I teach chiropractors and dentists to chuck the magazines out of the reception room and replace them with testimonial and success story books, before-and-after photo albums, health-related books; to decorate the walls with framed patient testimonials instead of paintings. My contention is there's only three things that a patient should be doing while in the office: getting treated and getting well; getting educated; and getting motivated to refer. In other words, being sold. Being sold on the doctor, so the patient complies with and follows through on his instructions—the win for the patient, and so the patient refers others to the practice.

Fully Embrace Your Role as Salesperson

At a big event in Washington, DC, shortly after the 2008 presidential election, I met the newly famous "Joe The Plumber." My sense is that what you've seen of him on TV or heard on radio is real; he is a straightforward, sincere fellow with strong feelings about America. Thanks to his made-by-the-Obama-campaign celebrity, he likely has a small window, a brief opportunity to

> "I think that the failure of medicine, the failure to get adherence with what we suggest is because we think as M.D.s we are deities, because we wear The White Coat that patients will do what we say. That's one of the great failures of medicine. Even if the pills are free, in the V.A., and patients who have hypertension and know that it is a serious disease, only one-third of those patients take the pills as prescribed—and that's when the pills are free! Only two-thirds even fill the prescription to start with. So **our failure in medicine is failing to understand that we have to sell health**, and then making ourselves expert and proficient at that. Just telling a patient is not enough, if you don't get into the emotions of that individual, if you can't get that patient to really understand why it's important for them. So, for anyone to follow my path, I think you have to be good enough in delivering medical care, and then **be highly skilled at selling** your patients on doing what they need to do—whether it's actually doing the exercises you need to do, to prevent reoccurring neck and back pain, or making the right food choices—we are constantly selling patients. So, to come back to the question, selling is what we must do. If we don't sell, we don't get patients healthy. And the reason that my entire business outside the practice works as well as it does is that I am able to sell my concepts."
>
> —Dr. Michael Roizen M.D., Author of *The New York Times* Bestselling *YOU* book series and Chief Wellness Officer of the Cleveland Clinic—as seen on PBS and *Oprah*

capitalize. When I spoke with him I congratulated him on his new life as a personality with opportunity to influence, and on his book, and said that I hoped he was having success promoting it. He expressed the feeling that "being a salesman" wasn't for him and that relentlessly promoting his book wasn't something he was at all comfortable with. I held my tongue, but felt sorry for him. Unless he changes his attitude about this, he'll soon be nothing more than the answer to a trivia question.

It just doesn't matter if you are Donald Trump or the owner of a little restaurant in a small town, or Clint Eastwood with a movie you've sunk money into or a fledgling author with your first book or a famous doctor like Michael Roizen at the Cleveland Clinic or a dentist in suburbia, you'd better embrace the role of Salesman-in-Chief.

The Two Most Important Sales You'll Ever Make

I believe the most important sale you'll ever make in your life is selling yourself on selling.

The day you commit to a life of selling can be the day that turns your life around. When you start viewing *all* your activities in the context of selling, you'll get much more done, much faster, and much more effectively. You'll have greater clarity about what to invest your time in, how to set priorities, who to associate with, where to steer conversations. You will be bolder at self-promotion and promotion of your business. You'll be more confident, more capable of getting what you want.

The second most important sale is selling you on you. Do you really believe you have what it takes to succeed as an entrepreneur? How you feel about yourself and how you see yourself (self-image) combine to regulate what you permit yourself to do and be, much like the thermostat on the wall regulates temperature. No one can outperform his or her own self-esteem or self-image. (For more information about this important subject, I recommend the book I co-authored with Dr. Maxwell Maltz, *The New Psycho-Cybernetics*.)

How to Bridge the Confidence Chasm

For new entrepreneurs, and sometimes for experienced entrepreneurs, there can be a wide gap between the capabilities a person thinks he has and the capabilities he perceives necessary for the tasks ahead. Facing that chasm can be as intimidating as standing at the edge of the Grand Canyon and contemplating an Evel Knieval-like motorcycle leap.

It has consistently been my experience that people underestimate themselves and over estimate what's necessary for the success they seek. The multi-millionaire entrepreneurs that I know are not that much smarter or more knowledgeable than the average person on the street, nor are they gifted or somehow preordained for exceptional achievement. In many cases, they're not even as smart as most people. Believe me, I've met some pretty

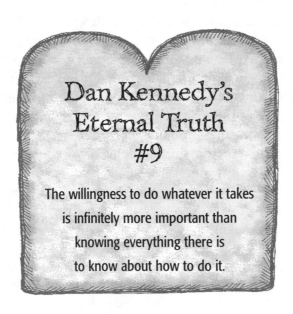

Dan Kennedy's
Eternal Truth
#9

The willingness to do whatever it takes
is infinitely more important than
knowing everything there is
to know about how to do it.

dumb rich people. Just about anybody *could* do what they do, it's just that few *will* do what they do.

One good way to bridge the confidence chasm is to make a point of discovering how little the so-called experts and superstars actually do know. You'll be shocked, as I was shortly after I'd determined that I would build a business as a professional speaker.

This is now some 30 years ago, but it's as fresh in my mind as yesterday. At the time, I had given a lot of speeches to sales organizations, clubs, and other local groups, was making about $10,000.00 a month in a way I believed to be primitive and difficult, and had decided it was time to hang around the real pros at the National Speakers Association to find out how this business was really supposed to be run. By the end of the first afternoon workshop I attended, I was thoroughly depressed—not at how much I yet had to learn but at how little the "superstars" knew! I got over my disappointment when it dawned on me that I was a whole lot further along than I'd guessed and that I was clearly "qualified" to be a big success in this field.

There were many speakers there who were infinitely better than I was on the platform. But I could find none better at selling. I could find none taking a business-like, entrepreneurial approach.

Since then, I've had similar experiences with other groups. I've discovered, over and over again, that the chasm between my self-assessment and my perception of the expertise of the wizards is easily bridged.

The bottom line is that success really is simple. There are commonsense fundamentals that make up 80% of the essence of each and every business. These fundamentals are transferable from one field to another. Once you grasp these, it's not difficult to collect or hire the other 20% of specialized knowledge.

You can hire expertise and experience at surprisingly low cost. Some of the smartest people in the world are working for wages, employed by companies founded by "dumb" entrepreneurs. You can also learn what you need to know about the specialized aspects of any given business in a hurry. What you bring to the table, and what is not so easily duplicated or obtained, is entrepreneurial guts.

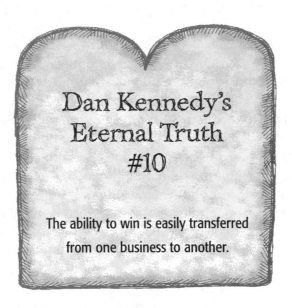

Dan Kennedy's
Eternal Truth
#10

The ability to win is easily transferred
from one business to another.

Earl Nightingale, one of the most famous success philosophers of all time, once pointed out that if there were no successful examples for you to observe, you could just as easily learn how to succeed from unsuccessful people! Note what they do, and then do the opposite. That idea applies to every business group I've ever been a part of or consulted in: about 5% of the people in the group rake in 95% of the money. The other 95% of the group represent sustained mediocrity. They have lousy work habits, poor self-images, vague and disorganized goals, waste huge quantities of time, and lack imagination and initiative. By carefully listening to them, you can identify what not to think about and talk about; by observing their actions, you can see what not to do.

The confidence chasm gets a lot smaller as you realize how basic bridging the gap is.

Another Important Sale

You can't sell what you haven't bought.

I'll often ask business people these questions:

- If you were the customer, would buying from you be the clear, inarguably best choice?
- Why should I do business with you instead of any of your competitors? In fact, why should I do business with you versus any and every other option available to me? (That's my original, proprietary, copyright-protected Unique Selling Proposition Question. You ought to pull it out of this book, write it boldly on a 4-by-6-inch card and tack it up someplace you see a lot.)
- Is your product or service a lot better than anything else out there? How?

It may surprise you to know that most can't answer these questions. They hem and haw, stammer and stutter, and, at best, mutter some goofy slogan.

If you can't answer these questions, you're probably not completely sold on the superiority of what you're selling, and if you're not sold, you can't sell.

In his great book *How I Raised Myself From Failure to Success in Selling,* Frank Bettger revealed that enthusiasm made the difference for him. But I don't believe in *acting* enthusiastic; I believe in *being* enthusiastic, and that requires good reasons. You need to structure or restructure your business, product, service, idea, or promise so that *you* are sold on the superiority of what you offer. After that, convincing others is easy.

To be convincing, you have to be convinced.

The New Economy Customer has come through some rough times. He has been recently, forcibly reminded that trust ought be granted cautiously and judiciously, and that money ought be spent only when receiving solid, exceptional value in return. The lesson was dramatized by Bernie Madoff, but delivered to at least 35% of the population by the stock market and the collapse of so many brand-name, big companies and institutions thought invulnerable. The lesson was delivered to millions of home owners and real estate investors. This customer has inner scars. He will not casually or easily trust or spend. Anyone asking him to do so must be completely convinced and masterfully convincing.

CHAPTER 8

KEY PEOPLE FOR
YOUR COMPANY

Your friends may come and go, but
your enemies accumulate.

—Coach Bill Foster

Very few people want to go it totally alone. Even the
Lone Ranger had Tonto. Tarzan had Jane *and* a chimp.
There are many reasons for this urge to surround your-
self with others, some good, some not so good.

Some entrepreneurs build up excess staff, for example, out of
feelings of insecurity, a feeling that theirs is more of a real business if there are a bunch of employees milling around. Many
want associates and employees to counter the stark loneliness of
entrepreneurship compared to the camaraderie of a corporate
environment. Others need a cheering section. But these are all
poor reasons for taking on partners, associates, or employees.

One day a client of mine returned home to meet with his
accountant after an arduous, week-long business travel adventure. After the meeting, he fired his 14 employees, put his

6,000-square-foot office complex up for lease, and went home to announce to his wife that he was moving his business back into the spare bedroom where it had started a decade before. One year later, he has done about 40% as much gross business as the previous year, but kept more money for himself and his family. And he calculates that the extra hours of work he has to do for himself are offset three-to-one by time saved not dealing with his employees' personal problems, petty disputes with co-workers, and so on. Admittedly, he has erected a major barrier to growth. Sometimes, though, never-ending growth shouldn't be the objective. Big, public corporations are caught in this trap, very often to their detriment; adding products, making acquisitions, even engaging in accounting sleight of hand to meet Wall Street's thirst for year-to-year, quarter-to-quarter growth. You have no such imperative. You can make your own choices. Net, lifestyle, and sanity matter. It's okay for them to matter.

Another bought out his two partners, who were the "Mr. Inside" guys while he was "Mr. Outside" drumming up business. He had a lot of fear about how he would manage things without them, but growing differences of opinion had become intolerable. To his shock, employees, vendors, even clients began telling him "horror stories" they'd been unwilling to talk about when the ogres were there. He replaced the two partners, who had each been getting fat salaries plus percentage of profits, and each of their secretaries—four in all—with one new assistant, starting at only $35,000.00 a year.

Of course, not every business lends itself to such dramatic downsizing and simplified operation, but the point remains: too often, entrepreneurs take on people for the wrong reasons.

The best reason to add people to your venture is to contribute to increased *profits*. There was a time when I would have said that this was the only good reason, but there are others. You may choose, for example, to employ a person who makes your life easier, handles problems for you, and frees up some of your time for personal or family activities, even if, in hard dollars, that person represents expense, not profit. As long as you do that knowingly and deliberately, fine.

The other very good reason is to obtain creativity and experience you cannot provide. Most successful entrepreneurs develop and depend on a small circle of close, trusted associates from their network of partners, key employees, friends, family, even peers, for input, encouragement, and support.

Andrew Carnegie described the formation of such a team as "the mastermind concept." The greatest caution that Carnegie, and his protégé, Napoleon Hill, had to offer was about choosing the people you include in your mastermind group or groups. The need for harmony, these men pointed out, is crucial.

In the entertainment world, a great team of masterminds made the *Tonight Show* an enormously successful television institution: Johnny Carson, Ed McMahon, and producer Fred DeCordova. In the infomercial business, I'm proud to have been part of the "brain trust" at Guthy-Renker Corporation for a number of years, that yielded dozens of successful infomercials including the earliest ones that fueled their Pro-Activ acne treatment products business. You do not necessarily have to employ all the brains you use. For years, Greg Renker and Bill Guthy put together different project teams for each product or infomercial, putting some staff with many freelancers like me.

These days, the need to have everyone in the same place is pretty much erased. Teleconferencing, video-conferencing, the ease of communication, of transmitting files makes out-sourcing across the country or across the pond feasible even for the smallest business. Posting particular needs on sites like www.Elance.com, www.craigslist.org, and countless niched sites will almost instantly bring many people with relevant expertise to your virtual door, eager to work for hire, on a project basis. A number of my clients who are basically solo entrepreneurs have "virtual assistants" providing secretarial services from afar. I have clients who've had websites built for them by freelancers in India, brochures prepared by graphic artists in—of all places—Kosovo, and content written for their customer newsletters by a school teacher freelancing on the side, in Guam. While I admit some of this gives me the heebie-jeebies 'cuz I'm a control freak, I also detest having employees underfoot, so I've gradually moved to finding the most competent person for a job even if 1,000 or 10,000 miles away. This gives you access to a much larger talent pool. As example, for three years I published a promotional magazine benefiting myself and a group of clients. By going beyond any vendors in my local area, and by avoiding even the thought of hiring staff, I was able to have the first issues designed by a brilliant graphic designer who worked full-time for Disney, and lived part of the time in Los Angeles, part of the time in Tokyo. Later, once the format was established, I was able to move the project to a graphics team in Baltimore and reduce the costs substantially. In both cases, I never saw these people face to face, never had them underfoot. One of my Platinum Members has made himself something of an expert in this whole approach to getting more done with less staff, using virtual assistants and freelancers, tapping a global talent pool even if a small business, and outsourcing everything from ghostwriting of your blog to packing and shipping your products. His name is Ron Ipach, and if this interests you, I suggest looking into his how-to resources. You can contact Ron at www.LazySuccessfulLife.com.

With all that said, few business owners are able to outsource everything, and some businesses obviously require significant numbers of employees. I have had as many as 43 myself, although by choice, I limited myself to about 5 for many years, and in recent years have 1.5. However, at Glazer-Kennedy Insider's Circle,™ there are more than 30, and staff size has grown year to year in each of the recent years.

My best advice to you is this: if you are going to employ people, then recognize it comes with serious and ongoing, day-to-day responsibility. They are not machines that can be calibrated properly once, switched on, and left to run properly for hours, let alone days or weeks at a time. If an employee is to be productive and profitable it will be because you make them so.

Take Off Your Rose-Colored Glasses

Because entrepreneurs tend to be optimists, they generally view people in their best light. But that may be unrealistic and, regrettably, this attitude can lead to frustration more often than to fulfillment. As hard as it may be to understand, some people just do not want to be motivated, to be helped, to be coached, to improve. And, when you try to force it on them, bad things usually happen. Others perform well at one level but fail miserably when promoted and entrusted with additional responsibilities. Some perform well when there's little pressure but crack when there's much.

On more than one occasion, I have made the mistake of bringing on a partner with unrealistic expectations. In one case, I brought in a close, personal friend as an executive of a company I had acquired, but I did so without considering the full picture. I saw him as I wanted him to be, not as he really was, and I tried to make him into someone he wasn't prepared to be. The end result was the destruction of a friendship and significant expense to me.

Enduring, successful partnerships are as rare as pro athletes without rap sheets. DeVos and VanAndel at Amway come to mind, my clients Bill Guthy and Greg Renker, then my mind goes blank. Michael Eisner was unable to keep his close, partner-like relationship with Jeffrey Katzenberg together at Disney, and heck, that's "the happiest place on earth"! Certainly, we can roam through recent business history and cite far more partnerships and top leadership teams that have come apart at the seams than we can those with longevity.

Having had my 22 year marriage suddenly and surprisingly end, and it a double-whammy—wife and business partner lost— I have some cautionary advice about having a business partnership with your spouse. Although we were fortunate to be able to reach an amicable end to our relationship and maintain an ongoing business relationship, this is rarely possible. (We have even remarried after several years divorced.) So, by all means, hope for the best, but prepare in advance for the worst.

Do not permit anyone—not even your spouse—to become indispensable to your business. There should only be one person who is indispensable. You.

This applies to partners, associates, key people, employees, or vendors. The point of business is independence, not dependence. The minute you have to worry and hesitate about ending a business relationship or giving a troublesome or disappointing employee or vendor the boot, you know you've let yourself become hostage instead of emperor. It's dangerous.

If It's Not Meant to Be . . .

Very few business relationships go the distance. That's why the smartest entrepreneurs develop dissolution agreements at the start of relationships. I know that I will never again take on a partner without such an agreement.

When it becomes evident to you that you have a "cancer" in your business, you cannot afford to hesitate or procrastinate for even a day. Cut out the cancer before it spreads. If your relationship with a key person deteriorates and there is no hope for recovery, you cannot afford the luxury of keeping that person around, even for one more minute.

When you "divorce," do it as decisively, cleanly, and courteously as possible. Avoiding unnecessary animosity is important for many reasons. It's an energy drain. It can block sensible negotiation and settlement. Biting your lip until it bleeds for a few days while getting the person out is infinitely preferable to bleeding for years from vengeful negative attacks. If there's anything reasonable you can do to diffuse the other person's anger, do it. On the other hand, if bloody battle is unavoidable, make it quick. Do what you must do to protect your business. That *is* your responsibility.

How to Choose Your Key People

Many new entrepreneurs don't really *choose* key associates; they anoint spouse, unemployed brother-in-law, or buddy for no reason other than the fact that they are spouse, brother-in-law, or buddy. This is no way to hire your vice-president.

In any case, every entrepreneur needs one support person. I work with a lot of clients who are essentially one-man operations, generating from $1 to $2 million to as much as $20 million a year. In the information marketing/mail-order field, where I have lots of clients, this is very doable. However, every one of these still needs and has at least the one back-up person. The really smart ones have two, for reasons I'll discuss later.

Entrepreneurs tend to leap between extremes of refusing to delegate vs. delegating tasks wildly, sloppily, and hastily. The most important person in the entrepreneur's business life will be very good at running behind, scooping up the pieces, and making sure initiatives get implemented. This key person has to cheerfully accept all this responsibility and, often, read the entrepreneur's mind.

That calls for four strong characteristics:

1. Ability to accept responsibility
2. Relatively low need for reassurance and recognition
3. Ability to cooperate
4. Ability to confront problems with maturity

This person can't worry about who gets the credit for success or who to blame for mistakes. He has to be secure enough about his own worth to not need recognition from afar. He needs to be very results oriented.

This person also needs to be good at creating and fostering cooperation among others. Because the entrepreneur often moves very quickly and assertively, he sometimes runs over other people's sensibilities. Somebody has to clean up that mess, too. (OK, take out the word "sometimes" and substitute "almost always.")

Behind just about every high-profile, highly successful entrepreneur, you'll find several of these key support people. These behind-the-scenes people are much like assistant coaches of major basketball or football teams. The high-profile head coach does the interviews, has the camera's eye, and gets the glory (or the criticism). But the head coach couldn't get through a game without the team of assistant coaches.

Last, the entrepreneur's key associate has to have great maturity in handling of problems. This means no panic, no emotional overreactions, just the calm voice of reason. I know several entrepreneurs who have just such people working with them, and they are very fortunate. One real estate broker I know pays his executive secretary $125,000.00 a year plus perks. Some of the few people who know of this think it's outrageous, but it is good value for what she does—and good business.

One of the many high-profile speakers we've brought to our the annual Marketing And Moneymaking SuperConferences held for Glazer-Kennedy Insider's Circle™ Members is George Ross, the right-hand man, chief advisor, and chief negotiator for Donald Trump. Although George is a very accomplished entrepreneur in his own right, including the purchasing, improving profitability of and selling of radio stations, George is a lawyer with extraordinary expertise in real estate deal making. He has been with Donald Trump for decades, basically since the beginning. George gave our Members great insight into how their relationship works. To a great degree, Donald Trump finds a property with hidden or unexploited potential and sets the stage for a deal, then it's up to George to live with that possible deal over days, more often weeks, wrestling every one of a million details that Trump would have no patience for, and probably doesn't have the expertise to do. Trump's name is on the high rise and George Ross' isn't, and George has to be completely okay with that. If you want to be Trump, you're going to need a few George Rosses in key positions.

On the other hand, another of Trump's key executives, developed and moved up to greater and greater responsibility by Trump—a woman you were introduced to in the first couple seasons of *The Apprentice*—went lame and Trump didn't hesitate showing her the exit. She was important, but he had not let her become indispensable.

George Ross

George Ross has written an outstanding book on business, delving into many topics—from negotiation to "the Trump formula" for creating new, added value in acquired properties, which has application far beyond real estate. The book, *Trump-Style Negotiation: Powerful Strategies and Tactics for Mastering Every Deal* is must reading for every entrepreneur.

The Worst Number in Any Business—and What to Do About It

Here is an advanced piece of information that, until now, I've talked about only at my high-priced seminars for entrepreneurs: the worst number in business is "one."

One is a very bad number, anywhere you find it.

If *one* client accounts for a disproportionate percentage of your revenue or profits, that's dangerous. If *one* media produces a disproportionate percentage of your customers, you are subject to being summarily put out of business. If *one* product accounts for a disproportionate percentage of sales, you are horribly vulnerable to competition.

Clients leave even when they shouldn't. When I ran a custom manufacturing business, a large client left us even though there were no quality or service problems, we had many times bent over backwards to meet his emergency needs, even carried him for months at a time when he couldn't pay. He switched vendors to save one half of one cent per unit. He said, "Biz is biz." Another large client left us, bluntly, because the sales rep of the competing company was having sex with him.

Media gets taken away. TV infomercials were once legal, then outlawed, then legalized again. In recent years, businesses have been thrown into trauma by new laws severely restricting use of FAX for marketing purposes, e-mail for marketing purposes, and the Do-Not-Call List for telemarketing. More restrictions on e-mail and even regular mail are being proposed and worked on at state and federal levels. Entrepreneurs are easily lulled into the false security of today's media landscape being the same when they awake tomorrow morning, and those with short-term experience, short memories, or little understanding of business history are often very stubborn in denial of the profound unreliability of media. As I am writing this, a new president has recently taken the keys to the White House and he, his administration, and the current Congress are very, very, very enthusiastic about regulation and interference in business, and are riding a wave of public support that will last for an uncertain amount of time, thanks to Wall Street scandals, stock market losses, and severe recession. Nothing you use and rely on is safe. Anything could be changed, new rules imposed, new costs added.

Products get knocked off, patents expire, copyrights get violated. It is very hard these days to sustain product exclusivity, or a unique marketing approach. The internet has eliminated just about all opportunity to develop some advantage gradually, unnoticed by most. It has provided an open environment ideal for piracy. And it has virtually eliminated basic barriers to entry for competitors eager to copycat a good thing, nibble at a successful business' market share, attack it by discounting. One product, one marketing or sales method, one media that is super profitable for you will almost inevitably be made unprofitable for you, sooner rather than later, and sometimes abruptly.

But by far, the worst "one" in a business is one key employee. If you are crossing a massive, barren desert and have only one horse, even if he kicks you, bites you, bucks you off, and craps on you, you can't shoot him. But if you have two . . . .

My advice—which sadly, I haven't always followed—to my clients is: never have only one person fulfilling any critical, key role. Have none or two, but never one. That way if you must shoot one, you can.

A number of clients have ignored this advice and told me how much they wish they hadn't, how much cheaper it would have been to pay the two salaries than to cope with the mess of the one's sudden departure. One of my coaching members, an investment manager, is in this category. He let one key, trusted person have all the contact with clients, then when that employee had to be axed, he had to step in and deal with chaos, and even lost some clients. Now every client has equal contact with two key people.

Many other clients have followed the advice and thanked me profusely.

CHAPTER 9

WORKING WITH LAWYERS
AND ACCOUNTANTS

The first thing we do, let's kill all the lawyers.

—WILLIAM SHAKESPEARE, *HENRY VI*

I have spoken at a major conference for lawyers, and that company purchased my *Ultimate Sales Letter* and *Ultimate Marketing Plan* books to give to all the attorneys in attendance. In my personal coaching groups, I have had six attorneys, we have quite a few lawyers as Glazer-Kennedy Insider's Circle™ Members, and several have followed my lead and become marketing ""gurus" to their professions, notably including Bill Hammond, expert in marketing elder law practices and legal services for families with a person suffering from Alzheimer's, and Ben Glass III, expert in marketing personal injury practices. As a speaker, I have appeared on programs with famous lawyers Alan Dershowitz and Gerry Spence. I confess to admiring Spence's masterful persuasive abilities and I recommend reading his book *How to Win an Argument Every Time*.

With all that said, I still share most entrepreneurs' allergic reactions to them. Here and now, I apologize to all entrepreneurs for helping attorneys. I'm sorry. My defense? I take special joy in taking *their* money.

The relationships between entrepreneurs and their lawyers, accountants, and bankers tend to be rocky at best. Most entrepreneurs I know harbor intense dislike for these people, including the ones they pay, and all their colleagues. Believe me, I understand this dislike. On the other hand, I have faced the reality that you cannot survive in today's business environment without relationships with these people. It's okay not to like them, but it's still important to be able to elicit productive results from them as needed.

How to Be Litigious without Buying Your Lawyer a Yacht

I have been accused of being litigious, which means I have often threatened to sue and file lawsuits. I have, on a number of occasions, been quick to threaten and even quick to proceed; it's often proved to be the best way to avoid being pushed around. I've discovered that most people as well as many companies have no real stomach for legal warfare. They know how costly and time-consuming it can be.

When you are building a company, you, sadly, often find yourself having to defend your intellectual property or proprietary products, in conflicts with competitors or partners or ex-employees, having to enforce contracts others ignore, even having to defend yourself against misplaced regulatory interference. I have, over years, won battles with the U.S. Postal Service, a trade association I belonged to, individuals owing me money, and a major insurance company. In most cases, aggressive action on my part backed only by a knowledge of the relevant law and threat of litigation was sufficient; but in some, nothing but a real, honest-to-gum lawyer would do.

In the most recent years I have been more restrained in this than in earlier years. Some of that is the prevailing of a cooler head, a lot of it the opportunity to be much more selective in who I permit myself to be involved with. At this point, I command enough respect that many unfair uses and abuses of copyrighted or otherwise protected intellectual property can be stopped or reversed with nothing but a stern letter from me. However, still, there are times when nothing short of a lawsuit will do.

Al Capone is credited with saying, "You can get a lot with a kind word and a smile, but you can get a lot more with a kind word, a smile, and a gun." Some people only understand power and force.

What to Do If You Are in a Fight

One of the most time-consuming legal weapons is called "discovery." This allows you to subpoena opponents' records, interrogate them under oath, and serve them with written interrogatories that must be completed within a certain period of time. An interrogatory is a written set of questions, pages long, prying into every imaginable aspect of the opponent's business and personal life. If there is a possibility of your being awarded damages from your lawsuit, you usually have the right to discover, in advance, the nature and location of all the opponent's assets. You can ask for detailed information about income, bank accounts, and personal and family assets. Like an inventory of the wife's jewelry, the amounts in the kids' piggy banks.

With this approach, you can consume immense amounts of the opponent's time and force public disclosure of information he would rather not make public. Also, dropping a 200-page interrogatory on an opponent's spouse can make for a very interesting evening in their home. Used properly, the interrogatory is often the only shot you have to fire.

Some lawyers are reluctant to drop this big a bomb. I advise against employing timid or polite lawyers. If the time comes when you must sue somebody, it's important to find a lawyer who will go for the jugular. I cannot emphasize this enough. Once you find that a real fight is unavoidable, you do not want a lawyer who likes playing nice with his professional peers or proceeding slowly, cautiously, step by step according to some secret guidebook of professional courtesies and procedural norms. You want a guy with finger hovering right above the big red button, eager to push it.

In a number of conflicts, people have instantly become more reasonable and respectful as soon as they've realized that I was prepared to bring in the legal beagles and start discovery. I signify this by sending copies to my lawyer of the correspondence I have with the other party, and, sometimes copying that party my memo to my lawyer. Using only this method, I've settled a lot of problems in my favor. Of course, I must mention here that I am not a lawyer, and my comments here are not a substitute for legal advice.

Just for example, I used this method to settle a dispute with a trade magazine that had made a mistake with the photos in an advertisement we placed. When the magazine billed us, I wrote to the publisher expressing my dissatisfaction. When that got nowhere, I sent a second letter indicating my refusal to pay any amount and describing how the deficient ad had probably damaged us at a trade show. That second letter indicated a copy had gone to my lawyer. Soon afterward, I got an offer from the publisher to settle. That happened early in my career, and taught me that you don't need to let media you advertise in abuse you. Since then, I've gotten free make-good ads and money in excess of the original buy quite a few times from magazines and other media that placed my ads improperly or otherwise "made mistakes."

Why, you ask, did I do all the work myself? Why not just turn it over to the lawyer from the beginning?

First of all, although some of my companies have had lawyers on retainer, I have never had a blanket retainer arrangement. Putting "cc" at the bottom of my letter costs me nothing. Having a lawyer handle it costs me $200.00 to $400.00 an hour.

Second, I wanted to rattle my sabers, not actually wind up in battle. Keep in mind that your interests and your lawyer's interests rarely coincide. In the matter of the dispute I described above, I would have had to nudge, push, and check up on the lawyer a half-dozen times to get it handled. Lawyers tend to deal each day with only those matters that have escalated to crisis, so a case like mine would have been put on the back burner forever. Including value of my time, it would have cost me more than the spoils from my victory to get it done. The cliché "talk is cheap" does not apply to lawyers. For their own financial interests and by conditioning, they are not prone to swift solutions.

Using a similar threat of litigation, I have, at various times, stopped a competitive company's salesperson from spreading rumors, got an insurance company to pay off nearly $250,000.00 in claims on a technically lapsed policy, got an undesirable equipment lease terminated without penalty, reduced and compromised bills, and collected past-due balances.

My objective through all this has been to win cheaply and quickly. And, in 35-odd years of using this approach, I've wound up in actual lawsuits only four times: settling twice and litigating twice.

Your Turn Can Come

It comes as a seismic shock to many entrepreneurs how easily and frequently they can be threatened with lawsuits. Anybody can sue you at anytime for anything. Sure, you have recourse in most cases where the suit filed against you proves baseless, and you can demonstrate cash damages as a result. By that time, though, you've had your business and family disrupted, tied up money in legal fees and costs, and consumed a fortune in antacids.

When you get attacked, most lawyers will want to react slowly, cautiously, and by the book. I've found, however, that when threatened or served with a lawsuit, the best defense is a very fast, very strong, even a little wild-eyed-and-foaming-at-the-mouth, kick-butt offense. Push your lawyer to run straight at them.

Legal problems are a part of business. The old idea that nobody has legal problems unless they deserve them is as out-of-date as handshake agreements and leaving the back door unlocked while you take any evening stroll down to the ice cream parlor.

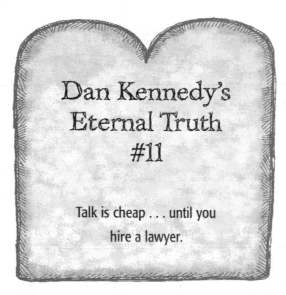

Dan Kennedy's
Eternal Truth
#11

Talk is cheap . . . until you
hire a lawyer.

When You Must Really Use a Lawyer

Keep this in mind: don't lose control. Don't be intimidated. Don't let yourself leave with a pat on the head, a reassuring word, and unanswered questions. You must understand everything about your situation. Take nothing for granted. Insist on being an informed participant in the strategy process. If the lawyer wants to tell you what to do rather than educate you about your options and their ramifications and help you make your decision, run.

You must manage your lawyer just as you would any other employee. Be very clear about fees, costs, and how the relationship is to work. Follow up on every phone conversation or meeting with a written letter, "just to confirm what we agreed to do," and use this memo to reference and enforce deadlines. Be polite and considerate, of course, but firm. You are the boss—act like it.

Some lawyers will work effectively with you in this kind of the relationship. Some will not. There are plenty to choose from.

Putting a Wall Around Your Castle and Alligators in the Moat

If you have or appear to have assets, are or appear to be successful, you are a target.

The business owner is in constant peril of lawsuits from employees, associates, investors, customers, vendors, and passers-by.

Most entrepreneurs are negligent, chronic procrastinators about asset protection. It is akin to home security systems: well over half are purchased and installed only after the home is burgled. However we are talking about more than the loss of your TV and having your undies pawed over.

There are more than 100-million lawsuits filed in the United States in an average year. We have more attorneys per capita than any other nation. Hundreds of thousands more are in law schools as I write this. They all need work. They all need somebody to sue. Like you.

It's a very good idea to discuss all possible business and personal insurance options with a very knowledgeable property-casualty, business insurance agent. If yours does not impress you as expert, and will not invest time in full understanding of your business, find one who fits that bill. It is also a good idea to educate yourself about asset protections, trusts, states with highest homestead protection for primary residences, etc., then to consult with an attorney expert in such matters.

If you are at all high profile, locally or nationally, you should also give some careful thought to your personal, family, and home security. The internet has made it frighteningly easy to invade your privacy and security, to find your home, even to access its floor plan. Identity theft is rampant. Not long ago, a client of mine well known in his area as a highly successful entrepreneur withdrew a large sum of cash from his bank, for legitimate reason. It is now believed but not, as I write this, proven that a bank employee tipped off criminals about this withdrawal. That same night, two armed men bashed in the front door of his home and held him, his wife, and his children at gunpoint. Unfortunately for them, the business he is so successful in is a martial arts academy; he is a big, strong, and extremely capable black belt who trains fighters competing in the extreme fighting matches on TV. His assailants left with broken bones and no swag. I have had other clients experience similar situations and not have them end as nicely.

Whether it is the thugs in Washington, DC, in Congress, targeting you, thugs in business suits with briefcases to whom contracts are meaningless and ethics comedy, disgruntled ex-employee thugs looking for a self-made golden parachute, or actual thugs with ski masks and guns, they are all around us. This is the world we live in.

Strange Creatures, Accountants

Accountants can be almost as maddening as lawyers to the entrepreneur, but for different reasons. The temperament and thinking of someone happy to sit in an office crunching numbers is diametrically opposed to the personality of the go-get-'em entrepreneur.

Still, you need a good accountant.

What makes a good accountant? The entrepreneurial joke is that you ask "What's this number?" And the good accountant says, "What would you like it to be?" That's amusing right up until the first tax audit. My own working definition, which may or may not be exactly right for you, is that a good accountant imposes a reasonable degree of discipline on your record-keeping and is very knowledgeable, informative, and helpful in the area of tax law—where your biggest risks and biggest costs can occur.

I have had good ones and bad ones, cheap ones and expensive ones, and my advice is find and hire good even if expensive.

The one mistake never to make is to put the bean counters in charge of making decisions about planting seeds or *harvesting* beans. Just as we entrepreneurs aren't very good at counting or keeping beans and a whole lot better at harvesting them, the accountants good at counting 'em are inept at planting or harvesting. A lot of companies are grown to a certain point by an entrepreneur, then turned over to accountant-types to manage. More often than not, they destroy it. It's quite common for an entrepreneur to sell a good company to a big, dumb company run by bean counters, then get to buy it back for a fraction of what he was paid for it in the first place! That doesn't mean entrepreneurs ought to continue with their hands-on, micro-management, antidelegation, control-freak style as a business grows from small to large and simple to complex either, but putting accountants in control is hardly ever an improvement.

Rear View Mirrors, Magnifying Glasses, and Binoculars

It's very important to understand that the kinds of numbers accountants and CPAs assemble and provide to you are Rear View Mirror numbers. They are historical. They tell you what has already happened in your business.

These numbers are useful in identifying what has gone awry that needs to be fixed, such as a type of expense that has grown in terms of percentage of sales and needs to be roped in, or a product or service insufficiently profitable vs. others. That sort of thing. But with these numbers you are always fixing problems that have already occurred.

Their numbers are also constructed more to satisfy tax authority requirements and meet general accounting norms than they are to help you manage your business more profitably. Yes, you need to know how to read balance sheets and income statements, but God help you if you try actually managing your business with them.

You need Magnifying Glass numbers to make good day-to-day, current decisions. That means what is happening, magnified, so you can clearly see and understand it. These numbers are foreign to most accountants. For example, two of the most important numbers in marketing are CPL, Cost Per Lead, and CPS, Cost Per Sale, and they need to be tracked by source. Most business owners cannot tell you what it costs them to acquire a new customer, or to sell a particular product. Another vital number is TCV, Total Customer Value. You decide whether your business has short or long customer life, one year or ten years. But you have to know what a customer is worth in order to determine how much you are willing to pay to get one. And you have to know the different values of different customers secured from different sources. These are the kinds of numbers that those of us in direct marketing understand, that most other types of entrepreneurs don't.

Incidentally, the entrepreneurs I've worked with over the years who make the most money and build the biggest fortunes are the ones who are very, very good at these Magnifying Glass Numbers. So good, I can't easily stump them with questions. My former client, now retired, Len Shykind at U.S. Gold, could, in moments, pull up any number you could ask for, with regard to the CPL or CPS from any of hundreds of different TV stations and dozens of magazines he advertised with, comparing day to day, month to month, time slot to time slot. A much bigger user of TV, Guthy-Renker, is comparably on top of these numbers as well as every number in the back end of their businesses. Bill Glazer, who has built Glazer-Kennedy Insider's Circle™ from small business to multi, multi-million dollar enterprise is, to be impolite, downright anal retentive about these numbers. They win big because they are. If you don't "Know Your Numbers," you cannot possibly manage for profit, and you'll likely have unpleasant meetings with bean counters telling you about beans lost after the fact.

This is difficult for most entrepreneurs, because we hate crunching numbers. I love working with clients who do it well even though, personally, I'm mediocre at it; better than most by small margin. The worst entrepreneur I've ever seen at it, bar none, was an early mentor of mine, who constantly insisted "If there's enough gross, there must be net around here somewhere." He was wrong. And broke a lot, even with gigantic grosses.

You also need Binocular Numbers. These are predictions and forecasts into the future that may affect current decisions. These, of course, are the hardest to come by.

One way I use Binoculars and approach this, for each year, is figuring up, listing, and forecasting all the income I can be reasonably sure of earning. The difference between that total and my goal must then be bridged. I can then start slicing that sum up, and assigning pieces of it to different sources of income, different promotions I'll need to do. This is how I plan my year's schedule of activities.

Finally, you need to consider all your numbers in some big picture context. There is an inside-Disney story about an ambitious, relatively new vice-president of something-or-other coming into the CEO with a list of proposed cost savings—and being summarily fired. Looking at costs in a vacuum, any idiot can see thousands of ways Disney could spend less. They paint white fences every night—why not once a week? The walkway from the lake to one of the resort's entrance has a large open lawn on either side, bordered with a row of neatly trimmed hedges. Imagine the savings to be had replacing grass with astro-turf, hedges with potted, artificial shrubs. The V.P. did imagine that, but that's not what the Disney folks mean when they use the term "Imagineering." They have been way ahead of so many other companies in understanding that they are in the experience business, so everything matters, and marketing is more than media.

The New Economy is *all about* customers' experiences. There are so many choices in every product, service, and business category, so much more access to choices, often from beyond local or traditional geographic boundaries, and consumers are more thoughtful and demanding for dollars spent, so creating and delivering extraordinary experiences leading up to, during, and after the sale, throughout the relationship, is essential. This is the context in which numbers crunched must be considered.

Who Can You Count On?

In these necessary relationships, with accountants, lawyers, other advisors, strive to make things the best they can be, but do everything you can to ensure against them turning to the worst they can be. And never lose sight of the fact that the only person you can completely rely on to protect your interests is you. The most successful entrepreneurs I know develop extreme confidence in their own judgment.

I teach that there are two things you NEVER delegate in a business. One is the marketing, the acquiring, optimizing, retaining, and multiplying of customers. That you want to be up to your armpits in, all the time.

The other is control of the checkbook. And, the important numbers affecting the checkbook.

I have had a number of private clients who each, at different times, ignored my pleadings and turned their checkbooks over to someone else: a comptroller, an accountant. All got screwed in

"Here's something else about God that any billionaire knows: He's in the details, and you need to be there, too. I couldn't run a business any other way. When I'm talking to a contractor, or examining a site, or planning a new development, no detail is too small to consider. I even try to sign as many checks as possible. For me, there's nothing worse than a computer signing checks. When you sign a check yourself, you're seeing what's really going on inside your business, and if people see your signature at the bottom of the check, they know you're watching them, and they screw you less because they have proof that you care about the details."

—Donald Trump, author *TRUMP: Think Like a Billionaire*

slightly different ways. I handle millions of dollars a year. I sign every check. By hand. And I pay attention to what I'm signing. I wouldn't do it any other way. I have always done so.

Another thing you want to pay attention to is your "white mail," which is any and all first-class mail containing correspondence from customers other than orders, including customer-service inquiries, complaints, and stories they write and share. To give credit where credit is due, I got this piece of advice from Gary Halbert, and it has served me well. For many years, even when personally running a fairly large company, I not only opened and read my own mail, I occasionally swept in, grabbed all the incoming mail, and went through every piece—especially correspondence from customers. If you don't, problems may be swept under the rug or mishandled, and eventually wind up biting you in the butt.

The bottom line is: you're on the hot seat all by yourself. It may look like you're surrounded by others, but don't be standing in their way en route to the lifeboats in a storm.

CHAPTER 10

WHY ENTREPRENEURS AREN'T MANAGERS—AND WHAT YOU CAN DO ABOUT IT

Never try to teach a pig to sing. You'll only annoy the pig and get yourself covered with mud.

—UNKNOWN

L et me preface this chapter with a personal confession. My ability to pick and hire good employees is roughly equivalent to my interest in having them. Zero. I am a far better golfer, and I can't play golf. At one point, I had 43 employees. I concluded I'd rather have a daily root canal. Consequently, I have structured my own businesses to function without them. In recent years, I've had only one. In a distant office, not underfoot. And one-half or less with me; a flexible hours, light-duty assistant, errand runner, files maintainer, fax sender. Many businesses require employees but would be better re-engineered to have fewer people.

I feel fortunate that for most of my life I have operated businesses with a minimum number of employees. Today, I have 1.5.

But I have had 5, 10, 43. I've had father, mother, and brothers as employees. I've had my share of managerial experience. I have some observations and opinions, based in part on my own pain and suffering, and in part on what I've learned from clients far, far more successful at managing employees than I.

At one point, I suddenly took over a company with 43 employees. The only management had been dictatorial and ineffective. There were massive quality control, productivity, and other problems. It was a hostile environment. I determined to do something about it all.

At the time, I had been doing a massive amount of reading about different management styles: Japanese management, open-door management, management by objectives, management by values, team building, and building ownership mentality. Exciting buzzwords, all of them. Once again, however, I discovered that most of the folks writing these theories never managed anybody. Or they managed only in their memories, from a time when people latched onto a good job and then did everything in their power to keep it; when getting sacked was a red badge of humiliation. Times are different now. Peoples' attitudes are very different now. Even given the high unemployment that had returned as I was writing this book, and the lines of people showing up for advertised jobs shown on TV newscasts, those with the jobs remained and remain surprisingly undetermined to do everything in their power to keep them.

Anyway, I waded in with all this terrific theory and got my head handed back to me, with bloody claw marks all over it. I sewed it back on, stuck it in there again, and pulled out a bloody stump.

What have I learned from that experience and from working with clients beset with management problems? The big secret. And here it is: all the theories work wonderfully with wonderful people. But trying to teach pigs to sing or chickens to soar is tough, tough work. Of course, you could simply only hire wonderful people. A good idea—in theory—but completely impractical. There aren't enough of 'em to go around even at times that over- all supply and demand favors employers. And today's Mr. Wonderful is tomorrow's green-eyed, knuckle-dragging, foul- smelling monster.

For example, I've done a lot of consulting work with chiro- practors. Typically, they have staffs of three to ten people who are all very important. Their contact with patients affects repeat busi- ness and referrals. Their attitudes affect the doctor's attitude, and these practices are attitude-driven businesses. I know doctors who bring their entire staffs to seminars, and there they are, smil- ing, happy, enthusiastic people, eager to do their jobs better. These doctors have incentive and bonus programs for their staffs. They set and work on team goals. They really have a team effort going. I also know doctors who have to pay and coerce their staffs to grudgingly go to a seminar. And there they are, stiff, frowning, restless, ants-in-their-pants, in and out of the room. These doctors try incentive and bonus programs and they fail miserably. If these doctors try to talk "teamwork," the staff mem- bers mutter "He's been to another seminar. It'll all blow over in a few days."

Using exactly the same management ideas, philosophies, methods, and strategies, one doctor will get incredibly good results; the other will be cut off at the knees.

Which brings us to several really tough, no B.S. management principles.

You Can't Teach a Pig to Sing

I repeat it again. You can apply the very same sound, proven motivational tools to ten people and get ten startlingly different results. Perhaps, theoretically, everybody and anybody can change and be inspired to change, but many "hard cases" just aren't worth the investment.

Hire Slow, Fire Fast

This motto hangs on the wall of the CEO of one of the four largest national chains of weight-loss centers. But his philosophy is, of course, the exact opposite of what entrepreneurs tend to do. We hate to fire anybody. We're optimists, so we believe that everybody can be saved. We keep trying, we keep giving them one more chance. By the time we finally fire them, they walk away wondering why it took us so long, as do the other staff members.

Then, we have this vacuum to fill. We need that work done. So we grab the first warm body who passes by. And, as they say, you have to kiss a lot of frogs to find a prince. I've gone through over 55 people to get 4 good ones. Am I inept? Well, most entrepreneurs I know who have a good team get there by hiring, firing, hiring, firing, catching and throwing them back, and only very occasionally finding a "keeper." Churning and burning is definitely not the worst idea you'll ever have, although, obviously, it's time-consuming and frustrating.

Forget the Idea of Ownership Mentality

The only people who have ownership mentality are owners. That's that. Why should it be any other way? The main reason that managing people drives entrepreneurs crazy is all our silly, stubborn hopes, beliefs, and assumptions that "they" are like "us." They're not. If they were, they wouldn't be working for us—they'd be competing with us.

Some years back, when I had five employees, I achieved a new peace of mind by recalibrating my expectations for the performance of different people in different positions. Each position has different responsibilities and different definitions of satisfactory performance and of excellent performance, and, in most cases, these positions do not require another you to meet these definitions.

I had two employees, for example, who just weren't "morning people." For years, it drove me bananas that they could not to get to work on time. It drove a business partner of mine right

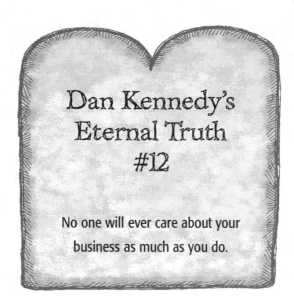

Dan Kennedy's
Eternal Truth
#12

No one will ever care about your
business as much as you do.

over the edge. It became his mission to end their tardiness; he tried everything and failed. Otherwise, however, these two were exemplary employees. They perfectly fulfilled the performance requirements of their positions.

We arrived at the big breakthrough. We made a new deal. We told these two they could come and go and work pretty much whenever they wanted to work as long as all of the work that needed to get done got done on time. If they meandered in at 9:45 A.M., nobody thought anything of it. I didn't even ask or pay any attention to when they were there and when they were not. I wiped an entire chunk of anxiety and aggravation right off my plate. And it worked out magnificently.

But, make no mistake about it, they only excelled at meeting reasonable expectations for their positions.

How Your Employees Sabotage Your Marketing

I walked into the Subway near my house about 1:30 P.M. on a weekday, to get a small sandwich and salad to go. There were two customers in a booth eating, no one in front of me at the counter. No "Sandwich Artist" visible. She emerged from the back room after several minutes, gave me a frustrated look, and greeted me:

"I can't get any work done today."

Gee, I was mistaken. I thought taking care of customers, making sandwiches, and stuffing cash into the register was her work. Bet the owner does too. But he and I are both mistaken. Make this note: what we think her work is and what she thinks it is, what we think are her job priorities and what she thinks they are—two different things.

As she was nearly finished putting my order together, two new customers filed in, one right behind the other. The look on her face was pure disgust. In a voice loud enough for us all to hear, she said:

"It's been like this all day, one darned customer after another. How will I ever get to do my work?"

If you think this sort of thing only goes on in other peoples' businesses, you're dumber than a box of rocks. It goes on in yours too, pretty much whenever your back's turned. If you'd like a lengthy FREE REPORT, reprinted from my *No B.S. Marketing Letter,* about the 12 ways employees sabotage your marketing—and what you can do about it—go to www.No BSBooks.com and look for the resources connected with this book, and with the *No B.S. Ruthless Management of People and Profits* book. For now, know that whatever you aren't watching over like a hawk, you aren't getting.

You Can Only Expect What You Inspect

This is an old management axiom and you've probably heard it before. Well, truth is truth, and if you want to stay sane, this is the way to manage.

Business owners don't want to believe their employees steal from them. Some don't even track their losses, they just stick their heads in the sand. And they're all wrong, because most employees steal at some time. "Theft" takes many forms. It can be cash or merchandise, but it can also be the sabotage I just mentioned above, or time theft, or covering up for inept vendors. In direct, outright theft of cash and merchandise, most businesses lose 50% to 100% as much as the owners' ultimate net, pre-tax profits. In indirect theft, much more. This is a massive problem and a giant opportunity most business owners live in denial about.

About 2% of the population are incapable of ever stealing; they would rather starve. Another 2% will steal for a nickel; they are incapable of being honest. The remaining 96% of people will steal if three factors are present:

1. need,
2. ability to rationalize their actions, and
3. opportunity to get away with it.

You cannot control the first two factors. Ask your employees if they need more money or if they need to take shortcuts in their work (another form of stealing), and most will answer yes. And most of us are pretty good at rationalizing our behavior. It often is expressed with words like "He just bought a new hot car and lives high on the hog. We do all the dirty work around here—he'll never miss a few dollars."

However, you can control opportunity, and that is why you can only expect what you inspect.

I took over a custom products manufacturing company once with a serious quality-control problem. Over 30% of all jobs had something wrong with them. In one month, that dropped to 5%. How did I do it? I simply took the time to walk around the plant at different times, almost every day, randomly pulling samples out of production and checking them. As soon as everybody knew that the risk of detection was high, the error rate dropped.

This isn't rocket science; it's simple. It's applicable to any business.

Identify, Keep, Reward, and Motivate

Mike Vance, one of the top executives of the Disney Corporation for a number of years and now a management consultant, says that management is all about "developing people through work, while having fun."

I agree with him—I'm not a cynic after all! I believe that smart entrepreneur-managers provide environments, opportunities, and encouragement for growth to whatever degree is possible. I believe sensitivity toward the nonmonetary rewards of work is important. And I believe in having fun and offering bonuses, incentives, team goals, compete-against-yourselves contests, and, of course, an overall positive attitude.

In all businesses, unhappy people do poor work. It is part of good management to create the right environment in the workplace. There are people out there who would kill for an opportunity to work in a good job, for somebody who respects and appreciates them, who lets them grow with authority and responsibility, and who includes them in a team effort.

Quality people respond to quality management techniques, so you'll be involved in going through people, weeding out the uncooperative, identifying the gems, keeping, developing, involving, and rewarding the keepers. Because everything is always changing—people, their circumstances, your business, and you—this process will continue as long as you remain at the helm. Don't resent it, and do it as effectively as you can.

Recent Discoveries About All Employees

As you might imagine, "employee problems" is a hot topic whenever entrepreneurs gather. My own mastermind/coaching groups talk about it a lot, and out of these conversations came a couple discoveries that I now believe are key hiring criteria.

In comparing notes, we realized that we have each had one to several employees over a span of years who were terrific. More importantly, in comparing notes, we discovered a "secret" commonality shared by every one of those rare, terrific employees. So, finally, here is some good news—a "trick" you can use to greatly increase the likelihood of hiring a productive person.

The hidden factor we unearthed is that all our best employees grew up in a family business environment. Their parents owned some kind of a small business, and they saw how hard their parents worked, they worked in the business too, they had exposure to dealing with customers and vendors and crises. The best of the best employees came from families that owned small restaurants.

I am sufficiently convinced of the validity of this factor that, if I were hiring people today, it'd be an absolute litmus test.

Another, similar "secret": the best employees to put in positions where they must handle incoming calls from new prospective customers or clients or otherwise interact directly with customers either have personal experience or have been around somebody with successful *direct* sales experience. That means they themselves or their father, mother, spouse, brother, or sister has sold something nose to nose, toes to toes, in homes or in showrooms, like vacuum cleaners, water filters, fire alarms, encyclopedia, pool filters. This experience will have gotten them over the all-too-common "squeamishness" about selling. Employees who have that squeamishness will consciously or unconsciously sabotage or at least "short" what needs to be done to achieve optimum sales in your business.

Finally, you want to hire people who can and will follow specific directions, particularly unusual ones. Most of my clients hire these days by advertising positions online, but then refusing to accept resumes by e-mail, often refusing resumes and requiring essays and answers to specific questions, response only by fax, driving candidates to recorded messages, and making them get through an obstacle course before even being considered. Some clients actually get hate e-mail from enraged job seekers! But they also thin the herd efficiently, and wind up with especially willing, intelligent, and attentive candidates. The success of their employees hired this way, with success measured by the employee earning continued employment, doing well, producing profits, is very high.

The Decision to Make

Too often, inmates are running the asylum. Decide it's your business. Never turn a deaf ear to input, ideas, information, or even properly voiced complaints from staff. But never, never, never accommodate them just to avoid conflict or to be accommodating or merely from fatigue. *You* make policy, *you* enforce policy.

Good People Can Make a Huge Difference

One of my coaching members, Lester Nathan, is the reigning expert advisor to America's independent pharmacy owners, on successfully competing with the giant chains. Lester routinely helps pharmacy owners increase profits by 200% to 500% within the first 12 months he consults with them. He accomplishes this with three "tracks," one of which is improving the quality, capabilities, and motivation of the employees.

My Platinum Member Jay Geier routinely increases chiropractic and dental practices by comparable numbers solely by focusing on training, incentivizing, motivating, and policing the employees who take incoming calls from new patients.

The common ingredient in their approaches is superior training. Truth is, most employees are tossed into jobs with little or no real training, no scripts, and then are not held accountable for doing things as they ought to be done. Incredibly, in many businesses, even salespeople are going without sales training!

If you are going to have people, then you need to commit to doing everything you can to get, grow, and keep good ones.

What Works for You Is What's Right

Throw out the textbooks. Five of the most successful CEOs I know have five dramatically different management styles. Their relationships with their people are different. Their beliefs about leadership are different. Their companies' environments feel different when you walk in. There *is* more than one right way.

Harold Geneen, who led the giant ITT, once said, "I have never come across a chief executive who tried, much less succeeded, running his company according to any set formula, chart, or business theory."

This is my most important message in this chapter on management: my way, that works for me, may very well fail miserably for you. You have to find your own way. Find a way that works for you; you must. Governing a business and a group of employees and vendors, and making decisions about it and them by the seat of your pants, by your thoughts of the moment, creates inconsistency if not outright chaos. You need your own set of definite governing principles, policies and best practices, and a set way of teaching them and enforcing them, with their purpose maximum profitability.

CHAPTER 11

HOW TO MANAGE YOUR
CASH FLOW

The bankers asked for a Statement.
I said I was optimistic.

—Mark Victor Hansen, co-author,
Chicken Soup for the Soul

I t's amazing what you can do with cash. There have been times in my entrepreneurial experience when as little as a few thousand dollars of cash would have made a million-dollar difference. I once saved a million-dollar business from extinction with $25,000.00. There have also been times when a million dollars wouldn't have helped. But more often than not, it is better to have cash than not!

Happiness is positive cash flow. Many businesses struggle through years of losses before achieving profitability, but survive thanks to positive cash flow. In business, cash flow buys the extra time necessary to win. Cash flow provides the staying power needed to invent, experiment, sort it all out, and, finally, wind up with a winning system. It's not all that unusual for one new product, one new ad, or one sales breakthrough to swing a company

Dan Kennedy's
Eternal Truth
#13

Cash is king.

from losing to winning. To outsiders, it may look like a lucky miracle. Actually, it's the logical result of a progression of experiments, failures, corrections, decisions, investments, and action.

In the year I rewrote this edition of this book, quite a few big companies the public and much of the investor community thought of as invulnerable and eternal were revealed to have shockingly thin cash reserves, and some even had their top executives sitting before Congressional committees literally *begging* for bailouts, claiming only days or weeks before being out of cash. It should have been unbearably humiliating. I suggested in my weekly political column that some of these so-called business leaders should adopt the Japanese response to such high dishonor: hari kari. A U.S. Senator echoed my remark a few weeks later, and got a lot of flak for it. But really, running these giants out of cash, existing like a poor person living paycheck to paycheck, unconscienable.

However, I have been there. I once took over a company running deep cash flow negatives and managed it with week-to-week, on-going cash emergencies, trekking to the bank frequently this can be done. Vendors competing for your business will use financing to get it. Instead of terms of "net 30 days," you may be able to negotiate paying in two or three installments, like a third in 30 days, a third in 60 days, and a third in 90 days.

- Conserve cash by leasing with deferred balloon payments.
- Refinance when you don't have to, to consolidate debt and reduce monthly debt service.
- If you have financed your business startup with personal collateral and guarantees and a patchwork quilt of financing sources, strive to replace that with conventional business loans and lines of credit, secured by the business, as soon as you can. With two years of profitability, growth, and a good payment track record, you can start working on this aggressively, shopping among banks if necessary.

Elsewhere in this book, I talked about different, superior kinds of leverage. I'll point out again here that most entrepreneurs think of leverage only in terms of OPM, Other People's Money—credit from lenders and vendors, which produces debt that must be managed, can be dangerously seductive and is usually costly, or capital from investors, which can ultimately be very costly. There are other options for financial leverage, notably OPR and OPC: Other People's Resources and Other People's Customers. It's important to think of these as forms of capital that do not create debt or sacrifice equity.

3. *How to Get Paid*

Many businesses suffer from some or all of the following credit-management deficiencies:

- Loose credit policies
- No credit checks before granting credit
- No enforcement of credit limits
- Late invoicing

- Credit given to those with past-due balances
- No standardized collection procedures
- Unwillingness to get tough

If you are going to grant credit, you need to have a plan to prevent problems and resolve them when they do occur. Making sales doesn't matter much if you don't get paid. Take the following steps to implement your plan:

- Develop strict credit policies.
- Make each customer complete a credit application.
- Check the references.
- Consider joining a credit bureau and checking credit files.
- Set credit limits for each customer.
- Send your invoices out promptly.
- Implement a collection procedure beginning with the first of three warning notices sent the 32nd day.
- Cutoff past-due clients, and only then negotiate a "deal" as you see fit. Do not keep granting credit to people who cannot or will not pay you.
- Get tough when you have to. Preserving the goodwill of a customer who can't or won't pay is silly. You may have good reason to occasionally make exception to this rule, but be sure the exceptions don't become the rule.

This is all common sense, isn't it? So why do so many entrepreneurs do such lousy jobs of collecting the money owed them? Because while wearing one hat, trying to negotiate with their vendors to get better terms, they develop great empathy for their customers. They find it difficult to switch attitudes when they switch hats.

A warning: invariably a business owner will play bank and carry a slow-pay account only to later have that client summarily leave him and switch to a competitor without a wisp of gratitude or loyalty. You do not buy loyalty by letting clients violate your credit terms.

You should also consider how and when you get paid. Many businesses are negligent or timid about demanding deposits or retainers, benchmark payments during long projects versus waiting until completion, incentivizing pre-pays. I was one of the leaders in teaching "pre-pay plan sales" to chiropractors, changing the relationship with the patient from pay-as-you-go to pay in full, in advance, for a multi-month treatment plan. Not only is this financially advantageous to the doctor in cash-flow terms, it increases the average case value because the patient doesn't drop out early, and it is beneficial to the patient because it compels complete compliance.

Others have opportunities to create auto-charge continuity plans, which effectively have consumers paying in advance of use rather than with or after use. A number of restaurants—even pizza shops—have implemented my club/continuity programs, where customers' credit cards are charged on the very first day of each month for coupons or certificates they'll use all month long.

4. Increase Cash Flow by Increasing Sales

Most entrepreneurs would argue that increasing sales is the first step to increasing cash flow. But sales alone aren't the answer. Driving up sales without a thorough approach to cash flow and profit management will wind up enriching everybody but you. You'll need more people, more equipment, more inventory, more freight, more postage, etc., and everybody will get richer—but will you?

Sometimes, it's even helpful to cut back sales volume, cut out the least profitable product lines or parts of a business, and alter the economics for the better—much like pruning a bush so it can grow straighter and stronger.

However, having said that, it is still probably your goal to make your business bigger, and that's fine. But remember there are usually more opportunities than there are resources, so choose those that provide the best margins and the best cash flow, not those that provide tightest margins and worst cash flow. In other words, grow sales *strategically.*

I once consulted with a manufacturer who was enjoying sales growth of over 25% per calendar quarter but so strapped for cash he was a walking ulcer. Over 80% of his sales were to three big chain store accounts, who routinely took 90 to 120 days to pay, and he was about to get his product line into a fourth comparable chain when I insisted he slam on the brakes. A year later, the business had again doubled, but the percentage in the chains was cut in half, as he focused on distribution to a lot of small independents who paid net 30 or in advance, and on private label manufacturing, for which he got paid 50% in advance.

I do like to see capital created rather than borrowed.

The story of my friend, George Douglas, exemplifies this kind of unique resourcefulness. George went broke in a big way in a direct sales business and wound up sitting in his bare house, all the furniture gone, and nothing left but a box of 48 copies of the book, *Think and Grow Rich,* and a dozen broken down auto-dialing (telephone marketing) computers. George had used these machines to set up appointments for his salespeople in his now-defunct business. He knew they could work and he believed in them. He used the books in his classes to motivate his salespeople.

George asked himself what resources he could draw on to get some cash. He repaired the auto-dialers so they could be sold as used but operable equipment. Then he got on the phone, calling insurance salespeople, real estate agents, and other salespeople, inviting them to a free seminar on using auto-dialers to increase business. He offered a free copy of *Think and Grow Rich* to anybody who came to the meeting.

He called and invited hundreds. About a dozen salespeople showed up. He nervously stood up in front of the group, explained how auto-dialers worked, how he used them successfully, and helped others use them. Then he gave a demonstration and offered a unique "rent-and-try-then-buy" offer on the machines he had in stock. That evening, George sold eight machines; in the first month he collected $800.00 for rentals. He discovered that he had a knack for selling this type of equipment.

In short order, he found a manufacturer of auto-dialers and convinced him to sell the machines at wholesale as George needed them, without an inventory requirement, franchise fee, or other up-front payment. In the next few years, he built a large business, with national advertising and sales representatives, selling these machines. He also used some of the profits from that business to invest in a new idea for computer software, and that, too, turned into a very successful business. He went from bankruptcy to big money without borrowing a nickel.

Only a few years later, he was grooming replacements to run his companies, personally working two weeks a month, and sailing the Caribbean on his yacht the other two weeks of the month.

Contrast this with the dot.comers who blew through millions and millions of dollars of capital without even coming close to

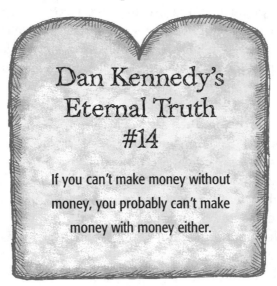

Dan Kennedy's
Eternal Truth
#14

If you can't make money without money, you probably can't make money with money either.

making even one honest dollar. Out of the giant dot.com boom with thousands of dot.com companies attracting millions and millions of dollars of venture capital, mere handfuls emerged from the crash, and ultimately became legitimate, profit-producing businesses. Amazon.com is a very notable example. While having money to build a business can be very useful, having money to burn usually encourages the burning of money. Businesses built more with ingenuity than with cash seem much stronger.

One of the key principles I talk about in my Renegade Millionaire seminars is that Renegade Millionaires are resourceful, not necessarily full of resources. This is why understanding and using the aforementioned OPR and OPC are so important.

5. How to Find or Invent a "Slack Adjuster"

Those in the used car business use the term "slack adjuster" to describe the occasional great buy they find somewhere, like a ten-year-old car in mint condition that they buy for $1,500.00 and can sell for $6,000.00, a 400% mark-up, far exceeding their normal mark-up.

A "slack adjuster" is something you sell that gives you a surge of extra profit to help pick up the slack.

In the appliance business, it's the add-on warranties they sell. In the finance business, it's "credit life insurance"—probably the worst insurance buy ever perpetrated on consumers.

One of my members owns a couple neighborhood hardware stores. Two years ago, he added Grille Shops, in which he sells all kinds of barbeque grills, including the incredibly expensive, elaborate "built-in" gas grills. He only sells two or three of the $5,000.00 to $10,000.00 grill installations a season, but they pick up the slack for a lot of $3.00 hammers.

It's worth noting that, almost without exception, no less than 5% to as high as 20% of any business' customers will buy premium or deluxe versions of the goods or services if offered. This is where slack-adjuster profit margins can often be created. Price strategies and MCF strategies go hand in hand. I conducted an in-depth seminar about "price, profits, and power" which is now available as an online course with video; you can find it at DanKennedy.com or e-mail Customer Service at that site and ask for information about it. A business' cash flow can often be multiplied and profits at least doubled with nothing more complex than better price strategies.

Two Commonly Under-Utilized Means of Boosting Sales, Profits, and Cash Flow

Well-run, sophisticated direct marketing/mail-order companies do two things well that a lot of other businesses miss altogether.

One is the instant upsell.

If you call and order from a catalog company, the person taking the order will usually end the call by asking you to consider one or several special offers of the day. If you call and order from seeing a TV infomercial, the person taking the order may offer you a second of the same item you're buying at half-price or an unrelated, extra item. In most of these cases, from 5% to as high as 20% of the customers say yes to one of these upsells. It costs a lot less to get the upsell than to get the person calling in to buy the first item; you're only adding minutes on the phone, not pages to a catalog or commercial time on TV.

Some smart businesspeople "get this," and incorporate it into their operations one way or another. One restaurant chain lists a recommended wine along with each entrée on its menu, and pays bonuses to its waitstaff on sales of its premium desserts. In movie theaters, you are "bumped up" from regular size to jumbo size beverages and popcorn tubs, because "it's only x-cents more"—but those x-cents provide a much higher profit margin than the core purchase.

Another way to think about this is, by failing to devise and use upsells, you leave 5% to 20% of the money readily available to you for the asking safely inside your customers' wallets instead of in your cash register where it rightfully belongs!

The other neglected opportunity is cross-selling. One chain of gourmet food shops has a checklist at each cash register, so if a customer is buying any kind of sausage without cheese, the clerk suggests a cheese, or if buying a cheese without a sausage, vice versa. A chain of menswear stores carefully tracks customers who've bought suits and ties but no sportswear, and sends them sportswear offers and coupons, and which have bought sportswear but no suits, and sends them offers and coupons for suits.

Pursuing these opportunities not only increases sales, but produces profitable sales and improved cash flow, because you are leveraging the same customers, not having to invest in acquiring new ones.

The Ultimate MCF Tactic: "Pre-Pay"

The fastest way to multiply cash flow is to get customers to pay in advance for goods and/or services to be delivered later, preferably over time.

When I took over a very troubled, cash flow negative manufacturing company, we immediately instituted a 5% prepay discount on repeat orders, 7% on new orders. Nearly 20% of our accounts switched to paying in advance, and it made a huge difference.

I mentioned the value of "pre-pays" in chiropractic practices. Pre-paid "plans" or "memberships" have been devised and successfully sold by Members or clients of mine who own martial arts schools, restaurants, resorts, clothing stores, carpet cleaning services, pest control services, and many other kinds of businesses. One photography studio owner I know sells five-, seven-, and ten-year pre-paid family portrait plans, the most expensive of which is about $30,000.00 in services and products if purchased piecemeal, discounted to $19,000.00 pre-paid. He says he usually sells only one, sometimes two, of these plans per month, but over the past four years, he's used these big chunks of money to first pay off some high interest credit cards, then pay cash for new equipment, and finally to invest in income-producing real estate.

The most interesting entrepreneurs to me are the ones who create their own capital from sales of pre-paid goods or services. I got to know Bob Stupak, who built the Vegas World Hotel and Casino (now The Stratosphere) from the ground up, paying for construction on each floor as money came in from his sale of pre-paid vacation packages. He turned an intangible into a tangible product that could be sold and collected for in advance of its use, and used it to build the hotel itself—without a dime of debt in construction loans.

Far too many would-be entrepreneurs are stopped in their tracks by lack of capital, when ingenuity would serve as a perfectly satisfactory substitute.

Through some or all of these methods you can multiply and maximize your business's cash flow, and, as a result, give yourself every possible opportunity to win big.

CHAPTER 12

HOW TO ACHIEVE PEAK
PRODUCTIVITY

The hurrieder I go, the behinder I get.

—Pennsylvania Dutch saying

A s a teenager, I worked summers as a groom at a harness racetrack, taking care of horses and shoveling manure. A lot of manure. Every workday started at 5:00 A.M., stopped around 1:00 P.M., started back up about 5:00 P.M. to get the horses that were racing that night ready, and finished after the races at 10:00 or 11:00 P.M.

During the day, I worked in aluminum-roofed barns that absorbed the sun's heat and cooked us pretty well. I filled wicker baskets with manure, about two per stall, anywhere from three to a dozen stalls, hauled the baskets the length of the barn, hoisted them up, and emptied them into the manure wagons. I fed, watered, and groomed the horses. I worked on their sore legs and feet. I walked them. I stacked bales of straw and hay.

All of it was hard work. Looking back, I have fondness and nostalgia for it all. So much so, I've returned, and now own about two dozen racehorses, even drive some in races at a major racetrack. But I do not shovel the manure. I'm not *that* nostalgic.

But, no matter how hard you have worked in previous jobs, you'll discover that running your business is even harder, more intense work. The pace and pressure of being the person in charge is unlike any other, and it requires masterful organization, control, and use of time. It requires that you have the ability to do many things at once. The multiple demands on the entrepreneur's time are extraordinary, and you need extraordinary measures to match these demands.

Time is the most valuable asset any entrepreneur possesses. Time to step aside and think. Time to network. Time to solve problems. Time to invent sales and marketing breakthroughs. *The use or misuse of your time*—the degree with which you achieve peak productivity—will determine your success as an entrepreneur.

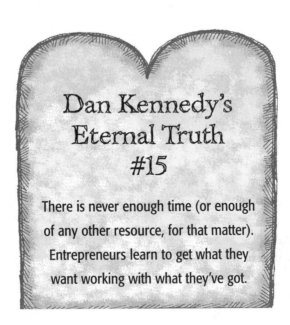

Dan Kennedy's Eternal Truth #15

There is never enough time (or enough of any other resource, for that matter). Entrepreneurs learn to get what they want working with what they've got.

Time may be the biggest problem in business, and the biggest societal concern of the moment. The Fortune 500 companies spend millions annually on time management training and productivity analysis. The market is clogged with time management systems and seminars. Despite all this, most business people I know are still woefully disorganized, behind in their work, running faster and faster to try to catch up. One research study I read about some years ago concluded that the average corporate CEO actually logs less than 90 minutes a day of genuinely productive time. Lee Iacocca told me he doubted it was that much! And I suggest entrepreneurs have even bigger problems with time than do corporate executives.

Imagine—in an eight-to-ten-hour workday, being able to count just 90 minutes of it as productive! Clearly, you can give yourself a tremendous competitive advantage if you can make more of your time productive.

Why Is Time Such a Problem?

To achieve peak productivity, you've got to know what it is, and when you're hitting it—and when you're not. Most people have no clue. Most people work harder and faster, without the ability to determine whether they're really getting anywhere.

I have devoted quite a bit of thought to defining what productivity really is—and what it isn't. The definition for peak productivity that I've developed is:

The use of your time, energy, intelligence, resources, and opportunities in a manner calculated to move you measurably closer to meaningful goals.

Once you understand and accept this definition, you'll be better able to choose what to do, what to delegate, and what to leave undone.

Why "Do It Now" May Not Be the Best Advice

The favorite affirmation of the late self-made multi-millionaire and success expert W. Clement Stone is "Do it now!" Given that something should be done, and should be done by you, then "Do it now!" is good advice. Procrastination is insidious.

But many people erroneously accept the do-it-now idea as a prison sentence requiring them to try and do *everything* **now. Some things shouldn't be done now.** Some things should be deliberately assigned to next week or next month. Some things shouldn't be done at all. And, the busier I am and the older I get, the more I conclude that the greatest wisdom of all is in astutely choosing what *not* to do.

It's interesting how obligated most people feel to answer a ringing phone. They'll interrupt whatever they are doing to pick up the receiver, even if they are in the shower! When somebody calls the office and leaves a message, people feel obligated to call back, even when they don't know the caller! Now, with cell phones, people put themselves "on point" 24-7, without even a moment's peace. In fact, I'm lately seeing men in airport rest-rooms, standing at urinals, peeing and talking on their cell phones. Sad and pathetic. If you can't even pee in peace, you're not Mr. Important; you're Mr. Idiot.

Mobile communications technology—cell-phones, iPhones, Blueberries, wireless laptops, texting, etc.—is supposed to liber-ate you and enable you to conduct business anywhere, at any time. Not to enslave you and compel you to conduct business everywhere, all the time.

The same is true for faxes and e-mails and correspondence. When people receive these in the office, they feel obligated to reply, quickly. Because someone appears in the office doorway, they feel obligated to acknowledge them, to invite them in, to talk with them. And on and on.

It bewilders a lot of people that I, for example, will go days without checking my phone messages or opening my mail. And, at home, I'll often take the phone off the hook for hours to write, nap, watch a game, whatever. "Having that phone off the hook would drive me crazy," a friend said. "I'd be worrying the whole time about who might be trying to call me."

For some years, I have refused to take any unscheduled busi-ness calls and I operate entirely by clustered phone appoint-ments. I do not own a cell phone and I will not use e-mail. For a time, I was mocked, but of late, a number of famous CEOs are stating they've disconnected their e-mail. Even one of the top internet marketing consultants in America refuses to use it personally!

You have to shake off the shackles of ordinary and customary obligations and feel free to do whatever assists you in achieving peak productivity. Your only real obligation is to your optimum productivity.

I deal with this in infinitely more detail—and prove to you with examples that you can still control access to you, your time, and your life in ANY business—in my book *No B.S. Time Management for Entrepreneurs.* One very important reason you should get and read this book is to learn techniques you can use, to work interruption-free, to better organize, prioritize, and stick to your highest-value responsibilities and opportunities.

The Yes or No Test

> "Pragmatic means 'leads to money.' That's what business is all about."
>
> —GENE SIMMONS, KISS, AUTHOR *SEX, MONEY, KISS*–A FABULOUS, FRANK BUSINESS BOOK I ENTHUSIASTICALLY URGE YOU TO READ. WE WERE FORTUNATE TO HAVE GENE SPEAK AT A GLAZER-KENNEDY INSIDER'S CIRCLE™ MARKETING & MONEYMAKING SUPERCONFERENCE ATTENDED BY MORE THAN 1,000 OF OUR MEMBERS, ALL SIMPLY BLOWN AWAY BY THE EXPERIENCE.

These days, when someone asks me to do something, attend a meeting, talk with somebody, read something, whatever, I silently ask myself: *Is this going to move me measurably closer to a goal?* If not, I do my best to say no.

I think in terms of *investing* time. After all, if time is money, then you must either be spending or investing it. Would you knowingly invest your money in, say, a stock that promised no gain or dividends? No. You might choose to spend some money on things offering no monetary profit such as tickets to the theater, flowers for your spouse, or a vacation. But investing time in activities unlikely to pay any kind of dividend is stupid. You must be very astute at making these time-investment decisions.

So, always ask yourself, is this demand on my time a wise investment? Yes or no?

This definitely applies to a lot of the online activities that are perceived by too many as "free media"—instead of the enormous time suck they often are. During the months I've been finishing this book, Twitter has risen to the top of the public obsessions, and I'm often asked about it by clients. The other day, a client who makes about $600,000.00 a year and aspires to seven-figures asked if he should be Twittering every day. I said, give or take, your time must be worth no less than $2,000.00 an hour to have a prayer of meeting your goal (per the formula in my *No B.S. Time Management* book), and you have to behave like the kind of person whose time is worth no less than $2,000.00 an hour. If your little twittering 'n tweeting throughout the day adds up to just 30 minutes, you have to see $1,000.00 a day, or, against 250 business days a year, $250,000.00 of value there. And if there is, you should be eager to hire and pay someone very good at this $100,000.00 a year to be your ghost-writer, twittering 'n tweeting on your behalf. Are you ready, I asked, to write that check? And he had his answer.

What Now?

One of the classic problems faced by entrepreneurs is the absence of an imposed work plan. As someone else's employee, a work plan is imposed on you by your employer. Your adherence to that plan may be policed by managers and supervisors. You are held accountable for effectiveness in adhering to and accomplishing that plan. Deviations from the imposed plan are restricted, sometimes punished. That imposed plan causes you to behave in a disciplined fashion. For example, you get up at a certain time every morning to arrive at work at a set, acceptable time. Maybe you get all your expense reports in order every Thursday afternoon because you are expected to submit them on Friday. You get your monthly newsletter out to your customers because that's part of the imposed plan.

Now you're an entrepreneur. You are your own boss—you can smash that alarm clock with a sledge hammer and set your own hours. You decide what will be done, when and how.

But for many new entrepreneurs, when they get free of the job, they don't know what to do next. It's too much freedom. They wind up paralyzed, looking around for somebody to tell them what to do.

You have to set up your own work plan. I am most productive when I operate under a self-imposed work plan that creates at least as much discipline as any employer-imposed plan would—preferably more. You have to be tough on yourself and set deadlines. If you wouldn't accept an excuse from someone working for you, you can't accept it from yourself. If you're trying to set an example of leadership for others around you, you have to overdo it: be more organized than they need to be, be more punctual than they need to be.

In a typical year, I write two or more books for bookstore distribution, other information products and audio learning programs published and distributed by Glazer-Kennedy Insider's Circle™, I edit four monthly newsletters, I write for two online publications, I frequently contribute articles to others' newsletters, and, for fees, I ghostwrite a book or two for other authors. I also bill over a million dollars a year in fees and royalties for the direct-response advertising and marketing copy I write for clients. This workload is in addition to consulting, serving as a strategic advisor to several corporations, running an elite coaching and mastermind group requiring involvement with its 20 entrepreneurs every month, speaking, and supervising a stable of more than 20 racehorses and driving myself in over 150 harness races a year. I am also married, with grown kids and grandchildren. And I'm a noninsulin-dependent diabetic so I have to invest extra time in taking care of my health.

If I wrote only when I felt like it, when I was inspired, when the time was right, I'd be finishing last year's workload in my next life. No, I write when I am tired, when I am uninspired, when I am too busy, not just in my office but on airplanes and in hotel rooms. I write each and every single day, no matter what. I put myself under self-imposed work plans and deadlines to create discipline.

My friend John Carlton, a top direct-response copywriter, says the greatest of all inventions in all of recorded history was the deadline. Without it, nothing else would ever have gotten done with any of the other inventions.

Nobody's going to do this for you. You're on your own. You must impose deadlines and disciplines on yourself.

Refuse to Let Them Steal Your Time

Another prevalent problem entrepreneurs fight in achieving peak productivity is other people's disrespect for time. Most people don't value their time very highly, and, as a result, don't place much value on yours either. Given half a chance, *most* people will waste your time.

I am militant about guarding my time. I learned, for example, not to set up business meetings in restaurants. If I was going to a business lunch with someone, I'd have them first come to my office. When you arrange to meet people in restaurants, you waste a lot of time waiting for them because very few people are punctual. If they're late but they're coming to your office, productivity can continue until they arrive.

Back when I was in my office most days, I had all my incoming calls very carefully screened. This did occasionally

irritate people, but that only served notice to me that the irri-
tated person was not a very successful businessperson. He may
be able to afford to waste time; I can't. So, in my office, no calls
were put through nor were any messages even accepted unless
the caller fully identified himself and the reasons for calling.
My best guess is that there were a dozen callers a day who did
not get through to me and never did, because they refused to
identify themselves. Even at just three minutes a call, that
alone saved me 36 minutes a day. Give or take, 900 minutes a
year.

Now my screening methods are even more stringent.

My assistant asks people to send or fax me brief, introductory
notes before trying to get on the phone with me. Many times, she
can handle these matters and I'm not needed at all. When a conversation is warranted, it is via a telephone appointment with a
definite end time. This applies to existent and prospective clients
alike, vendors, media contacts, virtually everybody. Currently, all
my telephone appointments are organized into just two days a
month, and I knock them out one after the other with only a few
brief breaks between 8:00 A.M. and 6:00 P.M. The other days are
free of any telephone calls. I also work predominately in one of
my home offices, alone, protected from interruption. My assistant works from an office in a different state. She faxes me as
needed, we speak three to five times a week, and once a week,
she sends me a box of correspondence, magazines, newsletters,
material from clients, bills, checks, and memos, all neatly organized for me to handle efficiently. I meet with her face-to-face once
a year.

I know this sounds extreme. But it explains why I can get
more done than any ten other people—in less time than any one
of them. Extreme as it may be, hundreds and hundreds of clients
have seen the wisdom of it and emulated it, if not to the same
extent, to significant extent, including those in businesses or professions where most would insist it impossible.

Put a Stake Through the Heart of Every "Time Vampire" Who Comes Your Way

Time Vampires are people dedicated to sucking up your time. In the process, they also suck out a lot of your energy, leaving you white, weak, and behind schedule. These are the repetitive, frequent drop-in visitors. The employee whose favorite phrase is "Have you got a minute?" Or those vampires are infused with "meeting-itis." They're chronically disorganized. Each time one of these vampires drops by and hangs out, picture him or her sinking teeth into your neck and sucking out a pint or two.

Suppose, for example, you want to make $100,000.00 this year, which means your work hour is worth about $36.00, which is about 60 cents a minute. So when a Time Vampire sucks up 20 minutes in a meeting for something that could have been handled with a 4-minute phone call, that person just sucked over $9.00 right out of your wallet. If that happens 5 times in a week, you lose $45.00. Over 50 weeks, that's $2,250.00. If you have ten of these vampires hanging around, you're down $22,500.00 before you get out of the starting gate toward the $100,000.00 goal. That's nearly a 25% weight handicap; too much to overcome. That's also a simplistic for-sake-of-quick-example calculation. The true cost of that time sucked is much higher, as I explain in detail in *No B.S. Time Management for Entrepreneurs.*

The Secret of Secrets of Getting Rich

Perhaps you think I'm overdoing this—beating this drum too loudly. But let me tell you why it's impossible to over-emphasize the deliberate achievement of peak productivity. It is the secret of secrets to getting rich.

Exceptional success in any business is the result of strategically directing ever-increasing amounts of your time to the activities you're very good at and very excited about, to the highest value responsibilities, to only the best opportunities. When you start a business, you do it all. The trick is to stay at that stage as briefly as possible, and, as you grow out of it, to grow by directing increasing amounts of your time to those aspects of the business you have the most passion for and do best.

You can never make this happen if your time is being abused, wasted, lost, sucked up by vampires, and controlled by everybody but you.

CHAPTER 13

HOW ENTREPRENEURS ATTRACT
GOOD LUCK

The more we know about what we really
want, the better prepared we are to
recognize favorable chances and extract good luck.

—A.H.Z. CARR , AUTHOR, *HOW TO ATTRACT GOOD LUCK*

I t's very common for authors of business and success books to insist that there's no such thing as luck. This is not true. There is, quite obviously, luck. People do "get discovered." Coincidences do turn to gain. For example, when I was still flying commercial rather than private, who I got sitting next to me in an airplane was the luck of the draw, yet, a number of times, conversations with those people turned into business, opportunity, and income for me. Sure, I took the initiative to steer the conversation in productive directions, I was mentally prepared, and I was in the first class section of the airplane, but, still, the luck of the draw put the right person beside me.

So, I believe in luck, I believe we get lucky breaks, and I don't think there's anything wrong with looking for a little luck and acknowledging it when we get it. On the other hand, let's remember that the lucky rabbit's foot sure didn't bring much luck to that rabbit.

Like most other entrepreneurs, I deeply resent the tendency of liberals, liberal politicians, and liberal media pundits to equate success and wealth with luck. If you resent this too, you'll probably appreciate one of my political columns published online at BusinessAndMediaInstitute.org, reprinted here, at the end of this chapter.

I also pity the poor who are sold this pile of b.s., as a means of discouraging their initiative and responsibility and perpetuating their dependency on the welfare industry, government, and liberal politicians. Henry Ford observed: the harder I work, the luckier I seem to get. Others have echoed his sentiment. Opportunity, cooperation of others, success, and wealth are all attracted to people for reasons predominately within their own control—and luck, too. I spell out these attraction factors, which I call Wealth Magnets, in my book, *No B.S. Wealth Attraction for Entrepreneurs*.

Most entrepreneurs I deal with share a belief and cheerful expectation in luck, and try to do their part to facilitate it. They and I believe that an individual can learn to take certain actions that will, in effect, make him lucky.

A book summarizing a lot of scientific research done about "lucky people" is *The Luck Factor* by Dr. Richard Wiseman. It provides evidence that you can actually increase the good luck in your life, on purpose.

Using Your Subconcious Mind

The biggest secret to deliberately making yourself lucky does not come as a set of concrete instructions—it has more to do with your subconscious mind. There just aren't enough pages in this book to convince you of the awesome power of your subconscious mind or how it works. I can only urge you to make a study of it on your own. You might want to begin with the book *The*

New Psycho-Cybernetics by Dr. Maxwell Maltz and me. I have thoroughly satisfied myself that the subconscious mind can be programmed or directed to search its vast stores to select, compile, and provide appropriate information and then give you the "flash of inspiration" you need to solve a nagging problem, go to the right place at the right time, say the right thing, or do the right thing. This is a computer-like function and most people can accept it as logical and true, even if they don't make a practice of using it. It's certainly nothing new; Thomas Edison used to lock himself in a quiet room, give commands to his subconscious mind, and, as he described it, "sit for ideas."

But the properly programmed and energized subconscious mind can go much further than that. Many very successful entrepreneurs, some scientists, and some psychologists believe that it can actually reach out and get needed information from the combined intelligence of the universe, and that it can set up a magnetic field that actually attracts the people, resources, and ideas needed to accomplish a particular goal.

The programming tool for unleashing the full powers of your subconscious mind is definition of purpose. The clearer your picture of what you want, the more productivity you inspire inside your subconscious system. There are three main ways to put this to work and they all involve writing:

1. *Continually develop your goals in writing.* Paul Meyer, founder of the Success Motivation Institute, says "If you are not making the progress you'd like to make, it is probably because your goals are not clearly defined." There is power in continually sharpening the definition of your goals on paper. Clarity is power.
2. *Write out your business plan.* A written, detailed business plan combines goal setting, action planning, and problem solving. It makes ideas believable. Incidentally, I'm not talking about a business plan conforming to business school textbook standards or one prepared for the benefit

of bankers. I'm talking about a working document actually useful in growing and running your business. You should also have a written marketing plan and a marketing and promotions calendar, and you can build yours from my book, *Ultimate Marketing Plan.*

3. *Create and use daily checklists.* You wouldn't ever want to be on an airplane where the crew had reviewed the preflight processes by memory rather than by referring to checklists. Isn't your day and your use of your time equally important?

These three action steps have great practical value, but they also serve to communicate to your subconscious mind, in an organized manner, the seriousness of your objectives. Then wonderful things happen!

How to Be in the Right Place at the Right Time

Some years ago, I was navigating a troubled company through a turnaround and, fortunately, using all three of these action tools to the best of my ability. I put trust in my subconscious system (largely because there wasn't anything else around to trust) and, from time to time, got some very valuable "flashes."

For some time, I'd been thinking about the possibility of selling off part of the company's business in order to get new capital and strengthen the remaining business. One afternoon, a "flash" crystallized that for me; a plan came into my thoughts out of nowhere—to sell the manufacturing part of the company to a competitor in that arena then use that capital to make the retail marketing part of the company stronger. It was all so clear in my mind that, that moment, I picked up the phone and called that company's president, and asked for an appointment to fly into his city and meet with him to discuss a business proposition. The next day, I described my proposal—with no preparation, just as it came to me—and immediately came to an agreement in principle.

In just one week, the details were worked out, contracts signed, and an unprofitable part of my company's business was converted to a nice six-figure sum.

I later learned that I had selected the perfect time to approach this competitor. The president was right in the midst of deciding whether to more aggressively pursue additional business in the particular market in which we were competing or to abandon that market and pursue expansion opportunities elsewhere. Had I been even a week later with my call, decisions would already have been made, possibly making our deal unworkable. Had I been a month or two earlier, the president would not have been ready. My timing was perfect. A lucky break?

No. "Luck" like this is a result of having clearly defined goals, working hard, associating with people who could facilitate success, being involved in situations where opportunities can arise, and continuing personal education and improvement. Oh, and *doing* something.

Dan Kennedy's
Eternal Truth
#16

Even a blind hog finds a truffle once
in a while—as long as it keeps
poking around.

I frequently create ad campaigns and direct-mail campaigns that bring in millions of dollars for my clients, or that out-perform their prior campaigns by impressive margins. I've heard people commenting how "lucky" I am to have this "knack." Nobody mentions the other campaigns I do every year that get results ranging from mediocre to non-existent. (To be fair, I don't either!) But this sort of thing is neither "knack" or "luck"; it is work.

More importantly, it is like drilling multiple oil wells to hit one gusher.

It is also result of years of intense study and hours every week of continuous study, of building up massive reference files of advertising copy sorted by topic, product, and purpose, even of training and conditioning my subconscious mind to search its files and quite literally write copy while I sleep, that I pour out through my fingers on the keyboard only minutes after arising in the morning.

To have good fortune, you have to do enough to help the pendulum swing in your direction. Quarterbacks that complete a lot of passes and throw a lot of touchdown passes throw a bunch of interceptions, too, and practice intensely, study film, train their minds to accurately and quickly read defenses. Babe Ruth had more strikeouts than home runs. Edison had a warehouse full of failed, abandoned experiments. Just about every successful entrepreneur I know tries a lot of ideas every year and profits handsomely if only one or two succeed. Every such entrepreneur is also well prepared and in never ending preparation for his "lucky break" or "streak of luck." One of my best clients tested six different "brilliant ideas" for doing more business with his past customers last year. Five of these ideas flopped. The sixth has turned into a million-dollar-a-year money machine. My very successful *No B.S. Marketing Letter* is what everybody sees now. Few know it was preceded by my creating and publishing four different, much less successful newsletters and a magazine, all abandoned.

Luck Is a Product of Universal Law,
But It Needs Some Assistance

There are certain universal laws. Gravity, for example, works the same way every time, in every situation, for every one of us, whether we know about it or are ignorant of it, whether we think about it or not, whether we believe it or not. Drop ten pencils, all ten fall to the ground.

Some other laws aren't so easily proven. My friend the late Foster Hibbard taught that the more you give, the more you get. He said give: get was a universal law. I have certainly found that the more you give, the more "luck" you get. I now use and teach Foster Hibbard's method for implementing this idea: you establish "the habit of giving" by opening up a separate, dedicated bank account, your "giving account." Into it you deposit 1% to 10% of the money that comes to you from any and every source, and give that money away as you see fit, with no strings attached.

I'm here to tell you that giving away money this way is a fast path to wealth. It energizes the subconscious mind with a wealth and success consciousness unlike anything you've ever experienced.

I confess this was a very difficult idea for me to buy into. It's illogical. If you have $2.00 and give away $1.00, you've got $1.00 left. You haven't increased your wealth, you've decreased it, right? Wrong. When I first started this, I couldn't afford it. I didn't have any extra money. But I decided to test it, and I have now proven it works.

Let me say, though, that this works only when you strictly follow all the rules. You set up the account. You commit to a percentage. You put that percentage into your giving account every time you get money—no exceptions, no excuses. You give it away with no expectation of return. Try if for a couple of months and stay open to real serendipity and to new financial gain coming at you from the most unexpected sources.

I suppose the benefit you get from this is guaranteed by universal laws. But the benefit requires use of a deliberate process.

But I want to emphasize, there is a law of gravity; there is no law of luck, or as heavily promoted again in recent years thanks to the enormously popular video *The Secret*, law of attraction. Gravity is a law because it works whether you choose to participate in any way or not. Attraction, of luck, success, wealth or anything else, is more of a process than a law governing circumstance. It requires active participation. It does not impose its will on you; in fact, very unlike gravity, it will ignore you completely should you ignore it.

Some Practical Advice on Attracting Good Luck

Keep an open mind and get a lot of exposure. You are sure to attract good luck this way. It's a big mistake to get myopic. Many business people have tunnel vision and, as a result, they cut themselves off from opportunity altogether. Breakthrough ideas usually come from unusual sources, but if the clothing-store owner spends all day, every day in the store only stepping out to trade association meetings and conventions, he is letting luck come in through one very tiny hole. From business people like this, you'll hear things like, "We've never done it that way before . . . . That may be okay there, but not in our business." They close their minds and shut themselves off from the world.

Drive to your store or office by different routes. Every month, pick a magazine off the newsstand you've never read before and read it. Make a point of talking to cab drivers, restaurant servers, and others you might not normally strike up a conversation with. Give yourself little bits of exposure to ideas, experiences, and people outside the normal, narrow scope of your business and see what happens. Something will.

I think one of the best benefits delivered to Glazer-Kennedy Insider's Circle™ Members is our bludgeoning at, our chopping away at, provincial thinking by business owners. We put so many current, real-life examples of successful strategies moved from one business to other wholly unrelated businesses in front of our Members that everybody finally, firmly, fully "gets" that no business is different, that theirs isn't different; that their business is marketing; then they are mentally liberated to bring breakthrough strategies to their business rather than being bound by its norms, conventions and history. When this light bulb goes on and stays on above an entrepreneur's head, he becomes a very different breed of entrepreneur.

That Next Step

Don't let this book be just a "good read." Let it be the introduction to a new way of thinking about opportunities for your business. You can experience Glazer-Kennedy Insider's Circle™ Membership FREE at www.FreeGiftFrom.com/business.

Dan Kennedy's Business & Media Institute Column, 3/3/09

A Letter from a Working Person

Dear Chris Matthews, build your own business
and see if it feels like work.
By Dan Kennedy
Business & Media Institute
3/3/2009 11:59:50 A.M.

Imagine my surprise to hear Chris Matthews, on his February 26th broadcast, cheerily and enthusiastically announce that President Obama is "promising to tax the rich people in order to pay for health care *for the working people.*"

Dear Mr. Matthews: maybe you are a rich person who doesn't earn your money and doesn't work. Since I see you working on TV all the time, perhaps you secretly feel that cheerleading for Barack Obama isn't really "work." I'm willing to accept your critical self-assessment.

But I and all the other people I know earning over $250,000.00 a year—and into seven figures—well, we are definitely working people. Most of us work longer hours than our employees do, take more work home to do in evenings than our employees do, and work more weekend hours than our employees do. Many of us travel and spend a great deal of time away from our families. Many of us bear enormous executive responsibility and the stress that comes with it.

We also do more valuable work—not by accident, but because we have worked very hard to make ourselves more valuable. We have chosen to learn more and keep learning more; read more, play less;

develop expertise. And almost all of us worked much, much, much harder than the "average working person" for years, even decades, to create our businesses, master our crafts and skills, build our reputations, and finally put ourselves in positions to harvest our current high incomes.

As a matter of fact, our willingness to work more and work harder than most of those you designate as "working people" *might* just be the reason we now, finally earn much higher incomes. I know this is a troubling concept for liberals, but there it is: cause and effect.

So when you speak class warfare, it enrages us. Your dividing of Americans into separate groups, "working people" and "rich"—thus characterizing the rich as *"not* working people"—is *obscene.*

Oh, and just for the record, we already pay extraordinarily high taxes. More importantly, we pay an exorbitant share of the total U.S. tax burden—far, far in excess of the difference between our incomes and those paying less, little or none, and far in excess of our ratio to the population and our consumption of services.

We are Atlas already carrying the entire nation on our shoulders, and we are now tempted to shrug. You see, we could choose not to work if sufficiently antagonized, assaulted, and abused. And for every one of us who takes the next four years off, thousands can kiss their jobs bye-bye. If that's a surprise to you, I'd be delighted to explain it with specific examples.

We not only work harder than all those we provide jobs for, we also provide nearly all the capital and take all the risks to create businesses and build communities and retail centers and everything else that provide the majority of jobs. Those you see as working people create no jobs for themselves; we nonworking rich provide them all. If we put our capital on strike for the next four years—a strike already in progress—there'll be 16 to 20 percent or worse unemployment, a 3,000 or lower Dow wiping out all working peoples' pensions and retirements entirely, boarded up businesses as far as the eye can see, and no health care for anybody.

Yes, that's a threat.

Finally, a quick math lesson. There are no more than six million of us (give or take) that Obama has targeted for his grand panoply of stated income tax increases, backdoor tax increases via the taking away of real estate interest, charitable giving and other deductions, capital gains tax increases, etc. If you confiscated 100 percent of our combined incomes, you still couldn't pay for everybody's health care.

This is the most vile lie ever told to those working people. Why? Because every dollar of income stolen from me with taxes I retrieve plus three, to cover the taxes and overhead. I do so by: downsizing companies and cutting jobs, outsourcing jobs, not investing in expansion and creating jobs, and by raising prices. The last, raising prices, causes inflation, the biggest tax on working people and the only tax on poor people. Every tax-the-rich scheme costs far more than it gets. Nothing else could come close to the destruction guaranteed by abusively taxing the rich.

Some honest reporting about all this would consider the so-obvious folly of trying to force six million people to buy health care for 200-million; acknowledge that Obama is not merely returning top tax rates to Clinton or pre-Reagan points but that he is laying on myriad tax increases by removing deductions; and would stop smearing the rich as not-working-people. We ought to be thanked, daily. Better we should be encouraged to work at creating and building things, but right now we've set that aside to work at out-maneuvering Obama's tax assault, and watch how hard we work at that.

CHAPTER 14

WHY AND HOW TO BUILD YOUR OWN
MINI CONGLOMERATE

It's an impossible situation,
but it has possibilities.

—SAM GOLDWYN

Over the years I've often been asked how I managed to keep up with all my different businesses. It puzzled many people. But one of the things they didn't see is how my businesses and activities fit together, so that I viewed it as managing one synergistic conglomerate rather than wrestling with an assortment of different ventures.

Early on, some of my companies shared office and warehouse space, computer services, a telephone system, and some personnel. By sharing this way, each business entity got better things then it could afford on its own, and no entity spent more than it had to for its needs. There was synergy. For example, one company produced videos and serviced a number of my consulting clients with infomercial and promotional video production. It also produced videos that my publishing company sold. My publishing company's catalogs also advertised my consulting, copywriting, and speaking services. My speaking activities provided new customers for my publishing company's mailing lists. The books I wrote for other publishers, which were sold in bookstores, provided new customers for my company's mailing lists and provided consulting clients, so I counted my writing as a form of advertising.

I carefully and strategically started, acquired, and developed businesses and business interests that were profitable and valuable in and of themselves, but that also assisted each other, so that the whole was greater than the parts. Many savvy entrepreneurs follow this same pattern.

The current Glazer-Kennedy Insider's Circle™ business, while much larger, is much the same, in having a number of business "units" under one umbrella. Further, I still strive to make my outside business interests and activities feed and support Insider's Circle, just as I rely on it to feed and support my other interests.

On a bigger scale, consider the Disney empire. Its cable-TV Disney Channel, its Disney Radio network, and its magazines are good businesses in and of themselves, but also a huge promotional system for its parks, movies, videos, and products. Its character-licensing business is immensely profitable, and everywhere those famous characters appear, they silently, subtly advertise Disney. Their substantial mail-order catalog and online catalog business advertise their movies and parks and cross-promote their retail stores. Their retail stores promote their movies, parks, and time-share real estate, Disney Vacation Club. And on and on it goes.

This kind of "cross-fertilization," done carefully and intelligently, on a big or small scale, can make your business more profitable and a lot more fun. This is the way to create a big income out of a small business.

In media, the term "platform" is used. Disney has a very substantial platform—its magazines, its television and radio network, its websites, and its parks—nearly guaranteeing the success of many new products or services. These days, book publishers prefer authors with their own platforms for promotion, virtually guaranteeing a significant number of sales. That might be the number of Facebook friends, the size of an e-mail list, or influence in a given industry. For me, the entire Glazer-Kennedy Insider's Circle™ business provides a substantial platform: there is an online networking community, heavily trafficked websites, an opt-in e-mail list of hundreds of thousands of entrepreneurs, four newsletters reaching all the Members, monthly tele-seminars and audio programs, over 150 local Chapters meeting regularly, and two major international events a year. With this in place, we can roll out a book and confidently predict a sales number larger than 90% of all non-fiction business books ever achieve—not counting new people who find it on bookstore shelves, while meandering around Amazon, or by recommendation from a friend. In the other direction, the book will introduce many people to me and to Glazer-Kennedy for the first time. I'll get speaking engagements and consulting engagements directly. In far bigger numbers, new Members will start—in this case, with the free offer on pages 272–273.

Of course you're not an author nor do you have an international membership organization, so what does this have to do with you?

Three Strategies for <u>BIG</u> Income Even if Starting as a <u>Small</u> Business Owner

There are three important strategies every entrepreneur should strain his brain over, to find a way to put them to use for his business.

Strategy #1: You want to develop and control an effective promotional platform, and think in terms of owning that, not just owning a business.

It can be local or global, niched or broad, facilitated predominately online or offline. But it should be multi-media, reaching an organized audience of customers as well as new, potential customers, ready for your use to roll out a new product or service or promotion. You want to be a mini-media mogul with your own media conglomerate.

Let's assume you own a local fine restaurant or wine store. You decide to organize a food and wine cruise, which you will host. If you can put 250 people on the cruise, you'll net $125,000.00 and, of course, go free. If all you have to work with is the traffic through your store or restaurant, it could take months to forever to make that happen. But if you have thousands of people getting your twice weekly e-mail gourmet cooking, healthy eating, and wine education tips; if you have hundreds actively using your searchable database for cool recipes; if you have a mail-order business shipping wines and food-gift baskets all over the country as well as delivering client gifts for local businesses; if you have a monthly newsletter featuring famous celebrities' favorite recipes; and if you have made yourself into something of a celebrity . . . . selling out that cruise in 30 days is not only possible, it could be a snap.

So think about using your business to build your multi-media platform, then using your platform to not only promote and support your business but to make all sorts of other income opportunities possible.

Strategy #2: Think synergistically.

When you layer one business on another, and another on top of that, or create horizontal product or service extensions, it should all work together in closed loops, feeding on and feeding back to the main business. Be very wary of unrelated, nonsynergistic involvements' distractions, diffusion of resources and energy, and trade-offs, producing dollars in one place but costing them in another.

For example, so far, several financial advisors have chosen to acquire Kennedy's All-American Barber Club™ franchises in their local areas. The Barber Club clientele tends to be affluent, many are business owners and entrepreneurs, and the Club is much more than just a barber shop, so it is a perfect vehicle for the financial advisor to become known to and get to know potential clients for his practice. Conversely, most of his financial advisory clients are affluent men, so gifting them with rewards at the Club works, and they can more easily refer their friends there—and all roads lead to Rome. There are other local businesses with whom the Barber Club has similarly good synergy; but there are some with which it has none. In a similar way, most of the 150+ Glazer-Kennedy Independent Business Advisors operating our local Chapters and Kennedy Study/Mastermind Groups in their areas have other, full-time businesses that work synergistically with their Business Advisor status.

I always like businesses with vertical synergy opportunity, meaning you can build one business on the back of the first. For example, one of our Members, John DuCane owns Dragon Door Publishing, marketing a variety of books, manuals, DVDs, and courses having to do with health and fitness disciplines, including the very popular "kettle bell" training. His is basically a mail-order company selling products. It has spawned two other businesses: one, a training and certification program for personal trainers and coaches who want to teach John's disciplines in their local areas; two, a distributor and affiliate organization, selling his products. In a related field, in the martial arts industry, a Platinum Member of mine, Stephen Oliver, owns Mile High Karate, with academies in his own, local area and franchised academies throughout the country. Stephen chose to acquire the major trade and professional association in that industry,

NAPMA; the National Association of Professional Martial Artists, which publishes the *Professional Martial Artists* magazine reaching every martial arts school in the country.

In horizontal extensions, one of our Members, Dr. Barry Lycka, started with a private cosmetic procedures practice, then opened a retail day spa next door. Many chiropractors opt to own massage therapy offices. Restaurants add bakeries, party centers, catering. My client Dr. Tomshack has a nationwide network of franchised HealthSource® chiropractic clinics that, once established, he added a weight loss franchise to. Sometimes this can even involve multiple business owners in a joint venture. In our Membership, for example, there is an M.D., a dentist, and a nutritionist who jointly own a "stop snoring" sleep disorders clinic, primarily treating sleep apnea.

Think about how to reposition your present business within a synergistic spider web, with other opportunities created vertically and horizontally.

Strategy #3: Give yourself something other than your business to promote.

When you set out to directly promote a business, media wants you to buy advertising—they're not eager to give it to you for free in the form of publicity. Much of the public is immediately resistant to your outreach and messages, viewing you as just another salesman arriving at their doorstep.

I'll first use myself as example. I have written and had published 13 books. As the author of a book, a great many doorways to customers and clients have welcome mats in front of them. Radio program hosts, industry advisors and associations conducting tele-seminars, trade journals and mainstream magazines are all happy to interview me or get content from me they can use. If I simply want to directly promote Glazer-Kennedy Insider's Circle™ Membership, many of these doorways slam shut.

If you own several dollar stores in your area, you may find getting invited on all your local radio and television stations to be interviewed and promote your stores difficult. But if you have a new, free access website to help consumers in a tough economy, featuring 101 ways to save money at home, on clothes, when buying a car, dining out, etc., with contributions and ideas from many experts that you've gathered, and a forum for people to submit their best moneysaving ideas—with a $500.00 shopping spree awarded each month for the best one . . . . that you can promote much, much more easily than your four stores. As you can see, an idea like this links back to Strategy #1.

What else can you promote but your business? A website providing useful information and services like the one in my example, a book, a special report, results of a survey, an event, a cause.

This entire discussion has taken us back to differences between ordinary business owners and entrepreneurs. Remember, ordinary business owners think inward and provincially. Entrepreneurs think much more expansively and creatively.

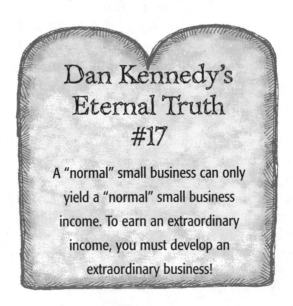

Dan Kennedy's
Eternal Truth
#17

A "normal" small business can only yield a "normal" small business income. To earn an extraordinary income, you must develop an extraordinary business!

How to Get Rich by Accident

The way to wealth as an entrepreneur is continually, creatively redefining and reinventing a business. Entrepreneurs need to be open to and alert for completely unexpected opportunities for alliances and ways to expand businesses on top of the business. When you can do this, you can *just about* get rich by accident.

The large mail-order marketer of office supplies, Quill Corporation, provides a good example. They got in the mail-order business completely by accident. They originally had a tiny, struggling retail business; to try and attract business, the owners experimented with sending out new product announcements and special offers on postcards. The response to their simple direct-mail campaigns was so good, they started selling directly rather than through the retail system.

The Miller Brothers started Quill in 1957 in a remodeled coal bin in Chicago with $2,000.00 they managed to scrape together. Today, they mail millions of catalogs a year, have a thriving e-commerce business, serve over a million customers, and generate hundreds of millions of dollars in annual sales. "Being in the mail-order business was never our intention," Jack Miller says. "It just sort of happened."

I had a client in the industrial chemicals business who discovered his employees sneaking bottles of one of their products out the back door and selling it to friends and neighbors. To their eternal credit, instead of putting an armed guard at the back door, they instead seized opportunity. They reasoned: if it's good enough to steal and sell to consumers, we ought to be selling it to consumers. Today, the sales of that one product bottled for consumer use and sold on TV, in catalogs, and in retail chains including Home Depot and Wal-Mart far exceed the entire sales volume of the original business.

Careful expansion and diversification, linking businesses within a business, building businesses on businesses, forming strategic alliances, and keeping the doors wide open to accidental, additional opportunity all added together can give the small-business entrepreneur a big income—a huge fortune.

The New Mandate of The New Economy

New Economy Customers increasingly reward the businesses of greater and greater and greater service to them. Amazon has become strong and successful by going far beyond bookselling, into countless other product categories, even into making its platform available to authors and small, self-publishers. My clients who are enjoying the greatest success are constantly finding ways to provide a better range of products and services to their customers. Convenience is key. The mini-conglomerate approach is a path to greater influence with your customers, value to your customers, and profitability for you by increasing Total Customer Value.

The New Economy punishes waste of resources. "Waste not, want not" applies to the nth degree. And the last thing you want to waste is customer value. The second most important thing not to waste is the full value in every advertising or marketing dollar invested.

The Antidote to Advertising

Yes, I'm an "ad man," but I recognize that for most business owners, advertising remains an expensive and frustrating mystery. I'm a marketing guy, but I understand that most business owners prefer other aspects of business, and are least comfortable with marketing. If this is you, and you find the entire responsibility of advertising and marketing to obtain new customers painful and problematic, there is a simple solution: do a lot more business with the customers you do get—so you need less of them. That begs a "mini-conglomerate" approach.

One of the greatest drains on a business' profitability is the high cost of acquiring each new customer, to replace those lost, and to grow. It can also be a challenge to capital. The antidote is doing more business with each customer you have. This puts the less-is-more principle to work for you. Personally, I've always preferred small numbers/big income businesses.

Recently, the automatic garage door at one of our homes turned Linda Blair from *The Exorcist*, opening and closing by whim, refusing to stay closed when asked, and emitting frightening noises at random. No spewing of green glop, but still. I picked a garage door service company out of the Yellow Pages, a service tech arrived, did a fine job, and that was that. Sad, I thought. They spent quite a bit of money to get me. Then they did so little with me. At barest minimum, some attempt should have been made to sell me an extended warranty and a routine service arrangement, so a tech periodically came, oiled, greased, tightened, and "whatevered" the door, the springs, the motor. But the opportunity for them was so much bigger than that. They had a capable person in my home who had gained my trust for himself and for his company by arriving on time, performing capably. If they owned or had strategic alliances with a garage cleaning, junk removal business . . . . a garage organizer company . . . . a house painting or gutter cleaning or door and window company or handyman service or car detailing or carpet cleaning, etc., etc., etc. business, they could have secured me as a customer for that at zero cost; the cost already paid for by the garage door company's advertising.

Two weeks have passed as of this writing, and no follow-up has occurred. No courtesy call from someone at the office to verify satisfaction—and offer or recommend additional services. No letter endorsing another kind of home services company with which they have a reciprocal relationship. Nothing. Nada. Zip. Safe bet, this company's owner is pretty clueless about TCV, Total Customer Value, and completely clueless about the mini-conglomerate approach. Fortunately, you are now well informed.

CHAPTER 15

USING YOUR BUSINESS AS A PATH TO FINANCIAL INDEPENDENCE

The only thing worse than not getting
what you want is getting what you want.

—OSCAR WILDE

W hy are you in business or getting into business? You might be surprised at some of the answers I get when I ask this question of clients or at seminars. You see, getting into business is actually pretty easy, even too easy for some people's own good. Getting in is often a lot easier than getting out. And getting in is definitely a lot easier than getting what you really want from being in business. For most, that's the tough assignment.

For starters, viewing your business as "the end" is a mistake. It's not an achieved goal; it is a means for achieving many other goals. For too many people, the desire to own their own business is so powerful and exciting that little thought is given to "what's next?"

You don't want to marry the business. Marry the goals.

Years ago, in connection with a writing assignment, I interviewed a woman in the muffin business in Atlanta. Her name has long since been forgotten, so I'll call her Margie.

Margie's experience provides a great example. Margie determined that she wanted to open her own muffin and cookie store. She researched the field, found a location she believed was viable, and developed some of her own creative recipes. She was very excited about her business plan. At night, she lay awake, staring at the ceiling, visualizing her sign—Margie's Famous Muffins and Munchies—over the door of her store.

After some struggle to get the money together, Margie opened her shop just as she had visualized it. Just one month later, she was in financial trouble. The location wasn't as "hot" as she'd believed, and there were other problems. But, by happy accident, the manager of a nearby supermarket chain stopped in and was so impressed with Margie's muffins that he asked her to supply products for resale in his stores. That was a big success, quickly requiring a full night-shift operation to meet the demand.

The retail store was losing money, but the wholesale baking operation was a success. Finally, Margie did the obvious and closed down the high-rent, unsuccessful retail location and put the wholesale baking operation in a cheap rental space. But she cried for a week over the death of her dream. By the end of that year, she was supplying more supermarkets plus numerous restaurants and made a huge net profit. By not having to be at her retail business every day, she had the opportunity to expand by selling new accounts. She's got the makings of an enormously successful business, but not the business she originally married, and that caused her quite a bit of emotional distress. Her emotional difficulties come from being too focused on *modus operandi* rather than being focused on life goals.

Don't Let Your Business Own You

It's ironic that in order to get what you really want from owning your own business—wealth, security, freedom, for example—you must do the most unnatural, difficult thing for an entrepreneur; you must systematically reduce the dependency of the business on you. Don't overlook this. This is *the* secret to becoming financially independent through entrepreneurship.

Most entrepreneurs have no understanding of this and give it very little thought until it's too late. They wind up being owned by their businesses. To their surprise, they find that they've traded one old boss for a plethora of new ones: stockholders, investors, and lenders, employees and associates, customers and clients, vendors and government agencies.

There's an old joke about the government bureaucrat descending on the small-business owner. He says: "We've received a report that you have some poor fellow working here eighteen hours a day, seven days a week, for nothing but a room, board, meals, all the tobacco he can smoke, and all the liquor he can drink. Is that true?" "Yes, I'm afraid it is," admits the owner. "And I'm sad to say, you're looking at him."

You're probably wondering about the security of your business. If the typical entrepreneur leaves the business alone for a week, it does a Jekyll-Hyde transformation. You have got to be there! I know many business owners who go years without a vacation. And, those who do go on vacation don't enjoy it. One half hopes everything's okay back at the ranch, which he checks every few hours by phone, and the other half is disappointed it if is okay; after all, how could it be without his indispensable presence?

I'm embarrassed for business owners connected to their businesses every waking minute, constantly, compulsively, truthfully fearfully jumping as if electroshocked every time their cell phone sounds its little ringtone, checking text messages and e-mails every other minute, their devices always at hand if not in hand. I tell men they have traded their testicles for an iPhone. Pathetic.

What is the point of being the Boss and the Owner if your every minute is dominated by things buzzing, beeping, pinging, and prodding you?

Too many people get into business only to discover they've acquired a new, tougher, more demanding, more stressful job, and they cannot see any way to change it. They tell me they see their stress climbing on the exact same ascendant line and pace as their success. Was that the goal?

The trick is to let the business mature—and the faster, the better. An immature business is entrepreneur driven. In its early days, that's okay and usually necessary. You are the business. From day one, though, if your business is to provide security, freedom, and wealth, you should be working at weaning the business from dependence on you and creating dependence on systems. My friend Ken Varga, who has built huge companies, says any business still dependent on your day-to-day presence after three years is not a business at all. It's a job.

I've appeared as a speaker on several programs with Michael Gerber, author of the best-selling book *The E Myth*. His advice is to systemize your business as if you would franchise it and replicate it in a hundred distant sites, even if you have no intention of doing so. Good, liberating strategy.

Getting Out of Your Own Way

Some people tie their egos up in their minute-by-minute, indispensable importance to their businesses. I have made this mistake myself: carrying data around in my head, making every decision myself whether for a dime or a dollar, being the first one at office in the morning, the last one there at the end of the day, the guy able to do every job in the place—and meddling in every one of them.

I was probably indispensable and irreplaceable. I was also stressed out—a nervous breakdown looking for a place to happen.

I started getting in the habit of stopping off "for a couple of drinks" after leaving the office and going home hours later, half-drunk. This is not the way to get your sense of importance satisfied.

Instead, you can be important and make the most meaningful contributions to your business—without sacrificing your health, family, and sanity—by freeing yourself from in-depth involvement in day-to-day operations, so you have more time for the few business-building things you do best. In my case, in my publishing company, what I did best was create new products or improve the ones we already had, create advertising and marketing materials, and deal with key clients and contacts. But if I gave equal time to purchasing raw materials and supplies, bookkeeping, organizing records and mailing lists, product quality control, and so on, I cheated the business out of my best and I cheated myself out of the business's best.

Be sure you're not cheating yourself and your business out of your best.

How to Help Your Business Mature

A mature business is some or all of these things:

- MARKET driven
- PRODUCT driven
- SERVICE driven
- SYSTEMS driven

For example, a retail store in a busy mall is driven by its market. Very little, if any, outside advertising or marketing is done; the business is designed to feed off the mall traffic. A manufacturer of a little widget that goes inside a bigger widget that makes the windshield wiper switch work is product driven. The bigger widget maker has to have the little widget; the little widget is only made by a couple of companies. A quick-print shop is service driven; its customers are usually concerned with and wooed by speed, convenience, and reliability.

In the beginning, these businesses will also be *owner driven*. The retail-store owner makes all the product, pricing, window-display, and other decisions for the store. The manufacturer watches over the widget making, hiring, firing, buying raw materials, keeping the customers happy, and so on. The copy-shop owner solicits accounts, deals with customers, and keeps the copy shop hopping.

Over time, these businesses can mature to a great degree. Each owner can isolate the one or two things he or she does best and delegate the rest. But the way to get to that stage is to develop your systems, and the development of effective *marketing systems* is the most vital job overlooked by most entrepreneurs.

For example, consider John G., a roofing contractor. He told me that he wanted to diminish his day-to-day work in the business, but as he is the one who brings in most of the business, he doesn't know how to go about it. He's been able to hire good crews and good managers and delegate all the labor, but, he asked, how do you delegate the prospecting and selling that gets the jobs?

The answer is to develop a marketing system that delivers predictable results from repetitive use. In John's case, we worked together to create a direct-mail campaign aimed at qualified leads (provided by a list broker), then a telephone procedure to convert a predictable number of those inquiries to appointments. Then, the big step, we worked on a standardized sales presentation using a flip chart, a video, and a cost-quoting computer program. This made it possible to hire sales representatives, train them quickly and easily, and put them in the field to secure just about the same number of jobs per appointments as when John dealt personally with all the customers. Bingo! This fellow was able to replace himself with a marketing system.

Over the next two years, not only did John achieve his objective of cutting by half his time devoted to the business, but the business was able to increase by nearly 30%!

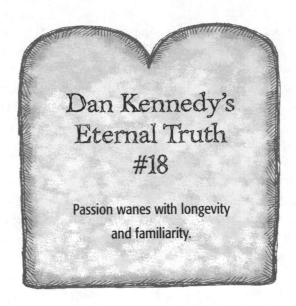

Dan Kennedy's
Eternal Truth
#18

Passion wanes with longevity
and familiarity.

The time to start thinking about all this is not 6 or 12 months before you'd like to change your role in your business. In fact, you should start planning for flexibility and change from day one. You must accept that the unbridled passions you feel for your business at the beginning, that has you happily there from dawn to midnight up to your armpits in work, will change as time passes. The activity you can't wait to get at today may bore the blazes out of you three years from now. It's smart to build your business in a way that allows you to satisfy your changing interests.

You can also think of this as a form of insurance. You could be injured or become ill. The statistics I've seen indicate that one of every three business owners experience some period of disability during their careers. For many, even with an insurance policy in their desk drawer, this can kill the business. Imagine, though, how much more likely it will be that your business can survive a period of months without you if you've structured it with systems from the very beginning.

The first thing you must do is ensure that the routine processes of your business are really routine. That means they happen by procedure so that just about anybody can step in and follow those procedures. You shouldn't have to have your nose in everything.

Second, you need to develop your business to the point where new customers or clients are attracted to your company by marketing systems, not through your direct personal efforts.

To Build Marketing Systems for Your Business

Consult the book *No B.S. DIRECT Marketing for NON-Direct Marketing Businesses,* for a detailed direct marketing blueprint and actual examples from a diverse variety of businesses . . . and Chapter 36 of *No B.S. Marketing to the Affluent,* which provides a diagram and a complete explanation of a fully automated customer attraction, capture, and conversion system.

Third, you must have a plan for directing more and more of your time and energy to the few aspects of the business you enjoy and do best and for reducing the commitment of your time and energy to the many aspects of the business you do not enjoy or do best.

How Does a System Work?

First and foremost, a system works without you being married to it 24 hours a day. Let's say that there have been a number of burglaries in your neighborhood, and you are suddenly more concerned than usual with making your home look occupied all the time. One way to do that is to stay home. Another would be to hire a house-sitter for the times you aren't there—in other words, delegating the responsibility. Or, you could get some simple, inexpensive electronic devices that can be set to turn different lights and appliances on and off at different times. That would be a system. Once in place, it works with little or no attention from you.

Systems deliver predictable and consistent results.

A marketing system is arguably the most important kind of system that an entrepreneur can ever give the business. One restaurant owner I know, Bill H., exemplifies the success of initiating such a system. He sends two letters and a postcard to residents of the neighborhoods surrounding his restaurant and to people in businesses around his restaurant. He has this system streamlined to the point that he has a formula for determining what percentage of response he will get from each mailing, and how many of those responses turned into reservations and revenue for his restaurant. This means he can guarantee his restaurant a certain predictable base of business each and every week. If, say, a seasonal slump is coming up, he can increase the number of letters mailed in order to increase revenue. He can go to sleep at night knowing that a certain number of new clients will call the next day, and, because this is an entirely mechanical process, he could go on vacation for three weeks and still guarantee a certain amount of business to his restaurant. His system gives him immense power, leverage of time, less stress and frustration, and better positioning with new clients.

Always strive to put systems in place; the right systems can totally transform a business.

CHAPTER 16

HOW TO GET A BUSINESS
OUT OF TROUBLE

One ought never to turn one's back on a threatened danger
and try to run away from it. If you do that, you will double
the danger. But if you meet it promptly and without
flinching, you will reduce it by half. Never run
away from anything. Never.

—WINSTON CHURCHILL

Hopefully you'll never need the advice in this brief
chapter. Hopefully.

I have been involved in a couple of business turn-
arounds and helped clients with others. I've also made a point of
studying some of the best-known, big-name turnaround experts,
and I can tell you that there is very little difference between getting one business or another out of trouble. Your options for
action are rather limited.

The very first, crucial step is honesty. You've got to forget all
about protecting your ego and blaming others. None of that matters when the kettle is boiling over. You have to diagnose and
identify problems, period. You need all the gory details. No one
can be allowed to hide anything; no one can be allowed to feel
they have to hide anything.

This is very tough to achieve. Everybody's natural responses are to cover their own tracks as best they can. If people can't or won't be honest with themselves and each other about the problems, either the people have to go, fast, or the business goes under. That's it.

As Long as There's a Pulse, There's Hope

The only absolutely certain death blow for a troubled business is running out of cash. There's little else that's irreversible.

Poisoned Tylenol® killed people but the business survived. Auto makers routinely recall thousands of cars with potentially lethal defects but they have survived—although as I write this, a few have had a myriad of their problems catch up with them. Regardless, crisis in business is common. Key people quit, big competitors move in, fires and floods happen, but businesses survive. I don't think there's any business problem that can't be beat as long as there's cash flow. During a turnaround period, profit and loss is even irrelevant. But cash flow is everything.

I've run a company completely out of cash on two occasions. Miraculously, this company got through both these situations. On one of those occasions, the company took five weeks to recover from a $47,000.00 checking account overdraft. I spent those five weeks walking around with just a few crinkled dollar bills in my pocket, coasting downhill in my car to conserve gas, jumping out of my skin at every phone call, just waiting for the final death nudge to come from somewhere. I've faced cash-flow problems since, but I learned my lesson. No matter the pressure, I will not take a business down to zero cash.

If you find your business in a cash-flow crunch, you must immediately become very tightfisted about parting with each penny. Pay bills in tiny pieces. Trickle it out. Negotiate new terms with vendors as fast as you can. Sacrifice some vendors if you must. Put tiny dabs of grease on the squeakiest wheels. But never,

never spend down to zero or, worse, below zero to appease the wolves. Let them stand out their baying and scratching at the door, but keep a few spare bullets in your gun at all times.

Forget "Kinder and Gentler"

Cut costs with the ax, not a surgical knife. If there's any turnaround mistake I've made more than once, it's being too gentle and conservative in the cutting. You can always put a person or function back in if you must. To start getting out of trouble, though, swing your ax in a wide arc. Cut everywhere. Spare no one, no thing. Cut, cut, cut.

In one turnaround situation, I let 38 people go in one day. I had more blood on my hands than the monster in a cheap horror movie. It was really awful. One of the top people asked me: "How do you know you can function without some of these people?" I said: "I don't." I really didn't. I didn't have time to sort out who was really important and who wasn't. I had to stop the cash hemorrhage first, to even get a minute to think. So I swung the ax with abandon. And I'd do it again without a second thought if presented with a similar situation.

Pull Together a Plan

Once you've done what you can to stop the cash from pouring out of the business' wounds, bring everything to a near stop for a few days, get the best brains together you can, lock yourselves up in a quiet room without interruptions, and pull together a plan.

Without a plan, you'll make the mistake I made in the first turnaround crisis I dealt with. I started out by instantly reacting to each and every new problem that reared its ugly head, each howling wolf as it appeared at the door. I'd drop one thing to face the other, then turn from that to the next noise in the dark. Pretty soon I was spinning around like a top. One night, long after everybody else had left, I was in my chair behind my desk, sweaty, bone tired, exhausted. I realized I was completely out of control.

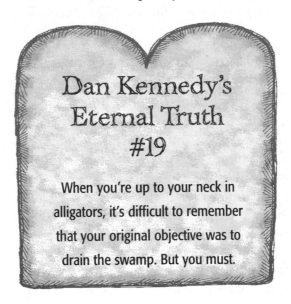

Dan Kennedy's
Eternal Truth
#19

When you're up to your neck in alligators, it's difficult to remember that your original objective was to drain the swamp. But you must.

Then I shut the door and put together a believable, step-by-step business plan with a lot of details for the first six months and more general ideas for the next six. With this battle plan in hand, I had confidence; I had the ability to engineer cooperation from others. Then I placed a limit on the amount of time each day dedicated to problems. When we hit the quota for the day, that was it; the rest of the problems had to stand in line until the next day. Each day, I set aside a certain amount of time to implement the business plan. With plan in hand, I restored order and kept myself out of the padded room.

Don't Hide

If your business owes a lot of money to a lot of creditors, you'll be tempted to hide. Big mistake. You or someone you give this responsibility to must keep the lines of communication open for those creditors and be as truthful as possible with them. When you can't promise a payment amount and date, don't; promise what you can, even if that's only the date and time you'll next communicate.

Target the creditors hurting your cash flow most for comprehensive renegotiation. Take your new business plan and meet in person if possible. At the least, phone or fax them, and shoot for the very best deal you can get.

For example, let's say you owe XYZ Company $20,000.00, all past due. You might get that $20,000.00 switched from a trade payable to a long-term, five-year installment note, interest only for the first year, and agree on new purchases to pay one-third with order, one-third on delivery, and one-third in 30 days. This takes $20,000.00 out of your current struggle altogether. Otherwise, you'd be whacking away at that $500.00 or $1,000.00 at a time, the creditor would never be happy, and getting needed goods would probably be next to impossible.

Facing trouble head-on, more often than not, earns respect and promotes cooperation.

Don't Take It Personally

Okay, your business is in trouble and you were captain of the ship while it smashed into the rocks. That's bad. But everybody makes mistakes. You're not the first, you won't be the last, and there is no shame in screwing up. The only cause for shame would be giving up without a fight. If you are genuinely trying to do the best you can, there's nothing to be ashamed of.

Beating yourself up or letting somebody else beat you up as a person is uncalled for and, obviously, unproductive. You have to be able to step out of the emotion and be a tough-minded turn-around consultant for your own business.

Direct Your Energy to Business Re-Invention

Even if it's only an hour, grab a certain amount of time each and every day and go to work on reinventing your business. Get to the very core of the problems. During a turnaround, you'll be doing a lot of patching work, and that's okay, but while you're patching up cuts and bruises you need to be the visionary designer of a whole new and improved operation.

Don G. had a chain of six restaurants that wound up in deep trouble. While he did all the things we've been talking about with the entire chain, he also took just one of the locations as his "new" model, and made major changes there, literally inventing a new and different restaurant operation, from A to Z. After a year, the entire company had limped its way back into positive cash flow, largely through debt restructuring and cost cutting, and although the entire business was still operating at a net loss, the new model was consistently profitable. Don now had a model to duplicate in his other five locations, which allowed him to again restructure debt, get some new investment capital, quickly make over the other five locations, and by the end of the second year of the turnaround, chalk up several hundred thousand dollars in profit.

At this point, the local beer distributor who supplied his restaurants bought into his company, contributed enough capital to wipe out all the high-interest debt, and open four more locations. Three years later, they sold the entire business to a national food-service company and walked away millionaires.

If Don had waited until he had his entire turnaround process implemented to go to work on his core business's reinvention, all these good things would not have happened, and he might have run out of time and money before ever getting to try his new plan.

CHAPTER 17

A FEW FINAL THOUGHTS ON
THE NEW ECONOMY

As I was completing this book, we were deep in a difficult, complex recession, I think, to be blunt, being made worse not better by the flailing about, idea-of-the-week government mucking about, and President Obama's monstrously ambitious agenda for political, economic, and social transformation. The nature of book publishing involves months of lead time, between the collecting of thoughts as words on these pages and realities on the ground. To that end, you can always access my most current comments directly connected to this and my other books at www.NoBSBooks.com, and more generally, via my newsletters, e-mail up-dates, and blogs for Members accessed with the free offer on pages 272–273.

Forward looking, I have talked mostly in this book about the evolving, emerging, probable New Economy, not the recession.

Hopefully, by the time you read this, we will all be New Economy Entrepreneurs rather than recession warriors. But whether that transition is still in progress or virtually completed, if not now, soon we will be doing business in that New Economy.

Ultimately, the single most significant fact is that the entrepreneur must be smarter, more strategic, more creative, more customer-centric, and more disciplined and determined than ever before. Given the presumed and probable tax burdens required by the unprecedented, gigantic deficits, it is going to require three, four, maybe five times as much income to create net wealth as was required in the past decade or two. The legacy of the recession and the government spending it spawned is a debt to be discharged through inflation, a type of tax imposed on all, and a plethora of increased and new taxes to be imposed on business, on high income earners, and on wealth creation. This is what it is, and neither rage or depression will alter its reality. If you intend to use entrepreneurship as a pathway to personal and financial independence, you have to recognize that path is much steeper than before. This means you must be much smarter about the allocation of every resource you own, borrow, rent, or otherwise assemble. Of *every* resource. If you would go back and read this book a second time through this single prism, you will see that most of my recommendations are directed at optimum results from resources.

There will always be rich, and most, as always, will get rich from scratch, through their ingenuity, initiative, and enterprise. There probably won't be fewer either. All efforts to flatten the economic pyramid have failed and will fail for good and rational reasons. The numbers are and will forever be 1% very rich, 4% rich, 15% doing very well, 80% dependent on today's wages to pay yesterday's bills, or on government subsidy or outright welfare and care. Further, in every separate population—everybody in your category of business, industry, or profession; everybody in your age range; everybody in your town—sorts itself the same way: 20%/80%. The fact of the top 20% is a permanent fact of life. Those in that 20% and what is required to be there with them has changed, is changing, and will change. But the 20% is unchanging reality.

Choosing to be an entrepreneur is, to my way of thinking, a courageous and noble choice. Without us, nothing else could occur. We provide the overwhelming majority of jobs, new jobs and new types of jobs. We create the products and deliver the services that make family and home life better and safer, people healthier, life more interesting and rewarding. Those of us who become rich, quick or slow, through our entrepreneurial efforts make an even greater subsequent contribution to society, by providing the investment capital required to, as example, turn medical research into breakthrough drugs, technology, and treatments brought to market; turn blighted neighborhoods into renovated, rebirthed, vibrant communities made livable. We also provide enormously important support for educational institutions, hospitals and medical centers, cultural institutions and charities. Finally, of course, we carry a disproportionate share of the tax burden paying for everyone's government services—as I was writing this, roughly 40% to 45% of the entire federal income tax load was being lugged by only the top 5% of the income earners. It's a very, very good thing we're around!

I have spent my entire life as an entrepreneur and as a teacher, coach, consultant, advisor to entrepreneurs, and I consider myself a champion advocate for entrepreneurs. I understand you and appreciate you, and it's in that spirit that I've invited you numerous times in this book, and again one final time now, to join me in a continuing dialogue and relationship, by accepting the free gift offered on pages 272–273. In The New Economy, we in the entrepreneurial community will be more important than ever. We have much work to do and many bills to pay. There is and will be greater, grander, more expansive opportunities than ever before, as well as tougher challenges to our autonomy and prosperity than ever before. It's no time to go it alone.

Businesses Launched During Recession and Emerging New Economies

TRADER JOE'S started as a chain of small convenience stores under another name during the slow financial period of the late 1950s. In 1967, the company changed its name to Trader Joe's and began carrying its own privately branded foods and beverages. It now boasts hundreds of stores.

GENERAL ELECTRIC was established by Thomas Edison in 1876, in the middle of the six-year recession following the financial panic of 1873.

SPORTS ILLUSTRATED was founded in 1954, at the tail end of a recession.

WALT DISNEY started the company we know as Disney today just as the Great Depression was beginning.

HEWLETT-PACKARD was born in a garage at the end of the Great Depression.

IHOP opened its doors in 1958, and began national franchising just three years later. BURGER KING started with a single restaurant in 1954, and during the recession in 1957, introduced its signature burger, The Whopper.

MICROSOFT was birthed in 1975, in the mid-70s recession attributed to the Carter administration, by Harvard drop-out Bill Gates.

CNN began as a cable station—not a network—in recession-plagued 1980. MTV began a year later, while the economy was still in a serious slump.

W. CLEMENT STONE, author of *The Success System That Never Fails*, started a door-to-door, office-to-office insurance sales organization in the depths of the Great Depression, built it into Combined Insurance Companies of America—for a time the largest company of its kind, and sold it for a fortune, creating billionaire personal wealth.

AMAZON.COM, originally named something different, that no one could spell correctly, was launched in a recession.

The Only Time You Have Is "Now Time"

RECESSION BOOSTS *SOME*. Family-owned Skinner Baking Co. in Omaha saw **sales rise 18% from '07 to '08**. In December, a big 25% jump. Its ovens are running 6 days a week vs. 5 before and **they are hiring (!)** to keep up with demand. They supply coffeecakes, cinnamon buns, etc. to supermarkets. They've been in biz since 1911, so their V.P. thinks he understands why they're up: "This is comfort food." The owner of Bathroom Magic in Fairfax, Va. reports **'08 revenues up 75% vs. '07**, and '08 being the best year he's ever had. Why? People who, in boom times, would bring in contractors to

completely re-model their bathrooms, in these times, choose a service they would otherwise sneer at: the one day bath make-over, with
refinishing glaze and fit-over components . . . to re-finish a tub like
new, just $425. The economy lets him get mass-affluent and even
affluent customers—"When the economy goes down, my business
skyrockets," he says. Interstate Batteries **opened 43 new stores in
'08—hiring to staff them**, on top of the existent 125, and expanded
the variety of batteries carried, although they're known for car batteries. "October and December were the **best months in the company's history**," reports the president of this 56-year old company.
Why? "With the recession, whether it's cars or laptops, people are
keeping what they own and trying to extend the life of their products." (Source: larger article, with more examples in *USA TODAY*
2/2/09). OK, go ahead and get it out: your business is different. *Your
business isn't designed to get a boost from the recession*. Duh! You
can fix that. *Any* restaurant can create comfort food menus, comfort
food nights. And since more people are staying home to eat, expand
pre-prepared meal offerings—didja notice Pizza Hut's pushing
lasagna? *Any* remodeler, contractor, furniture seller could reach up to
more affluent customers than he normally attracts with value packages and/or develop new, reduced price offers for present market.
Any retailer can alter or expand his product line to support a message right for these times. The question is not: how can I excuse
myself from business modification so I keep my excuses for suffering? . . . not: how can I survive the recession? **The question is**: how
can I be nimble, agile, creative, modify my business, alter my marketing to get a boost from recession?

Reprinted from *NO B.S. MARKETING LETTER*, March 2009

Buying When Everyone Is Selling

In tough economic times, the world is rampant with distress merchandise and cash is king. One such distress acquisition by John Paul Getty was the Hotel Pierre in New York City. The Hotel Pierre had a prestigious location with a full view of Central Park. However, in 1938 the prolonged Depression had taken a severe toll on the revenues of the Pierre. The hotel was in serious financial difficulties, so although Getty had no understanding of or interest in the hotel industry, he knew a bargain when he saw one. Discovering that he could buy the virtually new hotel for one-fourth its original cost, he realized that there was a huge upside potential with very little downside risk. He immediately paid $2.35-million cash and began using it as his East Coast home. Fifteen years later, when friend Frank Ryan called him with an offer of $17.5-million—over 7 times his cost—he took the offer on the spot and walked away with a $15-million cash profit. Many such cash deals were made over the years. The more deals he made, the more deals were offered. Garth Young of Signal Oil described his chief competitor Getty as a man who "could see further than any other guy I knew".

Whatever It Takes

Jeff Bezos' mantra was: "Work hard, have fun, and make history. Wake up petrified and afraid every morning. I know we can lose it all. It's not a fear. It's a fact." During the early years, he wore every hat in the organization and seldom left the office. Dana Brown, head of ordering, often worked through the night ordering books. When the orders were finally transmitted at 4:30 in the morning, no one else was there except Jeff. She admitted to working 15 to 18 hours a day and told the media, "Jeff was always there. I never saw him go home."

Another observer said of Jeff: "He is the most single-mindedly focused person I've ever met. It's all he cares about. He lives, eats, breathes Amazon.com."

A worker at Amazon said: "You can work long, hard, and well. At Amazon, two out of three won't work."

From *Entrepreneurial Genius* by Dr. Gene Landrum, www.GeneLandrum.com.

Gene created the popular restaurant chain Chuck E. Cheese, has assisted with numerous high-tech startups, and is a specialist in the psyche of the super-entrepreneur. He is the author of nine books probing the entrepreneurial mindset. He has appeared as a speaker at Glazer-Kennedy Insider's Circle™ events and on our audio learning programs.

ETERNAL TRUTHS

Dan Kennedy's Eternal Truth #1

Every successful achievement begins with decision.
Most unsuccessful lives are conspicuously absent of decision.

• • •

Dan Kennedy's Eternal Truth #2

If it's work, it won't make you rich.

• • •

Dan Kennedy's Eternal Truth #3

Failure is part of the daily entrepreneurial experience.

• • •

Dan Kennedy's Eternal Truth #4

How you deal with failure determines whether or not
you ever get the opportunity to deal with success.

• • •

Dan Kennedy's Eternal Truth #5

You cannot trust your own judgment.
Test, test, test. Then test some more.

• • •

Dan Kennedy's Eternal Truth #6
Live by price, die by price.

. . .

Dan Kennedy's Eternal Truth #7
We're taught that you can't judge a book by its cover, but
we can't help but judge a book by its cover. You will
be judged that way, too.

. . .

Dan Kennedy's Eternal Truth #8
No one will ever be a bigger expert on your
business than you.

. . .

Dan Kennedy's Eternal Truth #9
The willingness to do whatever it takes is infinitely more
important than knowing everything there is to know
about how to do it.

. . .

Dan Kennedy's Eternal Truth #10
The ability to win is easily transferred
from one business to another.

. . .

Dan Kennedy's Eternal Truth #11
Talk is cheap . . . until you hire a lawyer.

• • •

Dan Kennedy's Eternal Truth #12
No one will ever care about your business
as much as you do.

• • •

Dan Kennedy's Eternal Truth #13
Cash is king.

• • •

Dan Kennedy's Eternal Truth #14
If you can't make money without money,
you probably can't make money with money either.

• • •

Dan Kennedy's Eternal Truth #15
There is never enough time (or enough of any other
resource, for that matter). Entrepreneurs learn to
get what they want working with what
they've got.

• • •

Dan Kennedy's Eternal Truth #16
Even a blind hog finds a truffle once in a
while—as long as it keeps poking
around.

• • •

Dan Kennedy's Eternal Truth #17

A "normal" small business can only yield a "normal"
small business income. To earn an extraordinary income,
you must develop an extraordinary business!

• • •

Dan Kennedy's Eternal Truth #18

Passion wanes with longevity
and familiarity.

• • •

Dan Kennedy's Eternal Truth #19

When you're up to your neck in alligators,
it's difficult to remember that your original
objective was to drain the swamp.
But you must.

• • •

Other Books by This Author

No B.S. Sales Success for the New Economy (Entrepreneur Press)

No B.S. DIRECT Marketing for NON-Direct Marketing Businesses (Entrepreneur Press)

No B.S. Marketing to the Affluent (Entrepreneur Press)

No B.S. Ruthless Management of People and Profits (Entrepreneur Press)

No B.S. Wealth Attraction for Entrepreneurs (Entrepreneur Press)

No B.S. Time Management for Entrepreneurs (Entrepreneur Press)

Ultimate Marketing Plan (Adams Media)

Ultimate Sales Letter (Adams Media)

NO RULES: 21 Giant Lies about Success (Plume)

How To Make Millions with Your Ideas (Plume)

The New Psycho-Cybernetics (Prentice-Hall)

Zero Resistance Selling (Prentice Hall)

Websites Associated with the Author

www.FreeGiftFrom.com/business

www.DanKennedy.com

www.NoBSBooks.com

www.RenegadeMillionaire.com

Index

OK

Special Opportunity for Readers of "No B.S.® Business Success"...

The Most Incredible
FREE Gift Ever

($613.91 Worth of Pure Money-Making Information)

Dan Kennedy & Bill Glazer are offering an incredible opportunity for you to see WHY Glazer-Kennedy Insider's Circle™ is known as "THE PLACE" where entrepreneurs seeking FAST and Dramatic Growth and greater Control, Independence, and Security come together. Dan & Bill want to give you **$613.91 worth of pure Money-Making Information** including TWO months as an 'Elite' Gold Member of Glazer-Kennedy's Insider's Circle™. You'll receive a steady stream of MILLIONAIRE Maker Information including:

* Glazer-Kennedy University: Series of 3 Webinars (Value = $387.00)

The 10 "BIG Breakthroughs in Business Life *with Dan Kennedy*
- HOW Any Entrepreneur or Sales Professional can Multiply INCOME by 10X
- **HOW to Avoid Once and for All being an *"Advertising Victim"***
- The "*Hidden Goldmine*" in Everyone's Business and HOW to Capitalize on it
- **The BIGGEST MISTAKE most Entrepreneurs make in their Marketing**
- And the BIGGEEE...Getting Customers Seeking You Out.

The ESSENTIALS to Writing Million Dollar Ads & Sales Letters BOTH
Online & Offline *with Marketing & Advertising Coach, Bill Glazer*
- How to INCREASE the Selling Power of All Your Advertising by Learning the 13 "Must Have" Direct Response Principles
- **Key Elements that Determine the Success of Your Website**
- HOW to Craft a Headline the Grabs the Reader's Attention
- **How to Create an Irresistible Offer that Melts Away Any Resistance to Buy**
- The Best Ways to Create Urgency and Inspire IMMEDIATE Response
- *"Insider Strategies"* to INCREASE Response that you Must be using both ONLINE & Offline

The ESSENTIALS of Productivity & Implementation for Entrepreneurs *w/*
Peak Performance Coach Lee Milteer
- How to Almost INSTANTLY be MORE Effective, Creative, Profitable, and Take MORE Time Off
- **HOW to Master the "Inner Game" of Personal Peak Productivity**
- How to Get MORE Done in Less Time
- **HOW to Get Others to Work On Your Schedule**
- How to Create Clear Goals for SUCESSFUL Implementation
- And Finally the BIGGEE...How to Stop Talking and Planning Your Dreams and Start Implementing Them into Reality

* 'Elite' Gold Insider's Circle Membership (Two Month Value = $99.94):

- Two Issues of *The No B.S.® Marketing Letter:*

  Each issue is at least 12 pages – usually MORE – Overflowing with **the latest Marketing & MoneyMaking Strategies**. Current members refer to it as a day-long intense seminar in print, arriving by first class mail every month. There are ALWAYS terrific examples of *"What's-Working-NOW"* **Strategies**, timely Marketing news, trends, ongoing teaching of Dan Kennedy's Most IMPORTANT Strategies... and MORE. As soon as it arrives in your mailbox you'll want to find a quiet place, grab a highlighter, and devour every word.

- Two CDs Of The **EXCLUSIVE GOLD AUDIO INTERVIEWS**

  These are EXCLUSIVE interviews with <u>successful users of direct response advertising, leading experts and entrepreneurs in direct marketing, and famous business authors and speakers</u>. Use them to turn commuting hours into "POWER Thinking" hours.

* The New Member No B.S.® Income Explosion Guide & CD (Value = $29.97)

This resource is <u>especially designed for NEW MEMBERS</u> to show them HOW they can join the thousands of Established Members **creating exciting sales and PROFIT growth** in their Business, Practices, or Sales Careers & Greater SUCCESS in their Business lives.

Income Explosion FAST START Tele-Seminar with Dan Kennedy, Bill Glazer, and Lee Milteer (Value = $97.00)

Attend from the privacy and comfort of your home or office…hear a DYNAMIC discussion <u>of Key Advertising, Marketing, Promotion, Entrepreneurial & Phenomenon strategies</u>, PLUS answers to the most Frequently Asked Questions about these Strategies

* You'll also get these Exclusive "Members Only" Perks:

- **Special FREE Gold Member CALL-IN TIMES:** Several times a year, Dan & I schedule Gold-Member ONLY Call-In times
- **Gold Member RESTRICTED ACCESS WEBSITE:** Past issues of the *No B.S.® Marketing Letter*, articles, special news, etc.
- **Continually Updated MILLION DOLLAR RESOURCE DIRECTORY** with Contacts and Resources Dan & his clients use.

To activate your MOST INCREDIBLE FREE GIFT EVER you only pay a one-time charge of $19.95 (or $39.95 for Int'l subscribers) to cover postage (this is for everything). **After your 2-Month FREE test-drive, you will automatically continue at the <u>lowest</u> Gold Member price of $49.97 per month ($59.97 outside North America). Should you decide to cancel your membership, you can do so at any time by calling Glazer-Kennedy Insider's Circle™ at 410-825-8600 or faxing a cancellation note to 410-825-3301 (Monday through Friday 9am - 5pm). Remember, your credit card will NOT be charged the low monthly membership fee until the beginning of the 3rd month, which means you will receive 2 full issues to read, test, and** profit from all of the powerful techniques and strategies you get from being an Insider's Circle Gold Member. **And of course, it's impossible for you to lose, because if you don't absolutely LOVE everything you get, you can simply cancel your membership before the third month and never get billed a single penny for membership.**

EMAIL REQUIRED IN ORDER TO NOTIFY YOU ABOUT THE GLAZER-KENNEDY UNIVERSITY WEBINARS AND FAST START TELESEMINAR

Name _____ Business Name _____

Address _____

City _____ State _____ Zip _____ e-mail* _____

Phone _____ Fax_____

Credit Card Instructions to Cover $19.95 for Shipping & Handling:

_____Visa   MasterCard   _____ American Express   _____ Discover

Credit Card Number _____ Exp. Date _____

Signature _____ Date _____

FAX BACK TO 410-825-3301
Or mail to: 401 Jefferson Ave., Towson, MD 21286
www.In12Months.com